THE BOSTON TRADITION

JOHN SINGER SARGENT
Mrs. Fiske Warren and her Daughter Rachel, 1903
(cat. no. 63)

THE BOSTON TRADITION

AMERICAN PAINTINGS FROM
THE MUSEUM OF FINE ARTS, BOSTON

Carol Troyen

An exhibition organized by the Museum of Fine Arts, Boston and
The American Federation of Arts

THE AMERICAN FEDERATION OF ARTS

The American Federation of Arts is a national, non-profit, educational organization, founded in 1909, to broaden the knowledge and appreciation of the arts of the past and present. Its primary activities are the organization of exhibitions and film programs which travel throughout the United States and abroad.

Copyright © 1980
The American Federation of Arts

Published by The American Federation of Arts
41 East 65th Street
New York, New York 10021

LCC: 80-69210
ISBN: 0-917418-66-2

AFA Exhibition 80-3
Circulated November, 1980–August, 1981

Designed by Pauline DiBlasi
Type set by Dumar Typesetting, Inc., Dayton, Ohio
Printed by Eastern Press, Inc., New Haven, Connecticut

Cover:
JOHN SINGLETON COPLEY
Mrs. Samuel Quincy (Hannah Hill), ca. 1761
(cat. no. 9)

This exhibition and publication are supported by generous grants from Metropolitan Life Foundation, the National Endowment for the Arts, and the National Patrons of The American Federation of Arts.

Metropolitan Life Foundation is pleased to join the National Endowment for the Arts and the AFA's National Patrons in supporting this important exhibition of selections from the Museum of Fine Arts, Boston. The exhibition includes paintings by artists who lived, worked or exhibited in Boston from colonial times to the early twentieth century. Traveling for the first time as a collection, these paintings chronicle the development of Boston's rich artistic heritage. As one of colonial America's earliest cultural centers, Boston occupies a significant place in the development of American art. This exhibition and catalogue are the result of the joint effort of the Museum of Fine Arts and The American Federation of Arts to share "The Boston Tradition" with a wider audience.

Richard R. Shinn, *Chairman*
Metropolitan Life Insurance Company

TOUR

Des Moines Art Center
November 25, 1980–January 7, 1981

The Museum of Fine Arts, Houston
February 6–March 29, 1981

Whitney Museum of American Art, New York
April 21–June 14, 1981

Pennsylvania Academy of the Fine Arts, Philadelphia
June 26–August 16, 1981

CONTENTS

FOREWORD

The evolution of the exhibition and publication THE BOSTON TRADITION, American Paintings from the Museum of Fine Arts, Boston, has involved the talent, skills, and generosity of many individuals and organizations. First, we are indebted to collectors, curators, and donors of purchase funds, past and present, who have guided these great paintings into the collection of the Museum of Fine Arts, Boston.

The exhibition was first suggested to us by Theodore E. Stebbins, Jr., the Museum's Curator of American Paintings, who has also written the introduction to the catalogue. Its development and maturation is the work of Carol Troyen, Assistant Curator of American Paintings, whose scholarship and dedication to the project have been invaluable. She has selected the paintings in the exhibition while writing the description of each of these works and the central essay in the catalogue on the history of taste and patronage in Boston. Throughout its entire development, the project has been enthusiastically encouraged by John Walsh, Jr., Mrs. Russell W. Baker Curator of Paintings. The generous willingness of the Museum's Trustees to share these major works of art with the audiences of other museums across the country is deeply appreciated.

Critical financial support for the exhibition and publication have been provided by the National Endowment for the Arts, Metropolitan Life Foundation, and the National Patrons of the AFA. For the Foundation, it marks its first sponsorship of an art exhibition. Without the generosity of all these three, this project would not have been possible.

There are many on the AFA staff whose efforts must be acknowledged: Jane Tai directed the implementation of both the exhibition and book; Susanna D'Alton assisted her in all aspects of this endeavor; Jeffery Pavelka made arrangements with the presenting museums; Carol O'Biso, the AFA Registrar, was responsible for the care of the paintings throughout the tour; Pauline DiBlasi designed the handsome catalogue, and Steven Schoenfelder the poster and exhibition guide; Mary Ann Monet and Fran Falkin diligently proofread the manuscript; Sandra Gilbert coordinated publicity; and Walter Poleshuck secured the very important corporate funding for the project.

Finally, we wish to thank our museum partners who will be presenting the exhibition in their galleries: the Des Moines Art Center; The Museum of Fine Arts, Houston; the Whitney Museum of American Art, New York; and the Pennsylvania Academy of the Fine Arts, Philadelphia.

Wilder Green, *Director*
The American Federation of Arts

Jan Fontein, *Director*
Museum of Fine Arts, Boston

ACKNOWLEDGEMENTS

This exhibition coincides with a major building program at the Museum of Fine Arts, Boston. The renovation of the Paintings Galleries necessitates the removal of the Museum's unsurpassed collection of American paintings from public view. Thus the Museum has the opportunity to share some of the masterworks of this collection with other cities with rich cultural traditions of their own. "The Boston Tradition" was conceived by Theodore E. Stebbins, Jr., Curator of American Paintings at the Museum of Fine Arts; he has overseen this exhibition in all its many stages, and I am grateful to him for his unfailing guidance and support. The impetus for the collaboration between the Museum of Fine Arts and The American Federation of Arts came from Wilder Green, Director of the AFA, whose efforts on behalf of "The Boston Tradition" contributed enormously to its success. Jane Tai of the AFA has directed all aspects of the planning of this exhibition, and has graciously responded to my time-consuming requests and questions. The encouragement of John Walsh, Jr., the Mrs. Russell W. Baker Curator of Paintings, Museum of Fine Arts, has been invaluable to me, as were his many thoughtful recommendations from the outset of my work on the exhibition. This project has benefited greatly from the enthusiastic endorsement of Jan Fontein, Director of the Museum of Fine Arts.

My colleagues in the Paintings Department, especially Laura Luckey and Galina Gorokhoff, have good-naturedly assumed some of my responsibilities while I was preparing the exhibition, and I am grateful to them for their patience and encouragement. Several have contributed substantially to the content of the catalogue entries, and I would particularly like to thank Tanya Boyett, Anne Poulet, Scott Schaefer, and Diana Strazdes. The many facts discovered by Amy Lighthill about exhibitions and collectors in Boston during the nineteenth century greatly enriched the accompanying essay. Patricia Loiko, who typed the manuscript of the catalogue, provided many helpful editorial suggestions; her skill and dedication were invaluable in bringing the project to completion.

In the course of preparing for the exhibition, many unfamiliar paintings were brought up from the storerooms for a fresh evaluation; other well-known works were carefully examined and restored to sound and handsome condition. I am especially grateful to Alain Goldrach, Conservator of Paintings, and to Brigitte Smith, Associate Conservator, and Jean Woodward, Assistant Conservator, for their careful study and long hours spent treating these paintings. Equally essential was the painstaking work of James Barter, Technician in the Paintings Department, who repaired and secured the frames.

I have profited from the advice and experience of Linda Thomas, Registrar at the Museum of Fine Arts, who with the staff of the AFA arranged the insurance, packing, and transportation of the exhibition. Judy Spear carefully edited the manuscript of the catalogue. Janice Sorkow, Head of Photographic Services, assisted by John Woolf, spent many hours helping me to gather photographic material, and Wayne Lemmon, the Museum's photographer, obligingly provided excellent photographs of many of the pictures in the exhibition.

Many scholars, collectors, and dealers have generously shared with me their special knowledge of artists associated with the Boston Tradition, particularly Morton C. Bradley, Jr., Michael Brown, Helen Cooper, Dorothy Edinburg, Trevor Fairbrother, E. J. Fontaine, William H. Gerdts, Deborah Gribben, Jonathan Harding, Patricia Pierce, Jan Seidler, Robert C. Vose, Jr., and Andrew Wilton. Finally, I have benefited greatly from the generous assistance of two colleagues whose many contributions to this catalogue were always insightful and much appreciated: John Caldwell, who took time from his demanding work on the catalogue of American Paintings in the Metropolitan Museum of Art to read many of the entries and make numerous suggestions, and Alexandra Murphy of the Paintings Department, whose insights into French parallels for many American paintings in the exhibition greatly enriched my discussion of them, and whose essay "French Paintings in Boston: 1800–1900" (*Corot to Braque: French Paintings from the Museum of Fine Arts, Boston,* 1979) was the model for my own.

Carol Troyen

INTRODUCTION

No American city has been studied more thoroughly than Boston. Its important, often central, role in American history and American thought has been acknowledged and celebrated, and its historic places are national shrines. The economic and intellectual preeminence of the Massachusetts Bay Colony during the seventeenth century; the city's distinction during the eighteenth century, when its political and intellectual leadership led the way to Revolution; its architectural beauty and cultural greatness during the first half of the nineteenth century when the city and its environs nurtured the best American writers and thinkers of the time, including Emerson, Hawthorne, Thoreau, and Longfellow; and the richness of Boston culture in the years following the Civil War, that Henry James describes so evocatively—all these have been examined and reexamined. Indeed, Boston was once called "The American Athens," and it has enjoyed (if not always deserved) the appellation ever since.

Through its history Boston has also housed and patronized many of the nation's leading painters. Just as education and literature have been thought to be essential concerns of the city, so too has there been almost from the beginning a sense that art is somehow important; the purchase, ownership, and responsible disposition of fine paintings has thus been one of the continuing responsibilities of Boston families. Painters were surely never as important to Boston as its writers: nonetheless only here could one find a major suburb (Allston, Mass.) named during the 1860s after the painter, and one of the city's most important areas (Copley Square) named some twenty years later to honor its leading colonial artist. Yet the story of Boston's taste has not been told. Book after book has described the city's commerce and maritime trade, her religion and politics, her buildings and her writers, but we await a cultural and artistic history.

This exhibition has therefore two primary purposes: to share a group of the best American paintings from the Museum of Fine Arts with a wider public in Des Moines, Houston, Philadelphia and New York, during a period when our galleries are being rennovated and refurbished; and to remedy in part, at least, historians' relative lack of interest in Boston's art and its background. Through the catalogue entries and through Carol Troyen's essay, we hope to encourage further study of Boston painters and their patrons, their institutions, and their changing styles.

The paintings included here were selected on the grounds of quality and of appropriateness to our theme, the elucidation of Boston painters and patronage. We have defined our terms relatively narrowly, limiting ourselves to painters who worked in Boston and its environs, or were trained there, or whose art was adopted by Bostonians as their own. We cover two centuries, from John Smibert's portraits of Mr. and Mrs. Dudley of 1729 to Frank Benson's still life entitled *The Silver Screen,* dated 1921. Moreover, the content of the exhibition nicely mirrors the Museum of Fine Art's collection of American paintings, almost two thousand in number. Almost half the exhibition (thirty-four paintings) consists of portraits; these and the nineteen genre, historical and ideal subjects reflect Boston's traditional predeliction for figurative painting. There are also nineteen landscape and marine views, but interestingly enough only two portray Boston itself (Lane's *Boston Harbor* and Hassam's *Charles River and Beacon Hill*), with several additional views taken in such outlying towns as Medfield, Ipswich, and Gloucester. Local topography was left to the printmakers and watercolorists, while the Boston painter was free to depict the figurative, the ideal, and the exotic.

In addition, the visitor will find only two still lifes here, the Sharp and the Benson, a lack which again reflects historic taste, for Bostonians simply never enjoyed or bought still lifes in the way Philadelphians and New Yorkers did. Finally, there are just two "folk" paintings here—which follows from the nature of this essentially rural, unsophisticated art, rarely practiced or collected in Boston.

Fifty-six of these paintings were gifts or bequests to the Museum of Fine Arts, while eighteen were purchases. This reflects the great, continuing faith that Boston and New England families have had in the Museum. In terms of American art before the twentieth century there have—with the exception of Maxim Karolik—been no large-scale benefactors or collectors: indeed, fifty-three separate donors and purchase funds and one lender, are responsible for this group of seventy-eight paintings. Rather, there has been a steady stream of fine objects into the collection. The earliest acquisition represented here is the Allston, *Self-Portrait,* a bequest of 1884, while no fewer than ten of the paintings were acquired in each of the last two decades, including several important purchases.

The one multiple donor represented here (with twelve paintings) and the chief patron of the American arts in Boston's history, is Maxim Karolik (1893-1963). This great believer in nineteenth-century American painting has been called "the unlikeliest champion imaginable,"[1] and he *was* in many ways, as a Russian-born Jew, a boaster and egotist, and as an outsider who married the much older, socially prominent Martha Amory Codman. Karolik gave three major collections to Boston, one of furniture, the second consisting of about two hundred eighty American nineteenth-century paintings, and the third of American drawings and watercolors of the same period. The paintings collection, which concerns us here, was largely put together in a three-year period (1943–1945), and was given to the Museum later in the '40s and in a final bequest of 1964. Karolik's aim was to collect the then-unknown period between Stuart and Homer ("1815–1865"), and he was particularly moved by the realistic landscapes of the Hudson River School and related painters. Karolik was a pioneer; given the period, and his own disinclination to spend much money, he must be said to have collected brilliantly. His favorite painter was Martin Johnson Heade, whom he considered "*the* genius of our collection," and he bought over fifty of them. Heade is only one of the painters whose work he collected in depth—some with Boston connections, like Heade and Lane, most without—whose work would otherwise literally be unrepresented in the Museum's collection.

The present exhibition is as complete as we could make it, given the limitations of even the Museum's collection and the fact that certain paintings cannot be lent safely. We had aimed to begin at the beginning—that is, around 1670 when the "first Boston school," numbering about a half-dozen limners, portrayed Mr. and Mrs. Freake, the three Gibbs children, the Mason children and other Bostonians in a rigid yet charming Elizabethan manner. Unfortunately neither of our two seventeenth-century portraits is strong enough to travel, so the earliest pictures shown here are the portraits by Smibert from 1729. Other *lacunae* are a marine painting by Robert Salmon and a still life by John La Farge. In both cases we own fine examples, but unfortunately ones painted on fragile panels. Also unrepresented here is the Boston portraitist James Frothingham, for the same reason, and others including the early still-life painter Thomas Badger, the landscapist Samuel L. Gerry, and the later portraitist Charles Hopkinson, simply because we own nothing at all by them.

Looking at the whole, one comes to the conclusion that there are two quite distinct Boston traditions in American painting: one is the colonial period, which climaxed with the rise of the mature Copley in the 1760s, and may be said to have lasted nearly until Stuart's death in 1828, while the other is the modern era, which had begun by the time of Allston's return from abroad in 1818 and which may well continue today. Historians have noted that "in most realms of activity, Boston early outstripped every colonial rival."[2] Boston indeed was the most prosperous and most literate of our seventeenth-century cities, and she was the largest. As late as 1742, for example, Boston still led, with a population of 16,000, as compared to Philadelphia's 13,000 and New York's 11,000 (Charleston and Newport ranked fourth and fifth, far behind). As such, Boston drew the ablest craftsmen in the colonies, so that during the seventeenth century the state of cabinet-making, silversmithing and painting—all regarded as crafts on essentially the same level—was unsurpassed.

As noted above, a group of Boston painters flourished by 1670, a decade before Philadelphia had been founded. In the next generation, that of the Pollard Limner and others, there seems to have been a loss of energy, and the most creative of American paintings were being made by the "Patroon Painters" of New York's Hudson River Valley. However, with the arrival of John Smibert from England in 1729, Boston's leadership was firmly reestablished for several artistic generations. It was maintained with Feke, Blackburn, and then Copley during the 1750s, despite Philadelphia's rise at that time to become the largest American city, and despite the political unease which prevailed in Boston from the early '60s to the outbreak of Revolution in 1775-1776.

Copley, and thereby Boston, were unrivalled artistically during the '60s and early '70s. Copley's talent surely ranks as among the two or three most brilliant in American art history, yet we must remember that he was patronized only as a high-level craftsman; he might receive twice as much for a portrait as a gilder would for its frame, but that was all—there was no concept yet of artistic genius in Boston or in America, and Copley's only route to the upper class of the merchants and politicians, to which he aspired, was through marriage.

Economic and cultural disaster came to all the colonies in the years 1775–1790, but especially to Boston. Her population dropped from 16,000 in 1775 to 3,500 in 1776. With Charles Willson Peale and his family at work, Philadelphia became preeminent in painting (as it was economically) for a forty- or fifty-year period. American art elsewhere recovered by the early '90s, but Boston remained in the doldrums until Gilbert Stuart settled in the city, after having worked in New York and Philadelphia, in 1806. Stuart, like Smibert long before, brought the latest English style to the new nation, which remained England's artistic colony. He painted brilliantly at times here—one need only look at his *Bishop Cheverus* (cat. no. 19)—but still much of his best work had been done before he arrived in Boston. Nonetheless, he came—presumably because of Boston's well-known tradition of portrait patronage—and he established a dominant style that survived his death by many years. His younger contemporary Washington Allston was also drawn to Boston's culture; he came in 1818 after seventeen years in Italy and England, and as Stuart declined he succeeded to the role of Boston's chief painter.

Allston's poetic personality, his passion, his incredibly high ideals and long training in the European history-painting tradition, all endeared him to the city: he was the first artistic genius recognized as such by Boston. His art and his personality dominated the city's memory for the rest of the century. Thus, as late as 1881 Winsor's *Memorial History of Boston* comments: "Copley and Stuart are remembered as good painters, and nothing more. A halo of poetic memories surrounds Allston's life and lingers about his pictures."[3] Boston was nearly alone in seeing this halo, and at this point, during the 1820s, Boston diverges from the mainstream of American taste and enters what I would consider its modern artistic period. The proper Bostonian suffered no loss of confidence in his own taste during this time, but increasingly the art that *Boston* liked (usually the work of Boston painters) was *not* so highly acclaimed elsewhere. Boston's record from the beginning up through Stuart may be said to have been nearly perfect: the best American painters simply *were* the Boston painters. With Allston, the record grows spottier. Often artistic leadership and the artistic mainstream were elsewhere, and Boston's confidence in her artists was sometimes, though not always, misplaced.

Allston serves as a symbol for Boston's "new" taste—its concept of art as figurative, ideal, and moral, as something that stems from Europe, as depending more for its quality on the true spirituality of the artist than on its visual appearance—but he surely wasn't the single cause of it. Even in the city's golden age in the first half of the nineteenth century, during the heyday of the merchant princes and the literary renaissance, there were widespread doubts about art as dangerous and materialistic. One finds evidence of this in the writings of Emerson and Hawthorne. There were no regular art exhibits in Boston until 1827—far later than Philadelphia and New York. Most important, there appeared in Boston during the whole of the nineteenth century no single great collector, no Luman Reed, no Corcoran, no Thomas B. Clarke, who might have changed things. Carol Troyen, below, rightly describes

T. H. Perkins as the city's leading patron of the arts during this time, just as Thomas Wigglesworth was later in the century. But Perkins owned only Boston's favorites, Stuart and Allston, and a handful of other contemporaries (Robert Weir, Thomas Sully), in comparison to dozens of copies after old masters and English, Dutch, Italian, and French paintings and prints. With Wigglesworth, it was much the same: far less than half of his paintings was American, and almost all of those were by Boston painters. These included Heade, Lane, and Inness, as well as J. F. Cole, Winckworth Allan Gay, and Thomas Hewes Hinckley, so that it still would have been a wonderful group to preserve intact—but unfortunately no nineteenth-century Boston collection has survived, not even the institutional one formed by the Boston Athenaeum.

Boston liked literary and sentimental art, understandably as this was America's literary city (in 1850 two of the nation's five largest libraries were in Boston, and the city's average magazine circulation per capita was over twice that of New York and three times that of Philadelphia). When Charles Eliot Norton was first appointed as Harvard's art historian in 1874 it was as "Lecturer on the History of the Fine Arts as Connected with Literature." But harder to explain is Boston's growing taste for French art and French style in the years around the Civil War, as symbolized in the rise to prominence of William Morris Hunt, a brilliant but flawed figure in the Allston mold. Hunt and his French-trained friends were generously patronized, and even more successful was Hunt's introduction of the Barbizon school and especially J. F. Millet to Boston. Great collections of French art were quickly formed, and these survive today in the strong Museum of Fine Arts holdings in Millet, Monet, and many others. It is hard to know why Boston, the most English of American cities, turned so easily toward French styles at this time: in any case, Boston was sophisticated enough to collect ancient and modern art from every corner of the world, but it remained most reluctant to patronize the contemporary painter from New York, or heaven forbid, from elsewhere in America. Boston clearly had nothing against collecting as such, for its preeminent collections of Asian, classical, and Egyptian art were formed by individual citizens in the years after the Museum's founding in 1870: the problem was its attitude toward the work of the modern American.

Blinded, in a sense, by Allston and then Hunt, Boston missed the landscapes of Church and Bierstadt, the genre paintings of Bingham and Mount. New York had become the nation's art center by 1825, as it remains, and Boston rejected New York taste in every sphere (Boston etiquette books railed against loose manners in that city). Boston's open-mindedness had increased by the 1870s, and New Yorkers who painted to Boston's taste, such as Vedder and La Farge, became acceptable. Then during the late years of the century American art became more international, more sophisticated (in a sense more Bostonian), and the city had a last "Indian summer" of artistic preeminence and occasional national leadership. The chief Boston painters were still likely to move to New York, like Homer, Bunker, Hassam, and Prendergast for example, but the city patronized all four, and took others, such as the expatriate John Singer Sargent, to its heart. With the energetic early decades of the Museum School under Tarbell and Benson, a high level of craft and an appropriately sentimental style emerged, and for a time during the Gilded Era the "look" of Boston painting became nearly the look of American art.

In Boston, art was always accepted as essential to the culture, but it was seldom sought avidly. In the colonial period, through Stuart, Bostonians demanded and got the most up-to-date furnishings, architecture, and portrait styles: there was a constant search in Boston for the latest and best modern styles, and it may well have been America's most modern city. But in the last century and a half, during the time when Boston changed from a vibrant mercantile, political city to a literary, genteel one, the city's attitude changed drastically: now the best art was that which *felt* most like art of the past. Allston emulated Titian, Hunt followed his French masters, Paxton painted like a modern Vermeer, and Sargent echoed the eighteenth-century Grand Manner.

During the late years of the nineteenth century an evocative aesthetic was created in the hands of the best Boston painters, who skillfully portrayed a refined and limited world. Their work recalls a statement by Henry James's hero in his story, *The Passionate Pilgrim:* "I came into the world an aristocrat. I was born with a soul for the picturesque." But as time went on, Boston's genteel art became stylized and conservative. The position of the artist in its society declined; the painter was seen merely as a carrier of old ideas, incapable of innovation and true originality. Ironically, Boston's intelligence and her love of art blocked the way to modernism, to the myriad styles and enormous creative energies of the twentieth century. Modern style became the province of New York, as today. Nineteenth-century Boston was exposed to the paintings of Cole and Church, and found them inappropriate, just as today's collectors have rejected the art of a Roy Lichtenstein or a Jasper Johns. The reasons may have been the same: the contemporary work favored in New York seemed garish, bright, linear, and perhaps too materialistic, in comparison to the idealistic, intellectual, subtly colored paintings that Boston has favored for so long.

Boston's artistic tradition can be traced back over three hundred years. The arts here have seen periods of great energy, and times of relative inactivity—but as a whole, the work produced in Boston forms one of the great cultural legacies of America. Now in 1980, with the city again vibrant and prosperous, having preserved much of its old character and its fine early architecture, and having capitalized on its leadership in education, finance, and the technical industries, one looks to the future with interest. Just in the past decade the Museum of Fine Arts established a department of Contemporary Art (1971), and appointed a curator of American Paintings (1977). These are hopeful signs that the great collections of earlier American art will be cared for and built upon as they deserve; at the same time, trustees and staff are striving to bring the Museum and its collections into the twentieth century, and to prepare for the twenty-first.

Theodore E. Stebbins, Jr.
Curator of American Paintings

1. Brian O'Doherty, "Maxim Karolik," *Art in America* 4 (1962), p. 63.
2. Constance M. Green, *The Rise of Urban America* (New York, 1965), p. 4.
3. Arthur Dexter, "The Fine Arts in Boston," in Justin Winsor, *The Memorial History of Boston 1630-1880,* vol. IV, p. 392.

THE BOSTON TRADITION:
PAINTERS AND PATRONS IN BOSTON 1720-1920

In the twenty-eighth exhibition at the Boston Athenaeum, held in 1855, there was, in addition to the usual display of casts, statuary, and the Athenaeum's own collection, a gallery devoted to "Artists of Boston and New York." Included in that gallery were a group of tightly painted landscapes by the New Yorkers Cropsey, Durand, Gifford, and Kensett, and Frederic E. Church's spectacular *Andes of Ecuador* (1855; Reynolda House, Winston-Salem, N.C.), the first work by that painter ever to have been seen in Boston. Occupying a prominent position in the show was Cole's five-part *Course of Empire* (1838; New-York Historical Society), a work that had been popular in Boston since its initial exhibition at the Athenaeum the previous year. Also shown were romantic paintings by Allston, Stuart, and George Loring Brown, the perennial favorites of the Athenaeum exhibitions. But more significant was the inclusion of works by two painters who heralded the great impact of French paintings on Boston's artistic community in the ensuing decades: *The Fortune Teller* (cat. no. 41) by William Morris Hunt (1852; Museum of Fine Arts, Boston), lent by F. B. Brooks, and *An Interior* (now known as *The Knitting Lesson;* also Museum of Fine Arts), by Jean-François Millet, lent by the prominent Boston attorney Martin Brimmer.

The critical response to this exhibition indicates the beginning of the divergence in artistic direction and taste between Boston and New York in the years that followed. Although no notice was taken of the show in the Boston press, New York's *Crayon* was enthusiastic about Church's painting ("perhaps the best of his works"), while faulting *The Fortune Teller*, a monumental figure painting, for being painted in "the morbid manner, so popular in France," and finding Millet's painting of a poor French family "an earnest, though affectedly feeble peasant group."[1] The work of Hunt and his idol Millet, for which New Yorkers as yet had little sympathy, already had had an impact in Boston. Hunt's personal charm and social standing—he was married to the granddaughter of Thomas Handasyd Perkins, one of Boston's most successful merchants and the leading patron of the arts in the city in the first half of the century—gave him the ear of Boston's wealthiest men, and in the 1850s and '60s he became a crusader for the avant-garde French painting just then gaining public attention in Paris.

At the same time, another aesthetic was being introduced in Boston. Published in America in 1847, *Modern Painters* by John Ruskin (England's foremost art critic) was a celebration of the highly realistic yet mythic art of the Pre-Raphaelite painters, based on an appreciation of their medieval forebears, and was generally well received. Eight years later, James Jackson Jarves's *Art Hints* appeared in Boston, and was praised for its "fine, free, spirited" analysis of painting and architecture, comparable to that of Ruskin, "whose influence upon almost everything that has appeared on kindred subjects... may be traced, not only in the writings, but in the buildings and paintings of his day."[2] One of the earliest opportunities Bostonians had to see the work championed by Ruskin and Jarves came in 1858, when the "American Exhibition of British Painting" came to the Athenaeum. The show included many Pre-Raphaelite paintings, and was nearly as well attended and profitable in Boston as it had been in New York. However, it elicited some skepticism from Boston's critics, who poked gentle fun at Ruskin for having "discovered that Art was only rightly to be seen from a nut-shell." Although they admired some of the pictures, they were disturbed by the British painters' subordination of "central ideas to a skillful, thoughtful rendering of unimportant details," which they felt was "not the kind of subordination which should characterize high art."[3] In addition, during the 1850s, the New York painters who exemplified the Ruskinian "truth to nature" aesthetic in America were shown to some acclaim (though few were bought) in Boston.

Boston was given further opportunity to embrace the Ruskinian viewpoint in 1859, when the Athenaeum was offered a collection of Italian primitives assembled by Ruskin's American acolyte James Jackson Jarves. Formed with the profits of the Sandwich Glass Manufacturing Company, founded by his father, Jarves's collection was the forerunner of a type that did not emerge again in America until the end of the century. Jarves bought works on a grand scale, and with an eye to creating a historical survey of the period. He offered his paintings to Boston for $15,000, toward which $5,000 was pledged by a group of Athenaeum trustees, among them Martin Brimmer and Charles Eliot Norton, the future Harvard professor of fine arts and a staunch Ruskin supporter. Yet at this point, and despite their previous admiration for Jarves, Bostonians refused to act—neither an appeal to the rest of the trustees nor a drive for public contributions produced the remainder—and eventually the Jarves collection was sold to the Yale University Art Gallery in New Haven.

In refusing the Jarves collection, the Athenaeum indicated both a lack of interest in the early Italian painting Jarves had favored, and a reluctance to commit itself to having a permanent collection of historical scope. Founded as a library society, it would always consider its obligation to the visual arts a secondary function. More important, in failing to purchase the collection, Bostonians were expressing a growing disenchantment with Ruskin. The other kinds of pictures associated with the Ruskinian aesthetic, such as Pre-Raphaelite painting and the landscapes of the Hudson River School, soon would suffer the same fate. Increasingly, Bostonians found them gaudy, their painstaking realism antithetical to their own cultural tradition, the romantic idealism of Washington Allston and Gilbert Stuart: "There is such a thing as carrying realism too far. The followers of Ruskin seem to have had no sense of proportion: a pebble seemed to them as important as a whole mountainside."[4] Bostonians, furthermore, were skeptical of Ruskin's suggestion that modern painters were superior to old masters. Titian, Claude, and Poussin, disdained by Ruskin, were hallowed names in Boston, revered in their own right and as predecessors of painters like Washington Allston, Boston's most admired artistic personality. Because Ruskin's theories allowed the viewer to judge a painting on the basis of its fidelity to nature and the accessibility of its subject matter (rather than by its historical associations), they did find currency among some Americans, for they excused the cultural ignorance and lack of an artistic heritage about which they felt so defensive. In addition, his arguments could easily be used to support the belief that the future of western art was to be found not among the decadent cultures of Europe but in America: "It is *here*, in our fresh, healthy land, that the new and sublime advent of Art may be looked for"—a nationalistic statement all the more astounding for having been uttered by Augustine Duganne, a Frenchman transplanted to New York who wrote in 1853 of "Art's True Mission in America."[5] Although this sentiment echoed the theme of literary independence from Europe that Emerson had presented in "The American Scholar" some sixteen years earlier, when applied to the visual arts it was received with skepticism in Boston, which was justly proud of its nearly two-hundred year old cultural heritage.

Finally, the themes addressed by Ruskin in *Modern Painters* and other writings were increasingly suspect in Boston precisely because they had been adopted with such enthusiasm in New York. Long accustomed to regarding themselves as the nation's cultural leaders, Bostonians viewed with concern New York's ascendancy in the fine arts and the departure of increasing numbers of her artists for the more vital and receptive environment of New York. In reaction, Bostonians

sought their own viewpoint, their own cultural touchstone, one that was independent of New York and appropriate to its cosmopolitan and romantic artistic past. They found their spokesman in William Morris Hunt, who championed the art of Millet and the Barbizon painters as well as that of a group of young Americans, most of them Boston-born, who evolved styles influenced by those French artists. From the time of Hunt's arrival in Boston, Ruskin's teachings would become a minority viewpoint there, isolated in Cambridge with Charles Eliot Norton and his followers, and would not have any significant effect on Boston taste until the end of the century, when Isabella Stewart Gardner built her collection. Instead, Boston would seek its artistic models in France.

Boston's ultimate rejection of Ruskin's aesthetic, and its enthusiastic espousal of Barbizon art in the mid-1850s, marked the city's divergence from the styles and taste of New York that have come to be considered the mainstream of American art. During the succeeding decades, Boston would define its own tradition, one strongly oriented toward Europe, especially France, and based on a belief in the educational and moral value of art. The roots of this divergent tradition can be seen in the institutions, artists, and collectors who determined the standards of taste in the city from colonial times to the mid-nineteenth century.

In a series of articles discussing painters and paintings in Boston published in the *Atlantic Monthly* in 1888, William Howe Downes, the city's leading art critic in the late nineteenth century, claimed for Boston an artistic tradition then over two hundred years old: "It is at least as interesting to know that a city which has given birth to and adopted so many eminent painters, may trace the beginnings of her art almost as far back as the middle of the seventeenth century."[6] Boston's artists, as well as her historians, were proud of this heritage: the studio of John Smibert, the city's first professional painter, became virtually an academy of the fine arts in the late eighteenth century, for after his death it was occupied, and its contents studied, by leading painters of several successive generations, among them Copley, Trumbull, and Allston. In the seventeenth century, despite the myth of Puritan hostility to the arts, Boston was the new world's most influential artistic community. At least six artists have been identified and associated with paintings made in Boston between 1660 and 1700. These artists were all portraitists painting in a manner analogous to provincial styles in England; many of them came to New England with fully devel-

FREAKE LIMNER
Robert Gibbs, 1670

Robert Gibbs was born into the wealthy merchant class, which, with religious leaders, dominated patronage of the arts in seventeenth-century New England. Gibbs (here four and a half years old), his brother, and his sister were painted in Boston in 1670 by the Freake Limner, whose skills at rendering fabric and decorative color rivaled that of provincial English painters from whom he undoubtedly learned his trade. (Museum of Fine Arts, Boston. M. and M. Karolik Fund.)

oped styles and often returned there after a sojourn in the colonies in search of more lucrative commissions. Some, like the mariner Thomas Smith (whose self-portrait, now in the Worcester Art Museum, is the most compelling of all of these rather flat and linear images), were engaged in other occupations and worked only secondarily as painters.

In the seventeenth century, paintings were collected not for their value as art, but rather, like the domestic arts, because they served a useful purpose: some were brought from England as mementoes of family left behind or, less commonly, were sent from New England to relatives in the old world. Important individuals like Reverend John Davenport (whose portrait is now in the Yale University Art Gallery, New Haven), were painted upon reaching old age to preserve their likenesses for their survivors. Judging from the number of portraits painted in Boston in the seventeenth and early eighteenth centuries, it was common practice, and not considered a sinful luxury, for members of the merchant classes to have their features recorded in oils. However, except for popular divines whose likenesses were reproduced at the instigation of the printmakers, it was considered frivolous, ostentatious, and even politically inexpedient to have a mezzotint made of oneself, as Governor Jonathan Belcher of Boston angrily wrote his son in 1734: "I am Surprised and much displeased at . . . your having my Picture done in a Copper Plate—how cou'd you presume to do such a thing without my Special leave and Order . . . such a foolish affair will pull down much Envy, and give occasion to your Father's Enemies to Squirt and Squib and what not."[7]

John Smibert arrived in Boston in 1729, bringing with him a command of relatively up-to-date high-style portrait conventions and a collection of European images that became the basis of the developing artistic tradition in Boston. The city's eagerness for a connection with contemporary European culture is indicated by the fact that, although there were already several artists, Nathaniel Emmons and Peter Pelham among them, practicing their trade in the city, Smibert received over eighty commissions during his first four years in Boston. Smibert's own collection—copies of Raphael, Titian, Poussin, and Van Dyck as well as engravings after the work of many sixteenth- and seventeenth-century masters—represented an artistic tradition known firsthand to only a few well-traveled Bostonians. During the 1730s, clients and the curious, eager for culture, streamed through his studio. Mather Byles, a young visitor during the first winter of Smibert's residency in Boston, was so impressed by the sight of portraits from life and copies after old masters that he composed an eighty-line poem, "To Mr. Smibert on the sight of his Pictures"[8] in enthusiastic tribute to Smibert's collection. His appreciation for Smibert's contribution to the cultural life of Boston (he credits him with bringing civilization to a barbarous land) was no doubt intensified by his own limited exposure to works of art, but the fact remains that with the exception of color shops containing a few prints or private homes with family portraits, Smibert's studio was the only place a Bostonian in the 1730s could see fine paintings, art books, and prints.

Smibert continued to serve as Boston's connection with contemporary European art through the 1730s. In 1735 he had a shipment of prints sent from England, including Hogarth's *Harlot's Progress*, first published in 1732. The prints were well received: Boston's taste, in this instance, did not lag very far behind England's, and Hogarth's images inaugurated an interest in satiric prints that would continue in Boston through the nineteenth century, as exemplified by the popularity of the comic etchings of David Claypool Johnston.

Smibert's presence in Boston generated an active pursuit of the arts. The city's leading merchants—the scions of the Winslow, Amory, Hancock, and Oliver families, who were Smibert's first patrons—all acquired paintings, for the most part family portraits. There seems to have been a sort of friendly competition among them, for they had themselves painted by every portraitist who came to town. The silversmith Edward Winslow was painted by Smibert in 1729; his son Isaac was painted by Feke, Blackburn, and Copley; Thomas Hancock was painted by Smibert and (posthumously) by Copley, who also painted his nephew and heir John in 1765; Daniel Oliver and his sons were painted by Smibert, Emmons, Blackburn, Copley, and the Philadelphia painter William Williams. These men did not otherwise collect works of art, but they considered their family portraits important possessions, displaying them in their best parlors.[9]

The interest in European culture that Smibert's painting stimulated in Boston grew in the next generation; equally extraordinary was the increase in artistic activity, particularly among native-born painters, in the city over the next fifty years. With a population of only about 14,000, Boston was able to support three artists of major reputation (Robert Feke, Joseph Badger, and John Greenwood), as well as several engravers and heraldic painters, during the 1740s and '50s. The arrival of Joseph Blackburn around 1750 refreshed Boston's understanding of styles and fashions in European portraiture. He was the first of Boston's artists to be able to support himself solely with his income as a portrait painter[10] and paved the way for John Singleton Copley, who significantly altered the role of the artist in colonial society.

By the 1760s, Copley had achieved sufficient recognition and success as a portrait painter to be restless in an environment in which "was it not for preserving the resembla[n]ce of particular persons, painting would not be known in the plac[e]."[11] He aspired to escape the tyranny of portrait commissions and become a painter of historical subjects, which he knew from prints and from correspondence with associates in England to be a higher art. He had lofty ideals concerning the dignity of his profession, and chafed in provincial Boston, where art was regarded as "no more than any other useful trade . . . like that of a carpenter, tailor, or shoemaker, not as one of the most noble arts of the world, which is not a little mortifying to me." Yet this bitter comment hardly applied to his own case, for his financial success advanced the status of the artist considerably. By 1773, Copley was one of the largest property owners in the city, owning all the land between Charles, Beacon, Walnut, and Mt. Vernon Streets, Louisburg Square and Pinckney Streets—eleven acres in a newly fashionable residential area. He began life as a tobacconist's son, but his success as a painter and his marriage to the daughter of one of Boston's richest merchants elevated his social status to the extent that, on a visit to New York in 1771, he was entertained as an equal at the home of his patron, Samuel Verplanck. In the 1750s and early '60s, his patrons were, for the most part, middle class: men like Joseph Mann, a local baker, or Moses Gill, a brazier. But by the late '60s and early '70s, his clientele was made up chiefly of upper-class citizens

JOHN SINGLETON COPLEY
John Hancock, 1765

Copley painted this portrait and a companion picture of Samuel Adams at Hancock's request in the years preceding the American Revolution. The images of the two political leaders were used to rouse patriotic fervor both before and after 1776, being displayed at Faneuil Hall, Boston's public meeting place, and as the chief attractions of "the large and elegant collection of historical paintings" shown at Daniel Bowen's Columbian Museum (Boston's first public gallery) in 1891. (Museum of Fine Arts, Boston. Deposited by the City of Boston.)

like the Goldthwaits and the Winslows and of cultural and political leaders like Mercy Otis Warren and James Warren. Among Copley's achievements was to bring art in Boston beyond a mere imitation of European styles to a highly creative development of that tradition, which in paintings like the remarkable portrait of Samuel Adams (ca. 1770; Museum of Fine Arts, on deposit from the City of Boston), are no less sophisticated for their dramatic emotional power.

In 1774, intending to fulfill his ambition to become a history painter and to match his talent against that of English masters, Copley left Boston for Europe, visiting Italy and France before settling in England. He was the first of a long line of Boston artists to seek artistic education in Europe. His departure coincided with the out-

break of the Revolution, and also marked the beginning of a period during which Boston was noticeably less hospitable to the fine arts.[12] The half-dozen painters working in Boston during the 1780s and '90s were not innovators for the most part, but continued in Copley's manner. Some of them, such as John Johnston, were forced to supplement their incomes as portrait painters with other work; opportunists like Mather Brown left, leaving the field to less sophisticated painters, including Christian Gullagher and John M. Furness.

It was during this period and the early years of the nineteenth century that concerns about art were first articulated. John Adams was one of many who debated the value of art in American society; his often quoted question, "Are we not in too great a hurry in our zeal for the fine arts?" stemmed from the fear that art, associated in Adams's mind with luxury and the aristocracy, would corrupt the young republic. For thirty years after the Revolution, the legitimization of the arts and the determination of their role in contemporary society would be a complex problem for Bostonians. Collectors on a large scale were almost nonexistent at this time; private patronage continued, but with hesitation, for many feared with Adams that "from the dawn of history, they [the arts] have been prostituted to the service of superstition and despotism."[13]

The major exception to the decline in private patronage after the Revolution was James Bowdoin III. The Bowdoin family, who were merchants, diplomats, and land speculators, had been important patrons of the arts in the colonial era. James Bowdoin II had been painted by Smibert in 1735, and by Feke and Christian Gullagher; Bowdoin III had been painted as a child by Joseph Blackburn, and later by Edward Malbone and Gilbert Stuart, as were other members of the family. The family tradition continued well into the nineteenth century: in 1861, Mrs. Robert C. Winthrop, Jr., a collateral descendant of Bowdoin, was painted by William Morris Hunt (see cat. no. 42). However, the portraits by local artists appear as a minor aspect of a much more ambitious collection of European art, sought not as a family record but for its own sake. James Bowdoin III was America's first major collector of paintings, and his collecting established a pattern continued by the most prominent of Boston's collectors in the nineteenth century. The first objects he acquired were, ". . . some pieces of statuary for my Hall," and were, like Hancock's and Winslow's purchases two generations before, regarded as furnishings. But gradually he became interested in old master paintings and, while on diplomatic missions in France and Spain, began to buy copies of Van Dycks, Raphaels, and Poussins. Bowdoin's most exceptional purchases were drawings rather than paintings, and the Bowdoin College Art Museum, to which he gave his name, has, among other masterworks, a rare drawing by the sixteenth-century Flemish artist Peter Brueghel (*Mountain Landscape "Waltersspurg"*) as his legacy.[14]

In addition to Bowdoin's fairly isolated activity as a private collector, there was, at the turn of the century, a series of public commissions, as well as the development of public institutions for viewing works of art. In 1789, Bostonians celebrated the arrival of President Washington in their city by holding a grand procession, leading to ceremonies conducted beneath a huge triumphal arch at the State House. Copley would have been dismayed at the position of artists in the procession—and indeed their status had declined since his departure—for they marched after the Marine Society at the end of the procession, along with artisans, tradesmen, and manufacturers.[15]

Two years later, the Columbian Museum was founded on State Street. It was the first of several similar institutions in Boston that, like the Peale Museum in Philadelphia, was designed to display "a very extensive collection of artificial and natural curiosities," including a mammoth's skeleton, "elegant birds, in glass cases, preserved natural as the life," views of the East Indies, portraits of royalty, wax figures of historical personages (including, no doubt to his great chagrin, "John Adams surrounded by liberty and justice") and "a large and elegant collection of historical paintings," including Copley's portrait of John Hancock. Music was provided every evening on the concert organ and the price of admission was only fifty cents, a season ticket being five dollars.[16]

The proprietor of this miscellany was Daniel Bowen, an indefatigable entrepreneur whose operation survived two fires and competition from several similar institutions (including the Washington Museum, founded in 1803, which, like its namesake in Philadelphia, attempted to appeal to Boston's intellectual elite by showing wax figures of Shakespearean characters, and to the politically minded with "historical celebrations" of important Revolutionary war events). Bowen's museum remained until 1825, when it was absorbed by Ethan Allen Greenwood's New England Museum, one of two places in Boston where members of the general public could see paintings.

Pictures sent on tour and the generally popular panoramas were usually displayed in places such as Faneuil Hall on the waterfront, and later at Horticultural Hall, then on School Street. In 1815, Bostonians willing to pay twenty-five cents could see views of the battles of Champlain and Plattsburgh by Michel Felice Corné, and *The Landing of the Fathers of New England at Plymouth* by the popular local artist Henry Sargent. John Trumbull's *Declaration of Independence* was shown at Faneuil Hall three years later, and in 1829 Rembrandt Peale's great allegorical picture *The Court of Death* (now in the Detroit Institute of Arts) was on view in Boston. Touring tableaus such as these were extremely profitable and popular, especially if the pictures were large, had many figures (guides identifying the persons represented were usually provided at the exhibition hall), and depicted subjects from American history; these paintings furthermore exposed Bosto-

ROBERT SALMON
The British Fleet Forming a Line off Algiers, 1829

Robert Salmon, New England's
first professional marine
painter, came to Boston from
England in 1828. The next year,
he painted five huge (99 x 190
in.) panoramic canvases, including this view of the British
fleet, which were intended as
"drop scens." Semi-transparent

and lit from behind, these
paintings were the backdrop
for moving figures and changing light effects, a form of
entertainment which delighted
Bostonians in the 1820s.
(Museum of Fine Arts, Boston.
Bequest of Mary Lee Ware.)

nians to pictorial genres other than portraiture, and
kept them abreast of recent artistic developments in
other cities.

The vogue for touring pictures peaked in the 1840s,
when topographical panoramas replaced religious and
historical works in the exhibition halls. Robert Salmon
was one of the first to display such subjects, showing
*Boston Harbor from Mr. Greene's House, Pemberton
Hill* (now owned by the Society for the Preservation of
New England Antiquities) in the rotunda at Quincy
Market in 1829; the picture is about eight feet high and
fifteen feet long. The most spectacular of these paintings was shown in Boston in the mid-1840s: John Ban-
vard's *Moving Panorama of the Mississippi River*,
which he claimed was three miles long. The *Moving
Panorama* was displayed by means of a hand-cranked

apparatus that drew the canvas across the stage from
one mammoth reel to another; it took two hours to
pass before the audience.[17] One suspects that Bowen's
museum and the touring pictures provided as much
entertainment as edification for Bostonians and that
curiosity, rather than a desire for culture, accounted
for the huge attendance at these institutions.

At the same time, a different group of Bostonians
was gathering to form an organization of higher cultural aspirations. Dedicated to "the Improvement of
Taste and the Encouragement of Genius," the Anthology Society was founded in 1805 by eminent Bostonians such as the Reverend William Emerson, the
essayist's father, and William Tudor, Jr., a prominent
merchant and diplomat who would become Boston's
leading apologist for the fine arts. The society's activity
was centered around its literary magazine, the *Monthly
Anthology and Boston Review,* which was exchanged
for literary periodicals from other American cities as
well as from England and France, in hopes of fostering
scholarly communication. To further its goal of intellectual improvement, the Anthology Society also made
plans for a library with a reading room, an art gallery,
and a lecture hall; this organization, financed by large
bequests from private citizens, became the Boston
Athenaeum in 1807.[18]

With a charter based on that of the Anthology Society, the Athenaeum was similarly dedicated to the exchange of current ideas in literature and the fine arts. Its primary interest was literary and to that end, specific plans were made for the library and reading room; however, the charter also provided for "a Museum or Cabinet, which shall contain specimens from the three kingdoms of nature, scientifically arranged; natural and artificial curiosities, antiques, coins, medals, vases, gems, and intaglios; also, in the same or a different apartment, a Repository of Arts, in which shall be placed for inspection models of new and useful machines; likewise drawings, designs, paintings, engravings, statues, and other objects of the fine arts, and especially the productions of our native artists."[19]

If it had come into existence in that form, the Athenaeum's gallery would have resembled Bowen's museum or the Peale Museum in its combined display of the fine arts and "natural and artificial curiosities." There was, however little impetus for the formation of an art gallery in 1807, and in fact it would be twenty years before pictures and statuary were displayed to the public at the Athenaeum. That the Athenaeum ever included a picture gallery at all, and that it developed one in which works of art were meant as expressions of artistic personality, rather than as curiosities, was due to the efforts of two men: Thomas Handasyd Perkins, Boston's greatest collector after James Bowdoin III, and William Tudor, Jr., not a collector himself, but an eloquent defender of the fine arts.

To the charges frequently leveled against the fine arts—that they tended to corrupt society, that America's wealth was not sufficient to permit collecting, and that neither the level of taste nor of artistic production was high enough to merit the support of the arts—William Tudor responded in 1816 with arguments for establishing an institution of the fine arts.[20] The arts, he suggested, "purify, adorn, and elevate every country where they are cherished," and their cultivation would discourage corruption and the decline of society. He proposed the development of an institution that would be educational and self-perpetuating, containing casts of the statuary in the Louvre that artists would be free to study and copy and so improve their skill; the institution should also arrange annual exhibitions of the works of American artists, which would educate the public. The receipts from admission to the exhibition, suggested Tudor, should be used to purchase from the exhibition works by living artists for the permanent collection of the institution, thus encouraging, in a democratic manner, the production of native art.

To form such an institution, Tudor solicited money from wealthy private citizens like Harrison Gray Otis, to whom he presented another argument in favor of the support of the fine arts: the arts were, in his view, protection against the decline of civilization generally but also against Boston's decline in the face of the increased population and economic prosperity of cities like New York and Philadelphia, where art institutions (the American Academy and the Pennsylvania Academy of the Fine Arts) were already in existence: "The object here contemplated may, with a bold effort, go at once beyond them [New York and Philadelphia], and will produce permanent advantages. If we can make ourselves the capitol of the arts and sciences, and we have already so many powerful institutions that we may do it, our town will increase in that sort of society that is principally to be desired."[21] Although Tudor was unable to raise the $30,000 needed for the establishment of such an institution, his plan would be adopted by the Athenaeum for its Gallery of Fine Arts some ten years later; the men whose support he won—men like Isaac P. Davis, Theodore Lyman, Charles Codman, and T. H. Perkins—would become important collectors and patrons of the Athenaeum in succeeding decades.

The first step toward the realization of Tudor's goal came in 1823, when Augustus Thorndike presented the Boston Athenaeum with casts of eleven classical sculptures. By that time, the Athenaeum owned seven paintings, including two portraits by Gilbert Stuart, a copy of his portrait of Washington by Jonathan Mason, and *The Meeting of Rebecca and Abraham's Servant by Titian,* (then believed to be by Murillo). These paintings were acquired more for their historic than for their aesthetic value, a characteristic of the Athenaeum's early attitudes toward collecting, especially apparent in its acquisition of so many casts and old master copies in the 1830s and '40s. The year before Thorndike's gift, the Athenaeum moved from its original quarters on Tremont Street to a property on Pearl Street donated by James Perkins, one of the original proprietors of the Athenaeum (and brother of T. H. Perkins) whose major interest was the library. With the relocation of the Athenaeum, Pearl Street became the center for the arts in Boston: Washington Allston and Rembrandt Peale both had studios there, and Chester Harding's was close by.

In 1823, Thomas Handasyd Perkins contributed $8,000 for an addition to the Pearl Street building, which was to house a meeting room, a lecture hall, and, on the third floor, an art gallery. With Perkins's

WASHINGTON ALLSTON
Belshazzar's Feast, begun 1817

Allston labored for over twenty-five years on this enormous canvas. In the 1820s, a group of prominent Bostonians pledged $10,000 to encourage Allston to complete it, but the painting remained unfinished, and in ruinous condition, at his death in 1843. Nonetheless, its impressive scale and dramatic Biblical subject insured its continuing popularity: it was shown annually at the Athenaeum between 1845 and 1872, and was the centerpiece of the memorial exhibition of Allston's works held at the Museum of Fine Arts in 1881. (Detroit Institute of Arts. Gift of the Allston Trust.)

domination of the Athenaeum's building committee, the future of that institution's commitment to the fine arts was assured. Like William Tudor, Perkins was eager for the Athenaeum to arrange public exhibitions of works of art, and to sponsor a *de facto* academy for young artists by providing them with opportunities to study and copy casts and other works on display. He advocated exhibitions of both old master paintings and the works of living artists, and formed his own collection according to the same principles.

Thomas Perkins's interest in art can be traced back to 1805, when he began buying ornaments ("1 statue of Flora, 1 statue of Minerva, and two pedestals for the statues") as furnishings for his Pearl Street home. He was a shrewd Yankee businessman, and saw no particular value in original works of art when less money could buy "fine Copies of the best Old Paintings," by names that educated Bostonians would recognize. Perkins seems not to have had great interest in the sensuous aspect of his objects, but rather was concerned with their decorative and educational value. But he was nonetheless well known as a patron of local artists, "kindly aiding some who desired to improve by studying the great models in Europe, and liberally purchasing the works of those who deserved encouragement."[22] Among the Boston artists whose works he purchased were Gilbert Stuart, who painted Perkins's portrait about 1805, the landscape painter Alvan Fisher, and Robert Salmon, who painted several pictures for Perkins in the 1830s.[23] Perkins also owned three works by Washington Allston: a watercolor (now lost) of the ship *Galen*, on which Perkins and Allston returned together from Europe in 1819; the satiric composition *Poor Author and Rich Bookseller*, painted in 1811 (Museum of Fine Arts); and the dramatic *Saul and the Witch of Endor* (Amherst College, Mead Art Museum), which Perkins commissioned in 1820.

Perkin's devotion to the arts in Boston is also indicated by his participation, along with several other proprietors of the Athenaeum, in the subscription for Allston's *Belshazzar's Feast*. In 1826, to ease financial pressures on Boston's most revered artist, the proprietors of the Athenaeum offered Allston studio space in its Pearl Street building. The next year, sixteen members of Boston's economic and cultural elite advanced $10,000 to Allston for *Belshazzar's Feast*, the artist's masterwork and albatross, to be delivered when finished. They included James and Thomas Perkins, Isaac P. Davis, a prosperous ropemaker who was a close friend of Gilbert Stuart's, and who was credited by his contemporaries as being "one of the leading connoisseurs of works of art in Boston;"[24] George Ticknor, professor of literature at Harvard; and Samuel Appleton, a shipping magnate who was related by marriage to Henry Wadsworth Longfellow. It was hoped that the subscription would encourage Allston to complete *Belshazzar's Feast*, a grand allegorical painting in the manner of John Martin and Benjamin West; he had been working on it for ten years and, unable to satisfy himself with the composition, was always seeking the advice of others, rubbing out, changing, and repainting according to their (often contradictory) promptings. Pressure on Allston to complete *Belshazzar's Feast* increased through the 1830s, for it was believed that this grand moral picture could serve as the final legitimization of the arts to Boston's skeptics; as one of the first great history paintings produced in America, it would be a credit to Boston and a stirring demonstration of what American culture could sponsor.

Despite the efforts of Allston's friends and supporters, *Belshazzar's Feast* remained unfinished at Allston's death in 1843. It was first shown to the public in a rented hall in 1844 and thereafter almost annually at the Athenaeum. The shock of the spectators at viewing the ruin that the picture had become was poignantly expressed by Richard Henry Dana, who witnessed the unveiling of the picture in Allston's studio the day after the artist's funeral: "It was indeed a most solemn tragedy. . . . We felt that this had killed him. Over this he had worn out his enfeebled frame and his paralyzed spirit, until he had sunk under it. . . . Covered as the picture was with dirt and chalk marks, and with the king painted out, without cleaning, varnish or frame, the proprietors . . . would not understand or value the picture, and it would be vain and an injustice to Mr. Allston's reputation to subject it to such a test."[25]

But Allston's reputation in Boston was not diminished by the failure of *Belshazzar's Feast*. Instead he became a legend and a symbol of Boston's cultural hegemony. He had been beloved by his fellow artists, and served as a model and adviser to the younger generation of artists, who, like Benjamin Champney, followed his counsel concerning the benefits of a long period of study in Europe, and would remain faithful to his memory: "I have not had cause to change my opinion formed many years ago that up to the present time no American artist has equalled Allston in all the qualities that go to make a great painter."[26]

Allston was honored both for his mastery of color (in which he was compared to Titian) and for his dignity and gentility; many Bostonians would claim, with Julia Ward Howe, who met him as a young girl: "his living image takes precedence in my mind of [sic] all the shadowy shapes which his magic placed on canvas."[27] Allston's gentlemanly manner attained for the American artist the status Copley had longed for; he presented a new image of the artistic personality. No longer a mere artisan, the artist was seen as a romantic figure who served as a moral arbiter and suffered nobly for his art.

Allston provided local collectors with opportunities to buy pictures more interesting than the portraits and modest landscapes that were their normal fare. His religious and historical subjects were believed equal to European old masters, and Bostonians bought them in great numbers. The subscribers to *Belshazzar's Feast* were, not unexpectedly, his most loyal patrons: George Ticknor owned *The Valentine* (1809–1811; private collection), one of Allston's first images of contemplative young women; Isaac P. Davis owned the *Head of St. Peter*, a study for the *Angel Releasing St. Peter from Prison* (1814–1816; Museum of Fine Arts, Boston); Loammi Baldwin owned his early Italian landscape *Diana and the Nymphs in the Chase* (1805; Fogg Art Museum), a drawing, *Polyphemus Immediately after his Eye was Put Out* (now lost), his portrait, never finished (Fogg Art Museum), and the delightful fantasy *Flight of Florimell* (1819; Detroit Institute of Arts). Allston's presence in Boston also stimulated the patronage of local artists, who, after his model, began to be seen as a precious resource.

Finally, Allston satisfied Boston's longing for a tie with European culture. He had spent his formative years in Europe, and was intimately connected with the circle of young romantic artists in Rome at the turn of the century. Following his example, several generations of Boston painters and especially sculptors sought their artistic education in Rome; equally important was the exposure to contemporary trends in European painting that Allston provided Boston through his own works in the new romantic style.

Allston's deficiencies as a painter, glossed over by his contemporaries, were acknowledged by later critics like William Howe Downes, who suggested that his imagination was more literary than pictorial, and that his ideas ran ahead of his painterly ability.[28] These failings were attributed to a variety of causes—his melancholy, so paralyzing at the end of his life, ran counter to the Emersonian optimism that held sway in Boston at that time; his energy was drained by the many hours spent socializing with his friends in his Cambridgeport studios (a temptation to which many Boston artists fell prey)—nonetheless, Allston's reputation as Boston's "artistic lion" continued through the nineteenth century.

Although Allston was admired by artistic and intellectual circles in Boston from 1808, when he first returned from Europe (he would return to England in 1811 and remain there until 1818, settling permanently in Boston thereafter), it was not until the Boston Athenaeum opened its paintings gallery in May 1827 that the public had a chance to see his work. The exhibition consisted of 319 paintings, including miniatures, chosen by a committee headed by T. H. Perkins. The works were borrowed from local collectors and artists' studios, and many were offered for sale. Allston was represented in the exhibition by twelve paintings, including *Saul and the Witch of Endor*, lent by Perkins, and *Rising of a Thunderstorm at Sea*, lent by the painter Jonathan Mason (now in the Museum of Fine Arts). But the place of honor was given to Boston's other major painter, Gilbert Stuart, who showed eighteen pictures, including the monumental *Washington at Dorchester Heights*, presented to the City of Boston by Samuel Parkman in 1806 (now on deposit at the Museum of Fine Arts), and the five famed "Presidential Portraits," commissioned by the local framemaker John Doggett (formerly Coolidge family; now National Gallery of Art, Washington).

Many other local artists were represented at the Athenaeum's first exhibition; there were a fair number of landscapes hung among the portraits and historical pictures, including paintings by Thomas Doughty and Alvan Fisher, and two by Thomas Cole, *Col. D. Boone —the First Settler in Kentucky* (Amherst College, Mead Art Museum), and a landscape. Cole was one of very few non-Bostonians represented in the "living artists" section of the show; despite Boston's continued preference for local artists through the nineteenth century, Cole would always be admired.

The rest of the exhibition was devoted to "old masters," featuring the perennially popular, if spurious Ruysdaels, Van Mierises, Poussins, and Murillos (the *North American Review* alledged that of the 165 "old masters," less than 100 were genuine, and that estimation may have been generous); also included in the old master section were paintings by Copley and Benjamin West, the only American artists so honored, as well as works ascribed to Angelica Kauffman and Jean-Baptiste Greuze, a surprising indication of Boston's awareness of relatively recent European art.

To the Athenaeum's proprietors the success of the exhibition was a gratifying demonstration of Boston's enthusiasm for the fine arts. The attendance was high: twenty-five cents bought a single admission, fifty cents a season ticket, and, although actual attendance was not counted, revenues of about $4,000 suggest that as many as 10,000 people may have seen the show, a remarkable figure considering that Boston's population was only about 50,000 in the 1820s. With the revenues from admissions, the Athenaeum purchased works of art for its own collection, paintings such as Benjamin West's *King Lear*, which was acquired at auction in New York for $600 in 1828, and John Neagle's *Pat Lyon at the Forge*, the most popular painting in the exhibition of 1828 (both now in the collection of the Museum of Fine Arts).

The popularity of the 1827 Athenaeum exhibition is all the more remarkable considering the number of rival attractions visited by Boston's growing art-loving public. The New England Museum, founded in 1818 by the artist-entrepreneur Ethan Allen Greenwood, had absorbed the Columbian Museum in 1825; the combined collections were shown in eleven rooms on Court Street. Among stuffed birds, Indian and Asian curiosities, wax figures of the Incas of Peru, and other exotica, there were also works of art: "a marble statue of Venus by Canova, and various other full-length statues." Hanging in the entrance hall was Rembrandt Peale's *Roman Daughter in Prison*.[29] Peale was, after Allston, the most popular history painter in Boston. Although much of his life was spent painting portraits in Philadelphia, his birthplace, he established a studio in Boston in the 1820s (at "Mrs. Trott's" on Pearl Street), and frequently exhibited pictures there. Local patrons continued to prefer Stuart or Chester Harding for their portraits, but admired Peale's history paintings, which were large, dramatic (if not well executed), and pre-

sented moral themes always of interest in Boston. The popular *Washington at Yorktown Heights* attracted over 250 visitors a day in 1827.

In addition to Peale's *Washington,* Bostonians in 1827 had the opportunity to see a picture of another of their favorite heroes: J.-L. David's mammoth *Coronation of Napoleon* (a replica of the painting at the Louvre; this version from the Musée de Versailles) was on view at Faneuil Hall. The painting was guaranteed to appeal to those with a love of the sensational—at 750 square feet, it was claimed to be the largest picture ever painted—and to those with an interest in history, for as was customary with such multifigured pictures, a brochure distributed at the exhibition hall identified each participant. Contributing to the popularity of the picture was the fact that David was a name most cultured Bostonians recognized; the painting was one of a surprising number of relatively contemporary European paintings that were exhibited in Boston in the first third of the nineteenth century. François Marius

Granet's *Choir of the Capuchin Church in Rome,* one of some fifteen versions of the subject the artist painted in Italy, was in Boston between 1815 and 1820;[30] local collectors, inspired by the exhibition of works such as these, began to acquire contemporary European paintings, of which one of the most interesting is the Norwegian painter Johan Christian Clausen Dahl's *View of Dresden,* a rare example of Northern Romantic painting in America in the early nineteenth century, which S. A. Eliot lent to the Athenaeum exhibition in 1828. It was Washington Allston who instilled in Boston a taste for paintings such as these, for he knew Granet and other European romantics in Rome. Both the Athenaeum shows and the exhibitions held elsewhere enriched the general public's awareness of contemporary European art and, not surprisingly, local artists such as Henry Sargent were quick to apply the lessons found in such pictures to their own compositions.

With the inauguration of annual exhibitions at the Athenaeum, and the expansion of the collection of plaster casts culminating in the opening of a sculpture gallery in 1839, William Tudor's desire for an institution that would both preserve and promote the fine arts was fulfilled. A review of the third annual exhibition at the Athenaeum, appearing in the *North American Review* in July 1829, spoke with pride of Boston's showing in the fine arts, and of the positive influence of the exhibition:

> It was hardly anticipated that so large and good a collection could be made, for the third time, without the repetition of a single picture, and with so little aid from other places. . . . We take pleasure in saying, too, that the great merit of the collection is to be found in the works of all native artists. . . . Another pleasing fact is, the obvious improvement of those artists who have heretofore exhibited their works at the Athenaeum. They have all felt the influence of the exhibition. We think we perceive, too, in the increased number of those who visit the gallery, an indisputable evidence of the growth of a taste in the community, for the beautiful art which is there exhibited.[31]

In its early years the Athenaeum was as much a commercial gallery as a museum; its picture gallery was used for a variety of functions. In October 1827, John Vanderlyn, much encouraged by the successful Boston tours of his *Ariadne Asleep on the Isle of Naxos* (Pennsylvania Academy of the Fine Arts) and *Marius amid the Ruins of Carthage* (Fine Arts Museums of San Francisco) the year before, had rented the Athenaeum

gallery to display his *Panorama of the Palace and Gardens of Versailles* (Metropolitan Museum of Art, New York), but the exhibition was received so unfavorably that no rent was charged. Thomas Jefferson's collection, which would be sold at auction in Boston in the 1830s, was appended to the annual exhibition of 1828. Like the rest of the show, it contained the usual group of over-attributed old masters, including a portrait of Benjamin Franklin then attributed to Greuze but now called Duplessis (which the Athenaeum purchased), and a few American works, including Benjamin West's *Parting of Hector and Andromache* (probably the painting now at the New-York Historical Society).

In 1829, the Athenaeum's picture gallery was rented to Signor Antonio Sarti of Florence, who exhibited and offered for sale a collection of Italian old masters. Sarti's was one of many shows of European paintings held during those years; although in this case Bostonians were suspicious of the pictures and buyers were few, the weekly sales at J. L. Cunningham's Auction House (later the Corinthian Hall Galleries) at Federal and Milk Streets found many customers. The most popular pictures at such sales were romantic landscapes, especially those purported to be by Claude; Murillos were equally sought after. These buyers were not particularly concerned with originality; the Boston landscape painter George Loring ("Claude") Brown financed a trip to Europe in 1839 through commissions for copies of Claude's paintings. Bostonians' indifference to authenticity, and the huge demand for old master pictures, led to the sale of a great number of

(19) VENERATION

DAVID CLAYPOOL JOHNSTON
"Veneration," *Scraps,* 1837

The collecting boom of the 1830s and '40s led to a proliferation of fakes, forgeries, and over-attributed pictures on the Boston art market. Johnston made a series of engravings satirizing both the unscrupulous sellers and the self-styled connoisseurs; at the same time, the *Boston Evening Transcript,* tongue in cheek, suggested to its readers how to act like a connoisseur: "Wait till you hear the name of the painter. If its Rubens or any of them old boys, praise, for its agin the law to doubt them." (Museum of Fine Arts, Boston. Bequest of Sylvester Rosa Koehler.)

fraudulent paintings in Boston. This problem, recognized by the press, prompted David Claypool Johnson to publish a series of prints satirizing connoisseurs who, in *Veneration* (1837) admired what they variously claim to be a Claude, a Snyders, and Titian, and a Michelangelo: "nobody ever painted flowers like him, this is undoubtedly his *chef d'oeuvre*."

Cunningham's also held auctions of local artists' works; however, these sales were seldom very profitable to the artist. Robert Salmon's pictures, frequently sold at auction in the 1830s, brought only $10 to $15 apiece. Although Salmon and others preferred to work on commission from local patrons (Perkins paid Salmon $35 per picture), most artists, with the exception of the portraitists, were dependent on auctioneers and on mirror- and framemakers such as John Doggett, and on sign makers such as J. S. Cloutman of Washington Street, who also sold landscapes and marine views by local artists.[32]

Although the Athenaeum occasionally made efforts to assist local artists (as it did in 1828, when Isaac P. Davis organized an exhibition of Gilbert Stuart's works for the benefit of Stuart's widow), it was not a particularly advantageous place for a young painter to show his pictures. There was some prestige attached to being included in the exhibitions, but artists were forced to exhibit under unfortunate financial circumstances: admission proceeds went to the Athenaeum's purchase fund, rather than to the artists themselves. Nor were works selected by a committee that included artists, but rather by men like T. H. Perkins, who was more interested in old masters than in contemporary painters.

As early as 1828, dissatisfaction with the Athenaeum's system led artists to seek an alternative for exhibition of their works. That year the New England Association of Artists was formed under the leadership of the portrait painter Henry Cheever Pratt, and exhibitions of local work were held throughout the 1820s. Although the organization, composed for the most part of young artists not yet influential in Boston's cultural community, was unable to gather a great deal of support, it provided a precedent for the expression of dissent that led in 1842 to the formation of the Boston Artists' Association, which did achieve some independence from the Athenaeum.

Most of Boston's major painters, including Allston and Henry Sargent, were charter members of the Boston Artists' Association. The key figure was Chester Harding, whose gallery on School Street was the focal point of the organization's activities. Despite his cruder style, Harding had, by the 1830s, inherited Stuart's

mantle as Boston's most sought-after portrait painter. His gruff, backwoods manner was admired in England in the 1820s, and when he returned "Harding fever" swept Boston. One of his first Boston patrons was Abbott Lawrence, a leading textile manufacturer, who around 1830 financed the purchase of the School Street building that became Harding's Gallery. Exhibitions there were primarily of European pictures, notably two by Claude Marie Dubufe, *The Temptation of Adam and Eve* and the *Expulsion from Paradise* in 1834. Despite the catalogue's assurances that Dubufe's life-sized nudes were "perfectly chaste and beautiful in conception," and in fact redeemed by the moral subject matter of the pictures, they created something of a sensation in Boston. More acceptable to local audiences were copies "from celebrated pictures in various public galleries . . . made . . . with a strict regard to the style of each master," and the "modern European pictures" shown there in 1841, which, in addition to the usual Dutch and Italian masters, included works by Edwin Landseer, Thomas Lawrence, the marine painter Clarkson Stansfield, and other modern British painters.

At the same time, Harding was giving gallery space to American artists. In 1834, he held the first exhibition in Boston devoted exclusively to the works of local artists, and included paintings by Thomas Doughty, Alvan Fisher, Frances Alexander, G. P. A. Healy, Harding himself, and others. Some of the works were privately owned, but most were submitted by the artists and offered for sale. In 1839, forty-five of Allston's paintings were shown there, all of them from private collectors or other institutions, including the rival Athenaeum and the Pennsylvania Academy of the Fine Arts, which lent *The Dead Man Restored to Life*. Bostonians were pleased to have at last the opportunity to witness "the genius of a man whom it prates much, but knows little."[33] The exhibition, the first in America devoted to the life's work of a contemporary artist and the first of major significance in Boston to be held outside the auspices of the Athenaeum, lent support to the cause of local artists eager for recognition outside that institution.

The Boston Artists' Association, which grew out of the exhibitions at Harding's Gallery within a decade, was led by Allston, who served as the first president, and Henry Sargent as vice-president; Francis Alexander, Chester Harding, William Wetmore Story, and Fitz Hugh Lane were among the other founding members. The sole requisite for joining was professional status; however, a few patrons such as Thomas Gold Appleton, an amateur painter himself, were included as honorary members. The Association pledged to "seek

THOMAS CRAWFORD
Orpheus, 1843

When Crawford sent *Orpheus* to Boston from his studio in Rome in 1844, the sculpture arrived broken in several places. A local sculptor, Henry Dexter, was able to repair it, however, and *Orpheus* was shown at a special exhibition at the Athenaeum, where it elicited much chauvinistic praise: "It excells all the sculpture in America, and tweaks antiquity itself by the nose." (Museum of Fine Arts, Boston. Gift of Mr. and Mrs. Cornelius C. Vermeule III.)

the advancement of the Arts alone, for the Arts' sake" by providing "a systematic course of study for . . . [the] successful cultivation [of art];" and by seeking "the advantage to be derived from mutual cooperation and support."[34] The commitment to education, a theme that would recur in the bylaws of many of Boston's artistic institutions during the nineteenth century, met a serious need, for until this time the only training available to aspiring artists in Boston was that acquired through copying casts at the Athenaeum, the advice dispensed by Gilbert Stuart in his studio, and the lessons provided at drawing schools such as David Brown's, which flourished in Boston in the 1820s. The Association provided live models and later a drawing master; it also provided a forum for the exchange of ideas and techniques among the artists themselves.

An important indication that artists in Boston were attemping to improve their status was the standard of professionalism the Association insisted upon: the designation of a committee of artists, not patrons, to choose and arrange annual exhibitions, and the provision specifying that artists, not the organization, receive the profits from these exhibitions. Inspired in part by Allston's influence in Boston's cultural community, and by his example as a romantic figure, painters and sculptors were increasingly aware of themselves as people with special sensitivities and, as such, demanded to determine the standards and settings by which their work would be judged—demanded, in other words, independence from the patronizing Athenaeum system. Although the Association would exist as a separate exhibiting organization for only three years (it would join forces with the Athenaeum in 1845, for the competition was hurting them both), it made clear the need for alternative opportunities for exhibitions in Boston, and it would not be the last artists' organization to be formed in Boston to challenge mainstream taste.

The prevailing tastemakers in Boston in the 1840s and '50s, insofar as they were enthusiastic about American art at all, were enthusiastic about sculpture. The opening of the sculpture gallery at the Athenaeum in 1839 encouraged aspiring sculptors and mature masters alike, giving them a place to see and display statuary. In the 1840s, the Athenaeum embarked on a campaign to buy statuary, acquiring Hiram Powers's bust of Daniel Webster in 1841 for $500, and Horatio Greenough's *Venus Victrix* in 1842; these original works were placed in the sculpture gallery beside casts of such works as Michaelangelo's *Day* and *Night,* which T. H. Perkins had given the Athenaeum in 1834.

A series of exhibitions of sculpture held at the Athenaeum included, in 1844, a group of works by Thomas Crawford. This first one-man show by a native sculptor was sponsored by Charles Sumner, the distinguished jurist (later a senator), who arranged for a new gallery for the exhibition to be built adjacent to the Athenaeum's building on Pearl Street. Sumner was a minor collector of American paintings—he owned works by Allston, C. R. Leslie, and other American romantics—and, as was typical of his time, had assembled a large group of fraudulent and over-attributed European pictures. His most important contribution to the arts in Boston was his support of Crawford, and particularly his urging the Athenaeum to purchase Crawford's *Orpheus* (now in the Museum of Fine Arts), the centerpiece of the exhibition. The acquisition of the statue (for $500) did much to enhance Boston's reputation as a discerning cultural influence, for it was viewed as a major commitment to collecting original works of art and to supporting American artists.

In June of 1848, Hiram Powers's *Greek Slave* was shown in Horticultural Hall in Boston, after a successful exhibition in New York City. As with Dubufe's paintings fourteen years before, Powers's famous nude statue provoked charges of lasciviousness, but prompted by a catalogue accompanying the statue, Bostonians were appeased by the "edifying" qualities of the work and began to think of themselves as more sophisticated in the fine arts: "Every sensitive and ingenious art lover recognized high and pure ideal, which gives significance and vitality to the graceful form."[35] Thereafter, sculptors encountered less resistance to the exhibition of nude statues in Boston: Edward A. Brackett's erotic *Shipwrecked Mother and Child* (now in the Worcester Art Museum), first shown at the Athenaeum in 1852, was exhibited almost annually to great acclaim in the 1850s and '60s, and was praised by sculptor Horatio Greenough for its expression of "the decency and dignity of womanhood," although he wondered why spectators crowded so close to the sculpture to see it.[36] (Paintings of nudes did not fare as well in Boston, especially when no overriding moral content could be claimed for them. In 1859, William Page's *Venus,* now lost, brought from Italy by Charles Eliot Norton and a few other progressive art enthusiasts, so shocked the Boston public when shown at the Athenaeum that it was removed from exhibition only a few weeks after going on view).

Many of the sculptors admired in Boston were born locally but, like Greenough, followed Washington Allston's example and sought their artistic education in Italy, where marble and studio assistants were cheap, where examples of classical statuary were plentiful in the original, and where a sculptor could work in the aura of great masters such as Bertel Thorvaldsen. Thomas Crawford, who spent most of his working life in Rome, argued optimistically that European art was merely a stepping stone and that American art was nearly ready to overtake its old-world model.[37] But William Wetmore Story, another Boston-born sculptor, had conflicting feelings about America's receptivity to the arts and about the potential of art's flourishing there. At age twenty-six and without any formal training as a sculptor, he was awarded the commission for a monument to his father, Judge Story, erected in Mount Auburn Cemetery in Cambridge; despite this early support, he would later claim that Boston was an inhospitable place for an artist. Rome, in contrast, provided him with education and liberation, as he poignantly wrote Henry Jarvis: "I hate the more to leave Rome . . . How shall I ever again endure the restraint and bondage of Boston."[38] Yet in 1844, full of nationalist zeal, he argued for the need of American artists to be independent of Europe: "An American art would never be born of seeds sown in foreign soil."[39]

The idea of cultural independence had been proposed in 1837 by Ralph Waldo Emerson, who argued that such independence was necessary for great achievement: "We have listened too long to the courtly muses of Europe."[40] Underlying this desire for intellectual and artistic distance from Europe was a suspicion, lingering from John Adams, of the pictorial art forms born of subconscious creative impulses under the influence of "decadent" cultures. Art, Emerson pointed out in 1841, "has . . . its highest value as history"; its role is "to educate the perception of beauty." He valued the artist's moral insights rather than his aesthetic concerns, and believed that true artistic creation was not a special gift, but was present in every man: "When I came at last to Rome and saw with [my own] eyes the pictures, I found that . . . it [artistic genius] was familiar and sincere; that it was the old eternal fact I had met already in so many forms; . . . that it was the plain *you and me* I knew so well."[41]

Nathaniel Hawthorne had a darker sense of the visual arts, not even viewing them as an intermediary to higher perceptions, as Emerson did, but rather suggesting that creative passion led to destruction and disaster—a theme that Henry James would repeat seventeen years later in *Roderick Hudson*. In *The Marble Faun* (1859), which concerns a group of American artists in Rome, Hawthorne portrayed the Italian setting as decadent and corrupting, and the artist as at odds with nature: "The love of art differs widely in its influence from the love of nature; whereas, if art had not strayed away from its legitimate paths and aims, it ought to soften and sweeten the lives of its worshippers in even a more exquisite degree than the contemplation of natural objects. But, of its own potency, it has no such effect . . . It cannot comfort the heart in affection; it grows dim when the shadow is upon us."[42]

Neither Emerson nor Hawthorne perceived any spiritual connection between himself as an author and any painter or sculptor. Unlike New York City, where writers and artists were intimately associated and provided mutual support, writers in Boston kept artists at a distance and were, especially in the 1840s, uncomprehending of the artists' need to immerse themselves in European culture.[43] The greatest support for Boston artists, ironically, came from a group of collectors, themselves amateur artists, whose taste men like Story deplored but who, by virtue of their travels in Europe, would sometimes develop a sophistication surpassing that of the painters they patronized.

Among the most interesting of this group of upper-class Bostonians who began collecting in the 1830s and '40s was Thomas Gold Appleton, the dilettante son of the industrialist Nathan Appleton (himself a collector on a small scale) and the brother-in-law of the poet Henry Wadsworth Longfellow. Like Martin Brimmer, Quincy Adams Shaw, and other Boston-born collectors of his generation, Appleton was a Harvard graduate, was well-read and well-traveled, especially in Europe, and was quite comfortable financially. Unlike Brimmer, a lawyer, and Shaw, who made his fortune from mines in the Midwest, Appleton had no profession (although he was, like so many other Boston collectors, an amateur painter) and never married, but devoted his life to philanthropic activities, especially to patronage of the arts.

Appleton first went to Europe in 1833 and, like T. H. Perkins before him, began to acquire works of art to serve as furnishings. He sent home pictures to decorate the walls of his father's house, where Allston's *Rosalie* and some spurious old masters, including a Brueghel *Marine View,* provided the core of the collection. Appleton made copies of paintings in the Louvre with which to enrich his father's collection, and as Perkins had, began his own collection by buying copies, displaying conventional Boston taste (he admired Claude, Murillo, and Van de Velde, and bought a copy of Correggio's *Madonna of the Tribuna*); however, he expressed suspicion of modern European art, remarking prophetically, "I cannot abide Turner."

In 1844 and 1845, Appleton traveled to Europe with Perkins and, during the same visit, continued on to Greece and Constantinople with William Morris Hunt and his family. Appleton would renew his acquaintance with Hunt in 1852 in Paris, where he admired Hunt's *Fortune Teller* (already owned by a Bostonian, Frank B. Brooks, a member of another farsighted collecting family). Through Hunt, Appleton met the French painters Constant Troyon and Ary Scheffer, but his appreciation of living artists' work was still hesitant. When he bought the *Turkish Cafe* by the Barbizon painter Narcisse Diaz (now in the Museum of Fine Arts), he justified his purchase by calling it a French Rubens with a touch of Spanish in it.

Nevertheless, from this point, Appleton would become increasingly interested in contemporary art, both European and American. In the 1850s he bought works by Thomas Couture and Théodore Rousseau (no doubt with Hunt's advice), as well as a study head in the Couture manner by Hunt himself. He purchased landscapes by Winckworth Allan Gay, another Bostonian in Paris who studied with Troyon, and was among the first to patronize Elihu Vedder, buying his *Lair of the Sea Serpent* (now in the Museum of Fine Arts) in 1864. Appleton's connection with Hunt and other artists was crucial in the development of his own taste, and he would always value his friendship with artists—he went on sketching trips with John F. Kensett in the 1850s, and knew Frederic Church and F. O. C. Darley in New York.

Appleton was not the first Bostonian to patronize contemporary French artists. Charles Callahan Perkins, T. H. Perkins's grandson, was with Ary Scheffer in Paris in the 1840s and commissioned Scheffer's *Dante and Beatrice* in 1853. Nor was he the most devoted supporter of French painting in the 1850s; that honor goes to Martin Brimmer. But he was a pioneer in the appreciation of the Barbizon School, which swept Boston in the 1850s and '60s, and many prominent collectors would soon follow him to Europe.

The critical events for the development of American painting in Boston in the 1850s occurred in France, not at home. There Hunt and other transplanted Bostonians studied with the Barbizon painters Constant Troyon, Charles Jacque, and Jean-François Millet,

JEAN-FRANCOIS MILLET
The Sower, 1850

In 1853, William Morris Hunt bought Millet's masterpiece for sixty dollars. He brought it to America when he returned from Paris in 1855, and displayed it at the Allston Club exhibitions of 1866 and 1867. The tragic heroism of Millet's monumental figure made a lasting impression on Boston's art community, and echoes of the subject are visible in the works of Boston's most popular artists of the 1860s and '70s, among them George Fuller, William Babcock, and Hunt himself. (Museum of Fine Arts, Boston. Gift of Quincy A. Shaw through Quincy A. Shaw, Jr. and Marian Shaw Houghton.)

whose works they would eagerly promote, and whose styles they would appropriate and transmit to younger artists working at home. Hunt, the son of a Vermont congressman, had been suspended for practical joking after his first year at Harvard; his mother then took him to Europe to enable him to pursue a career as an artist. Like so many Bostonians, he went first to Rome, intending to become a sculptor. His studies with Henry Kirke Brown were unsuccessful, however, and in 1846, acting on the advice of Emanuel Leutze, whom he met in Rome, he next enrolled at the Düsseldorf Academy, but was uncomfortable with the discipline there. Hunt spent the winter of 1846–1847 in Paris, and would later describe his conversion to the art of painting with a romantic story indicative of the personal flamboyance that charmed whole generations of artists and patrons in Boston: "If that is painting, I am a painter," he ex-claimed upon seeing Couture's *Falconer* (Toledo Museum of Art) in the window of a gallery in Paris.[44]

Hunt then began to study with Couture. A year later he was joined by William Babcock, another Boston expatriate who would spend the rest of his life in France. Their choice of Couture, an unorthodox but well-known master whose method ran counter to that presented in the French academies of the day, was an interesting one. It may have been that their lack of formal training prevented them from attending the Ecole des Beaux-Arts, where several painters from New York were then studying. But it is also possible that unconventionality, freedom from the restraints that Boston represented, was what they sought, and that their long exposure to sculpture in Boston attracted them to the plastic style and statuesque figures of Couture and later J.-F. Millet, with whom both men worked in the early '50s. Both Hunt and Babcock would eventually develop styles based upon Couture's method (free painting without preliminary underdrawing, resulting in a rich, dashing, textured surface) and upon the heroic, moralizing subject matter of Millet. For this unconventional, unacademic art they fostered a taste in Boston.

With characteristic enthusiasm, Hunt not only admired Couture, Millet, and the Barbizon painters; he befriended them, lent them money, and bought up their paintings to send home for exhibition in Boston. His social position, increased in no small measure by his marriage in 1855 to T. H. Perkins's granddaughter, Louisa Dumaresq Perkins, enabled him to persuade many prominent Bostonians then in Paris to come to those artists' studios and buy their work. At Hunt's urging Appleton, bought paintings by Diaz, Troyon, Rousseau, and Couture, as has been noted. Edward Wheelwright arranged through Hunt to study with Millet in the 1850s and later wrote a moving account of his days with the French painter;[45] the landscapes he bought by Diaz, Ciceri, and Jacque were among the first Barbizon paintings ever to be shown in Boston, being exhibited at the Athenaeum in 1853. Martin Brimmer, who later became the first president of the Museum of Fine Arts, was Millet's first major patron, joined with Hunt in purchasing all the paintings Millet showed at the 1853 Salon. Among those works was *Harvesters Resting* (now in the Museum of Fine Arts), which, when Brimmer lent it to the 1854 Athenaeum exhibition, was the first painting by Millet to be seen in America, and the monumental *Sower,* perhaps Millet's most famous work, which Hunt showed in Boston at every opportunity during the next two decades (before selling it through Doll and Richards to Quincy Adams Shaw, who presented it to the Museum of Fine Arts).

Hunt's impact on taste and collecting in Boston was not limited to his importation of French pictures. He returned to America in 1855 and settled first in Boston and then in Newport, where he gathered around him a group of enthusiastic disciples—John La Farge, Edward Wheelwright, Thomas Gold Appleton, William and Henry James—all of whom were amateur painters at the time. Hunt instilled in them a love of the French aesthetic, which they would communicate to other Bostonians as they became the city's cultural leaders in the next decade. Hunt began holding art classes in his Summer Street studio in Boston about 1863 and attracted large numbers of young women, charmed, no doubt, by his full beard and bohemian aspect. Like Couture, Hunt advocated char-

coal drawing and uninhibited creativity, and, although one critic noted that Hunt aroused his pupils' enthusiasm for art more than he instructed them,[46] he produced several pupils in addition to La Farge who achieved some measure of artistic success: Elizabeth Boott, Maria Oakey Dewing, and Sarah W. Whitman.

Hunt was also an enthusiastic sponsor of numerous American painters who studied in France at midcentury, and counseled collectors like Brimmer to buy their works. On Hunt's recommendation, Henry Angell bought seven paintings by R. H. Fuller and six by J. Foxcroft Cole, both of whom painted in a Barbizon-inspired style. John B. Johnston, another French-trained painter promoted by Hunt, though now forgotten, was lauded in his own time as a "genius, whose small studies of cows were equal in color and characterization to Troyon's work,"[47] and was well represented in Boston's collections by the 1860s, Angell, Ernest Wadsworth Longfellow, and Thomas Wigglesworth all owned his pictures.

Thomas Robinson, who, like Cole, seems to have been more successful as an agent for French artists than as a painter, nonetheless produced heroic animal pictures praised for their "rude grandeur," which were admired by Hunt and were bought by Angell, Wigglesworth, Henry Sayles, and other Bostonians for whom he supplied French pictures. Like Hunt, Robinson and Cole were part of a long tradition of Boston painters who provided their patrons with European pictures. Both were associated with Seth M. Vose, the prescient art dealer whose Westminster Art Gallery in Providence was the first in America to show Barbizon pictures. Robinson, in particular, was working closely with Vose by 1855, and over the next twenty years made twenty-nine trips to Europe for him, buying paintings from the studios of Corot, Millet, Courbet, Troyon, and others. (Unfortunately, Robinson often drank and gambled away the money that Vose gave him to buy pictures; their association ended when Robinson, out of cash, attempted to deceive Vose by sending him fraudulent pictures.) In the early years, Vose offered his Barbizon pictures for less than $100, but had no buyers for them (the first American exhibition of Corot's works, held at his gallery in 1852, produced no sales), and Robinson often took his pay in artists' materials. But gradually the paintings began to sell: first for about $100; then in 1874 a Corot brought $400; seven years later, competition for these paintings and higher prices in France brought prices up to nearly $1,000 for a large canvas. The boom in Vose's business came as a result of the esteem in which he was held by

collectors and artists, especially Hunt, who had no formal business relationship with Vose but was an enthusiastic supporter of the gallery. Respecting Vose's
honesty and the great faith he expressed in the artists
he represented, Hunt sent many of his friends (Angell,
Brimmer, and Samuel D. Warren among them) to Providence to buy Barbizon pictures.

In addition to furthering the careers of the Barbizon painters, French and American, Hunt was probably responsible for the appearance and enthusiastic
reception of Frank Duveneck's and George Fuller's
works in Boston in the 1870s. He also persuaded Elihu
Vedder to come to Boston in the '60s, foreseeing that
his status as an expatriate and his imaginative, *outré*
imagery would appeal greatly to the descendants of the

supporters of dreamy Washington Allston. Martin
Brimmer was the first Bostonian to acquire Vedder's
works, purchasing *The Questioner of the Sphinx* (cat.
no. 49) from the artist in 1863 and an earlier canvas,
Fisherman and Genie, by 1861. (Both of these paintings
came to the Museum of Fine Arts after Mrs. Brimmer's
death in 1906). Henry Angell owned a Vedder (although he dismissed it as a minor work) and Dr. William S. Bigelow, who had inherited Allston's mysterious
Moonlit Landscape (cat. no. 21) from his father,
bought at least three works by Vedder over a thirty-
year period. Altogether, the Museum of Fine Arts owns
nine of Vedder's paintings, one of the largest groups of
his works in a public collection, and most of these were
purchased by Bostonians early in the artist's career.

Hunt's own paintings were eagerly collected during his lifetime in Boston, where he was, in the 1860s, a popular society portraitist. He also painted compositions derived from Couture, soulful, Millet-like figure studies and, late in his life, landscapes. Boston critics were aware of his stylistic indecision: "With all his genius and power, Hunt had no fixed manner of his own. . . . His works give the impression of great power in varied directions rather than of any such digested knowledge and fixed principles," but they admired him, as they had Allston, for his energy, his romantic lifestyle, and his ability to inspire other artists.[48]

Both artists and critics of Hunt's day credited him with effecting an artistic revolution in Boston. He was seen as a gifted painter who had "the uncommon faculty of communicating to others his own noble ardor and devotion to the artist's ideal. . . . The fact that Boston was prompt to recognize the best modern art was due to the teaching of Hunt more than any other cause. His own art was imbued with the modern spirit. He raised the art standard; he dignified the profession, and caused art to be respected as it had not been since Allston's day."[49]

That Bostonians associated Hunt with Allston explains in part his success as a tastemaker. His promotion of French paintings and of an American style born in France was a continuation of Allston's insistence upon an artistic connection with Europe, and it demonstrated once again that Boston's was a cosmopolitan culture. Moreover, the art for which Bostonians were now so eager was moral and inspirational. They admired the heroic content of Millet's pictures and, by extension, the American artists influenced by Millet and the other Barbizon painters were perceived as similarly uplifting.[50] The art Bostonians bought, French and American, was rich, yet simple; they found in it a literary content and a link with the revered art of the past ("They [Millet's paintings] have a Biblical severity, and remind us of the gravest of the Italian masters."),[51] but at the same time they saw in it a naturalism not at odds with Emersonian beliefs.

The interest in Barbizon paintings was also perceived as Boston's own revolution, a taste developing independent of the prevailing artistic fashions in New York. Competition between the two cities was expressed in terms of their rival styles: the meticulousness of the Hudson River School versus the freer style of French and French-inspired paintings. Underlying the rivalry was Boston's awareness that she was losing hegemony as America's cultural center. As usual, Hunt was at the center of the debate. New York critics like

the Ruskin supporter Clarence Cook called his work "an outrageous daub," "flimsy rubbish;" the Cambridge critic Charles Moore assailed Millet's work for "vague and inaccurate drawing" indicating his "shallow grasp of a subject." Hunt blasted right back, calling the Hudson River School painters "those sun-dried remnants of American art, who, like scarecrows, remain in a cornfield even after the harvest is past."[52] As early as 1848, Franklin Dexter, one of Boston's most thoughtful critics, had cautioned against the Ruskinian aesthetic then sweeping New York and gaining a foothold in Boston because he felt that such views would lead to cultural isolation and ignorance of the past. Dexter—and Boston—found a champion in Hunt, who provided an alternative to Ruskin's theories and developed Boston's own style, one that was literary, cosmopolitan, and romantic, values to which Allston had introduced Bostonians. With Hunt's ascendancy, Boston embarked on an artistic course entirely separate from New York's.

One of the most important by-products of Hunt's promotion of French and French-inspired American art in Boston was the formation of the Allston Club in 1866. The organization was short-lived, disbanding the following year after only two exhibitions, but it was successful, nonetheless, in challenging the established art institutions in Boston, the Athenaeum and the equally conservative Boston Art Club.

Founded in 1855 under the leadership of the portraitist Joseph Ames, the Boston Art Club held annual juried exhibitions of contemporary art, which initially complemented the old-master-dominated Athenaeum shows but became increasingly conservative in the 1860s, when it suffered financial difficulties. The purpose of the Boston Art Club was not the promotion of local artists, nor was the participation of artists essential; rather, it was a social club dominated by Boston's elite, with a special interest in art. Or, as described by founding member Samuel Gerry, "Ours is an *Art* Club, not an Artists. . . . The *palette* and the *palate* seem to thrive together."[53]

In contrast, the Allston Club was for artists, particularly those who (unlike Gerry) were interested in French art. Hunt was the organizer of the club and its president; Winckworth Allan Gay and Albion Bicknell were among the other officers; Vedder, Thomas Robinson, La Farge, and J. Foxcroft Cole were members. Collectors and the socially prominent were not excluded, but those involved were either amateur artists like Appleton and Edward Cabot, faithful collectors of French art like Henry Sayles, and dealers like E.

Adams Doll of Doll and Richards, who, with Vose, had done much to promote Barbizon painting in Boston.

It is clear why Hunt, Robinson, Bicknell, and other artists enthusiastic about French art and their own French training should feel the need for an organization dedicated to displaying contemporary art. Exhibitions at the Athenaeum had varied little during the previous ten years, showing more work from the 1830s and '40s than recent production. In 1866 the Athenaeum's annual exhibition included the Dowse Collection of Water Colors (small copies of old master paintings, presented to the Athenaeum by the Cambridge leather-dresser Thomas Dowse in 1858 and exhibited annually thereafter) and the Athenaeum's own statuary and paintings, reflecting the guiding influence of Isaac P. Davis and T. H. Perkins in the 1830s. The annual "Paintings in the Gallery," supposedly a selection of works new to the public, was dominated by C. C. Perkins's by then somewhat tired collection of old masters and no longer recent modern European works. Some of Perkins's paintings, like the *Dante and Beatrice* mentioned below, had been shown annually since the '50s, and as Henry James's sardonic comment makes clear— "Among the contemporary classicists, Mr. Hammerton [an English critic whose latest work James reviewed in 1868] mentions Ary Scheffer, of whose too-familiar *Dante and Beatrice* he gives still another photograph"[54] —Bostonians were bored with them. On the other hand, the Allston Club, whose ideals and allegiances were demonstrated by the two paintings the club owned (Courbet's *Quarry* [now in the Museum of Fine Arts], bought through the efforts of Robinson and Bicknell, and Joseph Ames's portrait of Washington Allston), was dedicated to the encouragement and exhibition of contemporary art.

The Allston Club's exhibitions were, like the Salons in Paris, international in scope and were chosen by a committee of artists and connoisseurs. The French bias of the selection reflected the contents of the most progressive Boston collections, from which many works were borrowed. In the 1866 exhibition of ninety-six paintings, fifty-five were French, including *The Quarry* and Millet's *Sower*. The exhibition was the largest public display of Barbizon paintings to be shown in Boston until that time, but the selection was apparently made without prejudice, for in addition to works by Millet, Corot, Diaz, and Daubigny were paintings by Frère, Lambinet, Bonheur, and other academic painters.

The American artists represented were, for the most part, Hunt's protégés. Thomas Robinson, who was described as the "pupil of Gustave Courbet," showed *Cow and Calf*—his perennial theme—and two other works; Vedder showed five paintings; William Babcock showed the Millet-like *Girl Before a Mirror*, lent by Henry Sayles; and La Farge was represented by two unusual works, *Flowers* (possibly *Vase of Flowers*, 1864; now in the Museum of Fine Arts), and a decorative panel entitled *Fish* (1865; Fogg Art Museum). Several paintings in the show, both French and American, were offered for sale through the Doll and Richards Gallery.

The disbanding of the Allston Club after only two years is difficult to explain. Vedder claimed that the high purchase price of the Courbet—$5,000—brought the club near bankruptcy, inasmuch as its premises, spacious rooms in the Studio Building on Tremont Street (where Hunt, Rimmer, Inness, and Ernest W. Longfellow all had their studios in the 1860s), with a billiard room and other social facilities as well as exhibition galleries, were expensive to maintain. In addition, during the club's second year, Hunt, who had been its guiding spirit, was traveling in Brittany with Vedder. But it is equally likely that the Allston Club's activities diminished after 1867 because the founders had made their point: by the late 1860s, the French aesthetic had won thorough acceptance in Boston. In fact, Bostonians collected French Barbizon paintings more eagerly than they did their American counterparts.

Albion Bicknell, writing from Boston in 1866 to Vedder in Rome, noted wryly that the Allston Club exhibition ". . . has created a sensation here. It is undoubtedly the finest exhibition in Boston. . . . French pictures are all the go and 'the natives' are doing nothing."[55] The overwhelming European content of several local collections bore out Bicknell's words. Henry P. Kidder, whose collection, formed in the 1860s and '70s, was considered distinguished enough to merit inclusion in Strahan's *Art Treasures of America* (a lavish volume that published important American private collections at the time of the Centennial), is credited with owning over thirty European pictures, mostly Barbizon and Hague School, but only one American painting, *Pontine Marshes* by Inness. Kidder actually had two additional Innesses (*Sunset* [1864] and *Italian Landscape* [1872], both now in the Museum of Fine Arts), but he seems otherwise not to have collected American pictures, and may well have become interested in Inness because of his success in adapting the Barbizon style. Similarly, Henry Sayles, whose collection was refined through his friendship with artists like Hunt and Robinson, and through his participation in the Allston

Club, amassed one of the earliest and most important collections of Barbizon paintings in Boston. He owned only a few American works, mostly early efforts by artists working in Boston like Bicknell, Vedder, and little-known figures such as J. C. Thom, who never achieved the success of their French contemporaries.

Unlike New York, where toward the end of the century Thomas B. Clarke put together a splendid collection consisting of only American pictures, and where patrons of the arts like John Taylor Johnston tended to buy American pictures precisely because they were American, Bostonians took pride (however defensively) in their more cosmopolitan approach: "Why should a man who loves pictures and is able to gratify his taste confine his attention to art of a single nation, even his own? Does one buy paintings from motives of patriotism?"[56] Consequently, if Bostonians did buy American art, they bought local works conceived in the French manner, especially after the Allston Club exhibitions, when Hunt's Barbizon aesthetic clearly overshadowed any remnants of the Ruskinian viewpoint still in Boston. Although Hudson River School painting, so popular in New York, had been exhibited with some regularity at the Athenaeum in the 1850s, it disappeared thereafter, and relatively few of those paintings were bought.

Of the Hudson River School artists, Cole had been well received in Boston in the 1840s and '50s, but his pure landscapes were far less popular than his grand allegorical pictures such as the *Course of Empire*, first shown in Boston in 1854, which appealed to the prevailing taste for pictures with moralizing content. John Kensett was also popular in Boston, perhaps due to his activity in Newport and his friendship with Thomas Gold Appleton. C. C. Perkins bought a *Sunset* in 1856 and showed it almost annually at the Athenaeum thereafter; Appleton owned *A Brook in Autumn* from about 1858, and Martin Brimmer bought a landscape by Kensett at about the same time. Bierstadt showed large numbers of paintings in Boston in the late 1850s, both scenes of Europe and those of the Far West. His work was sufficiently popular for the Athenaeum to buy *The Arch of Octavius*—a European scene, of course—in 1859, but most of his paintings in the shows were offered for sale or were borrowed from private collectors in New York. Very few of Bierstadt's paintings would remain in Boston, and of the twenty-six now in the Museum of Fine Arts, only one, the beautiful but modest *Thunderstorm in the Rocky Mountains*, came from a nineteenth-century Boston collection. All the rest were given to the Museum by Maxim Karolik in the 1940s.

The painters linked to the Pre-Raphaelite aesthetic fared even less well in Boston. Very few works by Asher B. Durand were shown there; Frederic Church rarely brought his paintings to New England, and even the spectacular *Icebergs* (Dallas Museum of Fine Arts) excited little attention when it was presented at a special exhibition at the Athenaeum in the spring of 1861, shortly after its successful tour of New York. And no Bostonian bought paintings by Church in this era, a lack reflected in Boston's public collections today.

The taste of Thomas Wigglesworth, an eccentric and eclectic collector, was broader than that of most Bostonians. In the 1860s he bought paintings by Martin Johnson Heade (who enjoyed a brief period of popularity in Boston during that decade, selling his pictures through Seth M. Vose in Providence), A. T. Bricher (also represented by Vose), Inness (including *Elms in Summer*, the only American painting in Wigglesworth's vast collection to come to the Museum of Fine Arts), and Lane; but in the late '60s and early '70s he became more interested in the American Barbizon movement and seems to have sold most of his Hudson River School paintings to buy Thomas Robinson, John B. Johnston, J. Foxcroft Cole, and J. Francis Murphy. He bought Troyon, Jacque, and other Barbizon painters in the '60s, and in 1879 acquired Courbet's *Young Ladies of the Village* (now in the Metropolitan Museum of Art, New York), one of the first major works by that painter to come to America; however, he was also interested in the kind of French painting more popular in New York, owning a Lambinet and Bouguereau's *Fraternal Love*, the latter now in the Museum of Fine Arts.

The only local patron to assemble the kind of collection associated with New York was Alvin Adams of Watertown, who owned pictures of a totally different class and scale than the modest French works collected by most Bostonians. Adams, whose fortune came from the Adams Express Company, a major shipper of arms and munitions during the Civil War, preferred Düsseldorf and Hague School pictures to Barbizon, owned a Tissot and a Boldini rather than a Millet, and championed New York painters—albeit minor ones—such as Casilear, Sontag, and Colman rather than Hunt and Inness. Many of Adams's pictures were very large; he preferred dramatic subjects (such as the violent shipwreck picture *Off to the Rescue* by M. F. H. DeHaas, a Dutch painter working in New York, which was seven feet wide) and was especially interested in western scenes. The focal points of his collection were two mammoth (twelve feet by six feet) landscapes by Albert Bierstadt, a personal friend. For one of these landscapes, *Among the Sierras* (ca. 1878, present location unknown), Adams is known to have paid $15,000. Although his flashy collection was greeted with disdain by most Bostonians, who criticized him for his lack of true connoisseurship, it brought about $60,000 when it was sold at auction some five years after his death. This is the largest sum ever to have been raised from the public sale of a private collection of works of art in Boston.

The Centennial was the high-water mark of appreciation for Barbizon paintings in America. New Yorkers, until then primarily interested in French academics and romantics like Ernest Meissonier and Rosa Bonheur, began to take notice of those painters championed in Boston. At the same time, Bostonians, ever conscious of their rivalry with New York, began searching for other artists to claim as their own. A series of exhibitions held in Boston around the time of the Centennial provided the city with new standard-bearers.

In 1875, a group of paintings by Frank Duveneck, who had recently returned from Munich, were included in the spring exhibition of the Boston Art Club. By this time, that organization, in its new quarters on Dartmouth Street, was the most vital art institution in Boston. Its activity had been revived under the presidency of the ubiquitous C. C. Perkins: it now had 800 members, held several exhibitions a year, and was praised for cultivating "a love of art and a good feeling among artists."[57] In addition to the five paintings shown by Duveneck in 1875, there were works by Frederic Vinton and other local portraitists, and the usual group of French and American Barbizon landscapes. Duveneck's works sold out; they were bought by Boston's most prominent collectors, including Henry Angell and Alice Hooper, whose family also patronized Hunt, John La Farge, George Fuller, and other local artists.

Duveneck's favorable reception was due, in part, to Hunt's teachings, which prepared Bostonians for the unorthodox; the press praised him for being "fearless in his realism" and noted with satisfaction that he avoided the superficial prettiness of which they suspected the artists popular in New York. Duveneck's pictures evinced "a deliberate rejection of the higher artistic function of beautifying, in favor of the more sordid end of astoundingly real representation . . . their appeal is that of a progressive man, and should be met with encouragement."[58] And even the conservative if eloquent critic Henry James, writing in *The Nation,* credited Boston with "the discovery of an unsuspected man of genius."[59]

That Duveneck, a painter from Cincinnati with a murky palette and heavy, Teutonic style should have been so welcome in Francophile Boston is something of a surprise. Even more astounding is the fact that the most beloved American artist in Boston after the Centennial was not Homer or Inness or La Farge but the little-known and rather awkward George Fuller. Once again, it was Hunt (or more properly, a group of his students, who came across the impoverished artist on his Deerfield farm while hiking in the area) who was credited with discovering Fuller. Hunt went to see his pictures, and subsequently encouraged Fuller, who began exhibiting at Doll and Richards in 1876. His work was an immediate success and, as Duveneck had been, he was hailed as Boston's new discovery. Boston's most progressive collectors—Mrs. S. D. Warren, Mrs. J. Montgomery Sears, Henry Lee Higginson, Quincy Adams Shaw—all bought his work, as did Thomas Clarke in New York.

Although Fuller is now seen as a minor, rather sentimental and conservative artist, he was honored in his own time for his visionary, inspirational subject matter. His paintings—generally of young farm girls with dreamy expressions (see cat. no. 55)—were widely praised; they were, in fact, a logical and consistent expression of Boston's taste. More than they admired Fuller's art, Bostonians admired the man. They romanticized his personality and saw him as New England's version of Millet: an artist-martyr who worked in isolation, sacrificing everything for his art. He was celebrated as a native son whose art expressed traditional rural values with roots in New England soil. Fuller was worshiped all the more when critics began describing him as Allston's successor; his vague, mysterious subjects were seen as an outgrowth of Allston's romantic themes and were believed to be similarly ennobling and uplifting. Even his laborious technique and the constant reworking of his canvases reminded Bostonians of *Belshazzar's Feast* and was viewed with reverence as a sign of the artist's struggle to convey his message, as the only manner suitable to his noble purpose. Finally, Boston took special pride in the fact that Fuller was a native: ". . . the recognition of his merit was complete at once, in New York and wherever his work was seen, as well as in Boston, though to us belongs the honor of acknowledging it first."[60]

William Morris Hunt died in 1879, committing suicide at Appledore on the Isle of Shoals, New Hampshire. One of his heirs as the molder of taste in Boston was John La Farge, a New York-born artist who had all the right credentials for leadership of Boston's artistic

JOHN LA FARGE
Bowl of Wild Roses, 1880

La Farge's most experimental works, as well as his most successful, were still-life compositions in oil and, from the mid-'70s, in watercolor. Delicately colored, intimate in scale, its brushwork daringly loose and free, *Bowl of Wild Roses* and works like it appealed to the same Boston sensibility that in the next decade would embrace Impressionism. (Museum of Fine Arts, Boston. Bequest of Elizabeth Howard Bartol.)

community. La Farge was the son of wealthy French *emigrés;* he was trained as a lawyer, but in the 1850s, he threw over his lucrative profession to go to Europe. He studied with Couture in Paris, and later was one of Hunt's first pupils at Newport, where he resolved to make art his profession. La Farge's training in French art made him at home in Boston; his landscapes in the Barbizon manner exhibited at the Allston Club and elsewhere in the 1860s were well received; and his ideal, subjective painting, freely brushed and born of feeling rather than of observation ("Any work of art which has been deeply felt by its maker is also naturally well painted")[61] was accepted as the proper successor to the visionary romanticism of Washington Allston.

In the 1860s and '70s, La Farge worked in many genres and with many different media, always experimenting but expressing his experiments in traditional subject matter with which Boston audiences felt comfortable. In 1872, his landscape masterwork *The Last Valley* (1867; private collection) was shown in Boston at Doll and Richards. Henry James labeled it the most important of the American pictures in the show, finding it "a remarkable picture, full of the most refined intentions and the most beautiful results, of light and atmosphere and of the very poetry of the situation."[62] La Farge's still-life paintings of the 1860s caused H. H.

Richardson to hire him some ten years later—despite his complete lack of experience—to design the murals for the interior of Trinity Church, where his brilliant color sense was manifest in complex decorations combining abstract, foliate ornament with Old and New Testament subjects. At the same time, he was developing techniques for stained glass (his first commission, a window for Memorial Hall, Harvard University, came in 1874, to be followed by work on a series of windows for Trinity Church), a medium in which his decorative abilities, his interest in scientific experiment, and his romantic fascination with medieval images and forms found a happy outlet.

La Farge's many artistic activities paralleled Boston's aesthetic interests in the 1870s. His delicate still-life compositions, intimate in scale and lyrical in mood, were at home in a city that had, for the most part, turned its back on the grandiose, sublime compositions of the Hudson River School that dominated the taste of New York. Small in scale, brilliantly colored, and decorative in design, they were avidly collected in Boston, and were especially admired by romantic, visionary artists, such as Elihu Vedder, who were so popular in Boston. To Vedder, La Farge was the most inspiring artist of his day, and his still lifes particularly evocative: ("This quality of subtlety is shown in those never-to-be-forgotten flowers, particularly in that

ENRICO MENEGHELLI
The Lawrence Room, Museum of Fine Arts, Boston, 1879

Many of the galleries of the first Museum of Fine Arts, in Copley Square, were arranged like a *Kunstkammer*, displaying a multitude of objects without segregation according to type or cultural context. The Lawrence Room, containing rare English paneling, medieval reliquaries, armor, and sixteenth-century portraits, was presented to the museum by Mrs. T. B. Lawrence, whose husband's original gift to the museum, a collection of arms and armor, was destroyed in the great fire of 1872. (Museum of Fine Arts, Boston. Gift of M. Knoedler and Co.)

damp mass of violets in a shallow dish on a window-sill, where the outside air faintly stirring the lace curtains seems to waft the odour towards you.")[63]

Boston's enthusiasm for La Farge's still lifes was also a part of the city's increasing interest in the water-color medium in the 1870s. The Boston Water Color Society was founded in 1885 (nearly twenty years after the formation of New York's American Water Color Society, with which La Farge exhibited from 1876), and showed works of such distinguished watercolorists as Childe Hassam and John Singer Sargent to an appreciative audience; at the same time, the Doll and Richards Gallery was becoming an important outpost for the exhibition of watercolors, and La Farge showed his watercolors there regularly from the late 1870s.

The decorative qualities that characterize La Farge's works in all media, gleaned from his sensitive and thoroughgoing study of the color and composition of Japanese prints, also mirrored a shift in the direction of Boston's taste in the 1870s and '80s. Several prominent Bostonians—Edward Morse, Ernest Fenollosa, Dr. William S. Bigelow, Henry Adams, and La Farge himself—traveled to Japan during this period. They brought back with them thousands of pieces of pottery, metalwork, scrolls, and prints that became the core of the Museum of Fine Arts' world-famous collection of oriental art and that sparked a vogue for *japonisme* that would persist beyond the turn of the century.

A similar taste for the decorative was influenced by the increasing incidence of "arts and crafts" design, beginning with H. H. Richardson's activity in Boston. The Boston Society for Decorative Arts was founded in 1879, and was followed by the American Society of Arts and Crafts, the first organizations of their kind in America; on the example of the Arts and Crafts Movement in England, spearheaded by Pre-Raphaelite painter William Morris, these groups advocated the encouragement of handicrafts, in particular the craftsmanship that flourished in the middle ages. The most important consequence of this interest had occurred in the early 1870s, when a group of prominent citizens were making plans for the foundation of a new museum in the recently developed Copley Square. On the advice of architect John H. Sturgis, they sought an "arts and crafts" model for their structure: they sent for the plans of the recently constructed South Kensington Museum in London, which had been built according to the "arts and industry" program of medieval-inspired style and oriental ornament. Ruskin's influence was gradually reappearing in Boston.

The two events that prompted the trustees of the Athenaeum to relinquish their authority over the fine arts in Boston and to encourage the founding of a new museum for the city were unlikely stimuli for an institution that considered itself a library society and incidentally ran a picture gallery. In 1869, Col. T. Bigelow Lawrence left the Athenaeum his extensive collection of medieval arms and armor. The collection could not be housed at the Athenaeum, which had reached its capacity for exhibition and storage of works of art, nor was there space on the Athenaeum's Beacon Street property to build the gallery for her husband's collection that Mrs. Lawrence offered to finance. At the same time, the Gray Collection of Prints, some 30,000 engravings assembled by Francis Calley Gray and bequeathed to Harvard University, was made available to the Athenaeum for exhibition. Again, although the Athenaeum's trustees were aware of the quality of the collection and of its educational value, they were unable to exhibit the prints for lack of space.

During these same years, the American Social Sciences Association formed a committee headed by C. C. Perkins and including Edward C. Cabot, the Athenaeum's architect and former vice-president of the Allston Club, and other prominent Bostonians. The committee was to study the value of art as an instrument of education. Their findings (consistent with William Tudor's belief, expressed over fifty years before, in art as a civilizing and edifying force in society) led the Massachusetts Legislature in February 1870 to establish "a body corporate by the name of the Trustees of the Museum of Fine Arts for the purpose of erecting a museum for the preservation and exhibition of works of art, of making, maintaining, and establishing collections of such works, and of affording instruction in the Fine Arts."[64]

This mandate for preservation and instruction re-flects Boston's long-standing beliefs in art as history and as education. As such, these principles did not differ significantly from those expressed in the charter of incorporation of the Metropolitan Museum of Art, enacted by the New York legislature at precisely the same time. But unlike the Metropolitan, which constantly sought popular support through public subscriptions during its initial years and which conducted delicate negotiations with the city (that is to say, with Boss Tweed) to obtain municipal backing, the Museum of Fine Arts neither solicited nor sought any public funds. A more important distinction between the policies of the two institutions is found in the appeal to potential supporters made by proponents of what would become the Metropolitan. An art museum should be welcomed, they argued, because among its other functions it would encourage "the application of the arts to manufacture" and would "furnish popular instruction and recreation." Beneath these noble aims was a profit motive, designed to appeal to the businessmen who would be major contributors: by improving the local artisan's design and workmanship and by elevating public taste by means of exposure to high-quality works of art, one could improve the level of consumption and the retailer's profits.[65] Such theories would have horrified Bostonians, where the association of the Museum with financial gain threatened to undo the hard-won belief in art as a force that

WASHINGTON ALLSTON
Elijah in the Desert, 1818

The Museum of Fine Arts had been encorporated for only a few months when it received its first gift, this well-known history painting by Washington Allston, one of Boston's best-loved native sons. The donors, members of the Hooper family, were responsible for returning several of Allston's paintings to Boston: they purchased *Elijah* and *St. Peter Released from Prison* in England, and the *Self-Portrait* (cat. no. 20) from the John T. Johnston sale in New York. (Museum of Fine Arts, Boston. Gift of Mrs. Samuel Hooper and Miss Alice Hooper.)

THOMAS ROBINSON
Cattle Plowing

Like many Boston painters of the 1870s, Robinson emulated the Barbizon masters so avidly collected there. *Cattle Plowing* was modeled after a monumental composition by the French animal painter Rosa Bonheur; it was one of the first American paintings to be purchased by public subscription for the Museum of Fine Arts. (Museum of Fine Arts, Boston. Gift by Contribution.)

---

countered such corruption. And in Boston, there was no talk of art providing public recreation; the Museum, it was hoped, would edify, not entertain.

The Museum of Fine Arts opened its doors at Copley Square on July 3, 1876. Its first president was Martin Brimmer, who would serve until his death in 1896. From the outset, the activity of the Museum reflected the taste, the interests, and the pride of Boston, representing especially the ideals of Brimmer's generation. The first special exhibition, held in 1874 at the Athenaeum (for the Museum's Copley Square building was not yet completed), was a group of paintings belonging to the Duc de Montpensier. After decades of admiring forgeries and over-attributed works, Bostonians at last had the opportunity to see a large number of genuine Spanish pictures, including works by Zurbaran, Veláz-

quez, and Ribera. The Athenaeum fulfilled its obligation to Harvard in a special exhibition of the Gray Collection of Prints in 1876 (the Lawrence Collection of Arms and Armor was lost in the great fire of 1872). Subsequently, the Museum in Copley Square embarked on a program of exhibitions honoring its native sons.

The first of these "one-man shows" was held in memory of William Morris Hunt in November 1879, a few months after the artist's death. The exhibition was the Museum's first "blockbuster," attracting large crowds (over 4,000 one Sunday), and four editions of the catalogue were printed. William Rimmer, the eccentric physician, sculptor, and instructor of drawing, was the next honored with a special exhibition held the year after his death in 1879. An exhibition of Gilbert Stuart's works, drawn primarily from local collections, was held that same year, another commemorating Washington Allston was mounted in 1881, and George Fuller's works were shown in 1884, a few months after his death.

In its early years the Museum of Fine Arts assumed the Athenaeum's responsibility for holding annual exhibitions of contemporary American art. The first, held in 1880 in conjunction with the Boston Art Club, was a juried exhibition consisting of over 150 paintings and sixty watercolors and, for the most part, showed the work of local artists, including J. Appleton Brown, J.

Foxcroft Cole, John B. Johnston, Ernest Longfellow, Ignaz Gaugengigl, Frank Crowninshield, and Otto Grundmann (the last two were members of the faculty at the School of the Museum of Fine Arts).

The core of the Museum's permanent collection was a large group of paintings lent by the Athenaeum in 1876, of which about one-quarter were American, including such works as Stuart's portraits of George and Martha Washington (now shared by the Museum of Fine Arts and the National Collection of Fine Arts, Washington), Trumbull's *Sortie from Gibraltar* (Metropolitan Museum of Art, New York), and Benjamin West's *King Lear* (Museum of Fine Arts). These paintings were displayed periodically in the Museum's galleries, as were a smaller group of pictures, including Stuart's *General Knox* and *Washington at Dorchester Heights* and Copley's portraits of Samuel Adams and John Hancock (on deposit from the City of Boston). The Museum's collection of paintings was supplemented by bequests from local collectors, of which the first was, appropriately, Washington Allston's *Elijah Fed by the Ravens*, presented in 1870 by Alice Hooper, and by works purchased by subscription or donated by Boston's artists. The first paintings to enter the collection in this manner—a Diaz *(Wood Interior)* and Couture's *Study for the Volunteers of 1792*—reflect the continued dominance of the taste for French art. The first American paintings to be acquired were also in the French tradition: George Fuller's *Arethusa*, sentimentally revered as his last work, and two Troyon-like pictures, *New-Born Calf* and *Landscape with Cattle* by John B. Johnston. Martin Brimmer's gift of three paintings by Millet ensured that Boston's taste of the 1860s would be enshrined in the Museum of Fine Arts.

By 1876, the Museum's trustees had fulfilled their obligation to the Massachusetts Legislature by providing for both the housing and the exhibition of works of art; the third aspect of that injunction, "affording instruction in the fine arts," was met at the same time. The desire for an art academy had been expressed in Boston as early as 1807, when the critic for the *Monthly Anthology* (probably William Tudor) called for an institution to "provide for the improvement and emulation of *artists,* and for the correction and refinement of taste in those who aim to be connoisseurs."[66] However, unlike New York and Philadelphia, Boston had never developed a real art school. In the 1820s, aspiring artists could take instruction at David Brown's drawing academy on Court Street. David Claypool Johnston taught drawing and painting at his own "academy" from 1838, as did his rival F. S. Durivage, who in-

structed amateurs in the use of mechanical aids to drawing and painting so that pictures could be made regardless of talent. (That course of instruction led to the School of the Massachusetts Charitable Mechanics Association, dedicated to the education and refinement of the mechanic.) Casts were available for study at the Athenaeum from the time of its opening on Pearl Street in 1827; later in the century, William Morris Hunt held classes and William Rimmer offered instruction in anatomical drawing. A few art schools had come into existence by the mid-1860s, but these institutions—the Drawing School of the Lowell Institute, and the State Normal Art School—were dedicated to auxiliary purposes such as the training of teachers of art in public schools, rather than to true artistic education.

At first, the School of the Museum of Fine Arts, founded in 1876 by the Museum's trustees with the advice of a committee of artists such as John La Farge, Francis D. Millet, and William Morris Hunt, had similarly limited aspirations. They hoped merely to create "a body of intelligent and instructed amateurs capable of guiding and influencing the public taste," and so to generate "a higher and more fixed standard of art."[67] The School opened in Copley Square in January 1877 with eighty students, among them figures who would become successful painters, such as C. H. Davis and Willard Metcalf, and dedicated amateurs such as Ernest Fenollosa and Charles Hayden, who in 1905 would give an endowment "for the purchase of modern paintings by American artists" to the Museum of Fine Arts. Otto Grundmann, a German-born artist of no great distinction but an able teacher and administrator, was appointed head of the School; Rimmer and Thomas Dewing were also on the faculty. The School would become in the 1890s the most vital artistic institution in the city; its initially modest ambitions would be elevated by its enthusiastic students and young faculty members like Edmund Tarbell and Frank Benson, who developed a journal, a series of exhibitions, and ultimately a style that would come to be identified with Boston.

Coinciding with the opening of the Museum in 1876 was a proliferation of artistic activity in Boston. In the 1880s, Vose Galleries, the Providence-based firm that in the preceding decade had been instrumental in exposing Americans to Barbizon paintings, opened rooms on Tremont Street in Boston. Among the American artists they represented were Martin Johnson Heade, A. T. Bricher, and Eastman Johnson, although by that time the demand for their work had greatly diminished in Boston. The demand for French paint-

ings had not, however, and Vose continued to be the principal adviser to the most distinguished collectors in Boston. In one year, 1889, Mrs. S. D. Warren bought about $22,000 worth of paintings from Vose, including Corot's *Portrait of Rude* (now called *Portrait of a Man*) and Couture's *Madame Couture (Woman in White)*, both of which she gave to the Museum of Fine Arts in 1891. Vose's arrival in Boston provided competition for the two major galleries already established there: Williams and Everett (founded in 1810 and thus the oldest gallery in Boston), which showed contemporary artists like George Inness, guaranteeing them an income in exchange for exclusive representation, and Doll and Richards on Tremont Street, which, in addition to showing French painters and artists like George Fuller, J. A. Brown, Thomas Robinson, and others painting in a Barbizon-influenced style, began in the late 1870s to show watercolors by Winslow Homer.

Although Homer did not live in Boston after 1859, his family remained there, and he always retained a special loyalty to the city, once declaring that Boston was the only city in the country ever to offer him practical encouragement.[68] In fact, Boston was never a particularly good market for Homer's *paintings*—although one notable exception, *Fog Warning* (cat. no. 58), was purchased for $1,500 by Grenville Norcross (a cousin of Homer's) in 1893 and given to the Museum

of Fine Arts that year, making it one of the first of his paintings to enter a public collection. Homer was more often successful with New York buyers: with a price tag of $1,800, *Lost on the Grand Bank* (coll. Mr. and Mrs. John S. Broome, Oxnard, Calif.) remained unsold for years after being shown at the St. Botolph Club in Boston, but went quickly for the sum of $2,850 at the Knoedler Gallery in New York when it was put on sale there in 1900.

But if Bostonians did not buy Homer's big pictures for large sums, as did New Yorkers Thomas B. Clarke and Catherine Lorillard Wolfe, they were faithful and consistent in their taste. They preferred Homer's watercolors (the Museum of Fine Arts now has forty-three, most of which were donated by local collectors), in part because La Farge had already made them sensitive to the decorative qualities of the medium, and also because watercolor was Homer's forum for coloristic experiments and often for lighter, less troublesome subject matter, toward which Bostonians seemed to gravitate at this time. The fact that Homer's watercolors were relatively inexpensive was also a strong consideration: many could be bought at Doll and Richards Gallery for about $100, a bargain compared to the four-figure prices Homer's oils frequently brought in New York[69] (although in the 1880s Bostonians willingly paid such sums for French paintings).

JOHN SINGER SARGENT
Isabella Stewart Gardner, 1888

When Sargent first came to
Boston, Mrs. Gardner had just
begun to assemble her remarkable collection of paintings,
and was already well known as
a patron of young artists. This
is the first of several portraits
Sargent made of her. The ropes
of pearls at her waist, her low-
cut dress, and the patterned
wallpaper which forms an
aureole around her head made
this painting the *succès de
scandale* of the 1888 St. Botolph
Club exhibition; it was later
installed in the Gothic Room
in Mrs. Gardner's Museum at
Fenway Court, where it hangs
today. (Isabella Stewart Gardner Museum, Boston.)

Homer's watercolors were bought by many Bostonians, including Dr. William S. Bigelow, who had a
special interest in Adirondack subjects; *The Blue Boat,
Hudson River,* and *Woodsman and Fallen Tree,* collected in the 1890s, were, with his many La Farge
watercolors, the core of Bigelow's bequest to the Museum of Fine Arts in 1926. David B. Kimball, who, with
his wife, would be an important patron of Monet and
Boston's Impressionist painters, bought Homer's watercolors in the 1890s, as did Desmond Fitzgerald, an
engineer who would become one of Boston's most active collectors of Impressionist painting and American
watercolor in the same decade. Perhaps the most energetic purchaser of Homer's watercolors in the 1880s
and '90s was Edward Hooper, then treasurer of Harvard College and a trustee of the Museum of Fine Arts.
He owned at least fifteen: farm scenes, Tynemouth and
Adirondacks subjects, and compositions from the Ba-
hamas. Many of these were shown at the Memorial Exhibition of Homer's paintings held at the Museum of
Fine Arts in 1911, which included seventy works,
drawn for the most part from local collections, of
which only eight were oil paintings. In contrast, the
Memorial Exhibition held at the Metropolitan Museum at precisely the same time showed fifty-one
works, of which almost half were oils.

Despite his popularity in Boston, Homer shunned

LEON BONNAT
Mrs. Francis Shaw, 1878

While in Paris in 1878, Mrs. Shaw commissioned the popular French artist Léon Bonnat to paint her portrait. It was admired in the Salon of the next year, and its elegant, restrained style briefly became the height of fashion in Boston. But when John Singer Sargent arrived in Boston in 1887, he introduced a more flamboyant, theatrical portrait style which immediately became more popular. (Museum of Fine Arts, Boston. Gift of Miss Clara E. Sears.)

the many social opportunities offered to him in the city, and spent most of his life in Prout's Neck, Maine. Other artists like Henry Hobson Richardson, Frederic Porter Vinton, and Daniel Chester French were (as Allston and Hunt had been) more disposed to mix art and socializing, and in 1879, along with William Dean Howells, T. Jefferson Coolidge, Henry Lee Higginson, and others, formed the St. Botolph Club, whose purpose was "the promotion of social intercourse among authors and artists, and other gentlemen connected with or interested in literature and art."[70] In addition to providing a comfortable clubhouse for its members, the St. Botolph Club hosted frequent exhibitions, usually of contemporary art, and became, at a time when the newly-formed Museum of Fine Arts was exhibiting

Boston's old masters, the center of artistic energy and controversy in Boston.

The club's first exhibition, held in May 1880, showed the American Barbizon artists (Cole, Robinson, Brown, Inness) long popular in Boston, along with John Singer Sargent's portrait of Carolus-Duran and works by the New York painters William Merritt Chase and J. Alden Weir. An exhibition of works by members of the Tile Club (a group of New York painters who met weekly from 1877 to design decorative tiles) was held the next year, and in 1884, 1886, and 1887, the St. Botolph Club showed artists associated with American Impressionism, including paintings by Chase, Hassam, Weir, and Twachtman. The club thereafter would play an important role in the promotion of

Impressionism, both French and American, in Boston, showing in 1890 and 1891 paintings such as Dennis M. Bunker's *Meadow Lands* (Museum of Fine Arts) and the work of the young Joseph DeCamp, Edmund Tarbell, Frank Benson, and others who would come to be known as the Boston School. And in 1892, the first exhibition outside of Paris of paintings by Monet (whose name was synonymous with Impressionism in Boston), organized by Desmond Fitzgerald, was held at the St. Botolph Club.

In 1882, T. Jefferson Coolidge had loaned his latest Salon purchase to the St. Botolph Club, and Sargent's *El Jaleo* became the artistic sensation of that year. Boston's interest in the painter would become even more pronounced in 1888, when Sargent paid his first visit to the city. During that time, the club held his first American one-man show, which included portraits of his many Boston patrons, such as *Mrs. Edward Darley Boit* and the famous *Daughters of Edward Darley Boit* (both now in the Museum of Fine Arts), *Mrs. Charles Fairchild* (the wife of a prominent banker and Sargent's first patron in Boston (private collection, Wisconsin), and the notorious portrait of Isabella Stewart Gardner, with décolletage so shocking that her husband refused to let it be seen again in public during his lifetime.

The Bostonians who patronized Sargent were, on the whole, a new generation and a new type of collector, interested in larger, flashier, more stylish pictures than had ever before attracted Boston's attention. The leading portraitist in Boston before Sargent's dramatic arrival was Frederic Porter Vinton, who made his reputation with dark, restrained, beautifully painted portraits of men, portraits that imbued them with a dignity appropriate to their social station and that were stylistically far removed from Sargent's brilliant, dashing images of leading socialites. And in the 1870s and early '80s, Bostonians who sought out European artists to paint their likenesses chose artists like Léon Bonnat, who worked in a quieter, less extravagant manner than Sargent or his European counterparts Paul Helleu, Giovanni Boldini, and Emile Carolus-Duran. The vogue for Sargent's portraits among prominent Bostonians was the closest they had come in a great many years to the taste of New York.

Sargent would return to Boston in 1890, when he received the commission for the murals at the Boston Public Library, and again in 1895, when he was so occupied with installing the first group of murals that he had time for only two portraits: Helen Sears (the young daughter of Mrs. J. Montgomery Sears, a prominent collector of French and American Impressionist paintings, whom he would later paint in London) and Gardner Greene Hammond. Hammond wanted Sargent to paint his children as well, but Sargent, busy with the murals, recommended Mary Cassatt in his stead. When Cassatt came to Boston to paint the Hammond children, it was also to further the cause of modern French painting: she became an adviser to Mrs. Sears, who bought Manet's *Street Singer* (now in the Museum of Fine Arts) on her recommendation.

JOHN SINGER SARGENT
The Frieze of the Prophets,
1892-1895

When John Singer Sargent received the commission to decorate the newly-built Public Library in Copley Square, he was only thirty-four years old but already the most popular artist in Boston. His theme for the murals was the evolution of religion; the segment for which this is a sketch was installed in the north end of the library's hallway in 1895. (Museum of Fine Arts, Boston. Gift of Mrs. Francis Ormond.)

In 1891, the St. Botolph Club showed a group of ninety watercolors (almost all privately owned) by nineteenth-century artists, French, English, Dutch, and American. In addition to the expected works by Homer, La Farge, Mauve, Troyon, and local favorites Dodge MacKnight and J. Linden Smith, there was a group of over a dozen English watercolors by Turner, Ruskin, Rosetti, and Burne-Jones, lent by Professor Charles Eliot Norton of Harvard. The Ruskinian aesthetic exemplified by these watercolors was beginning to emerge from isolation in Cambridge, where Norton and his circle had been its lone champion for many years. In 1880, the Museum of Fine Arts had held an exhibition of Ruskin's drawings, most lent by Norton, who eventually gave them to the Fogg Art Museum at Harvard. More important was the fact that Norton's pupils, themselves advocates of Ruskin's theories, were beginning to have an impact on Boston's cultural affairs. Among these were Henry James (a reluctant convert), George Santayana, and Bernard Berenson, who from about 1894 served as adviser to Isabella Stewart Gardner, the most dynamic collector of her day.

The first pictures Mrs. Gardner purchased were consistent with Boston's taste of the late '60s and early '70s; she bought a painting by Charles Jacque in 1873, a Diaz in 1876, and a Corot in 1880, all from local galleries. She also purchased paintings by La Farge and J. Appleton Brown during those years. But by the 1890s, her taste for old master paintings had been kindled. She acquired her celebrated Vermeer, *The Concert*, at auction in 1892, a Pesallino *Madonna and Child* (then believed to be by Filippo Lippi) that same year, and the Botticelli *Death of Lucretia* in 1894.[71] Her purchases, especially of the painters of the Italian Renaissance, were advised by Norton and Berenson, both of whom had a romantic, even religious attitude toward early Italian art and its power to instruct, inspire, and provide a moral example. In the 1890s, Mrs. Gardner would associate herself more and more with the intellectual circle that had nurtured the Ruskin-Jarves viewpoint in Boston, an increasingly powerful voice, if a minority one.[72]

Isabella Gardner patronized American artists in a limited way. Her taste ran to expatriates such as Sargent, Whistler, and Bunker, who were her friends; she also collected a group of younger artists, many of whom, like J. Linden Smith and Ralph W. Curtis, were amateurs. She used others, like Bunker and Louis Kronberg, as agents for the purchase of European pictures.

Mrs. Gardner's ambitious collecting, and her building of a fabulous palace to house her treasures, ran counter to the pattern followed by other Bostonians, which was to buy modestly and only what one's house could hold. Her ambivalent, defiant relationship with Boston society no doubt influenced her choice of objects, which were flashier and more exotic than what other local collectors were buying and were, by and large, not French; she bought her first Degas only in 1904, her Manets (with Kronberg's help) in 1910 and 1922, and owned no Millets or Monets.

Boston had no other patron of the arts like Mrs. Gardner. Of her competitors, only Mrs. Warren ever expressed a similar interest in old master paintings (Berenson nearly offered both of them Titian's *Rape of Europa* in 1896), only Mrs. Sears won nearly equal favor with Sargent, and only Desmond Fitzgerald (who, like Mrs. Sears, and before them Edward Wheelwright and Thomas Gold Appleton, was an amateur painter) had a like ambition to immortalize his collection; in 1913 he built an art gallery, open to the public, adjacent to his Brookline home. But Mrs. Sears, who was one of the first to patronize the Boston School (buying Tarbell's *Three Sisters: A Study in June Sunlight* [now in the Milwaukee Art Center] from an 1891 St. Botolph Club exhibition), and Fitzgerald, who deliberately sought out new American artists like the watercolorist Dodge MacKnight and was an early friend and patron of Monet's, had a strong interest in contemporary art. Mrs. Gardner did not; although her superb collection of old masters differed markedly in content and even in quality from that of other local collections (and was, in fact, comparable to the collections being assembled by men like Morgan and Frick in New York), her goals for a museum (artistic education through public exhibition of works of art) were traditionally Bostonian.[73]

An orientation toward modern art was not, after the turn of the century, characteristic of Boston taste. The Armory Show, which came to Boston in late April, 1913, after reasonably successful showings in New York and Chicago, stayed for three weeks and then disappeared as though it had never been. Pared down from over 2,000 works to 244 and bereft of all of its American pictures, the exhibition was vilified in the press (which called it "a chamber of horrors"), and its sponsors (among them Fitzgerald and Coolidge) disclaimed responsibility for the content of the show, explaining defensively that they neither approved nor disapproved of the art, but presented it as an educational service.[74] Although over 12,000 curious Bostonians saw the show during its three weeks at Copley Hall, its effect on patrons and artists was minimal: Boston collectors

bought only four or five objects from the show, the most important being a small Villon drawing (the first of the *Puteaux* series, bought for eighty-one dollars by Cambridge collector Walter Arensberg, who left the Villon and the rest of his collection to the Philadelphia Museum), and contributed little from their own collections although loans were solicited. There was little noticeable effect on local artists, either: Benson, De-Camp, and Tarbell, the major painters in Boston, continued to work in the same manner that they had practiced in the '90s, and the next generation of artists, for the most part their protégés, were faithful to the academic tradition, having little interest in abstraction or the innovative techniques of Picasso, Matisse, Villon, and others represented in the exhibition.

A few Boston collectors in the decades after the Armory Show bought modern works, American and European, and their collections now form the core of the Museum of Fine Arts' early twentieth-century holdings. John T. Spaulding, who acquired extraordinary late nineteenth-century French paintings during this period, also bought American pictures, among them Robert Henri's *Irish Girl* and Edward Hopper's *Drug Store* (both now in the Museum of Fine Arts), exposing Bostonians to a kind of direct

urban realism to which they were not accustomed. Robert Treat Paine II bought French paintings brilliantly, including Cézanne's *Self Portrait* (Museum of Fine Arts), and an occasional American picture by Bellows or Prendergast.

However, there were few other Boston collectors in this period collecting "modern" pictures, works inspired by Cubism or Futurism. The failure of modernism in Boston has been attributed to the city's reluctance to follow New York, to the absence of new money, often associated with patronage of the avant-garde, and concomitantly, to the absence of an environment hospitable to the many European artists emigrating to the United States, who chose instead to settle in New York. And according to Charles Prendergast, neither was Boston receptive to American painters working in a modern style: "You can't get a picture into the Boston Museum except you [sic] antecedents date back to the Mayflower . . . They are still hovering over old tradition."[75] The Prendergasts left Boston for New York in 1913.

An equally important reason that modernism had little significant impact in Boston was the continuing strength of the Boston School from the 1890s through the era of the Armory Show. A group of painters who taught at the School of the Museum of Fine Arts at the turn of the century, the Boston School included Frank Benson, Edmund Tarbell, Joseph DeCamp, and the slightly younger Philip and Lilian Westcott Hale and William Paxton. Most of these artists received their initial training at the Museum School in the 1880s and then studied at the more avant-garde Académie Julian in Paris. They specialized in portraiture and in figure paintings, especially of fashionable young women in tasteful interior or garden settings. The style they pioneered and transmitted to innumerable Boston painters in the teens and twenties was synthetic rather than revolutionary, combining the many artistic styles that had been popular in Boston in the nineteenth century. These artists' paintings were executed, for the most part, with the bright palette and dashing brushwork that Monet and others had made fashionable. Their simple, flattened compositions, and the oriental accessories that decorate many of the fashionable interiors they depicted, reflect the interest in Japanese art that was one of the most powerful aesthetic influences in Boston from the late 1870s. The most interesting ingredient of the Boston-School style was the soft golden light and emphasis on domestic settings derived from the paintings of the Dutch masters, especially Vermeer, which DeCamp, Paxton, and others saw in Paris and at Fenway Court. Although the emulation of these seventeenth-century painters had its critics (like Charles Hovey Pepper, who commented snidely, "A near Vermeer is a mere veneer"), it provided a link with art of the past that had always been important in Boston.

The Boston collectors who bought Impressionist paintings in the 1890s also patronized the Boston School. Desmond Fitzgerald owned five watercolors by Benson, a portait by Philip Hale, and a figure painting by Tarbell. Mrs. David P. Kimball, an early collector of Monets, bought Tarbell's *Mother and Child in a Boat* and Benson's *Girl in a Red Shawl* in the 1890s; both of these paintings are now in the Museum of Fine Arts. The Museum itself was an early patron of the Boston School, buying both DeCamp's *Blue Cup* (cat. no. 75) and Benson's *Eleanor* (cat. no. 73) in 1908, within a year of their execution.

Although its paintings won immediate favor in Boston, the Boston School was not without its detractors. Artist and critic Guy Pène du Bois, an advocate of the harsher realism of the contemporary Ash Can School, found Boston-School painting with its dreamy women and genteel interiors superficial and ignorant of current social changes: ". . . the Boston painters avoid all but the polite truths, and that means that their truths are perforce . . . perfunctory. They lend to art

airs of timidity not in keeping with that defiant independence which has produced great art in the face of tremendous privation and, worse still, opposition. They give it airs of a gentleman and that means airs of a particular class. They make it exclusive when it should be the reverse."[76]

Yet, whereas the Boston School painters were progressive neither in formal terms (that is, they did not experiment with abstraction) nor in their content, their goals were ambitious and their technical standards high. In applying Impressionist techniques to figurative subject matter, they were attempting to return Impressionism (or at least Impressionism as it was known in Boston through the landscapes of Monet) to humanistic concerns. That is, they endeavored to make art that focused on a central human presence and, as such, was classical and enduring. Their interests coincided with the avowed aims of Cézanne, soon to be avidly collected in Boston, who in the 1870s spoke of "making out of Impressionism something solid and durable like the art of museums."[77] This goal, evident in paintings like Benson's *Eleanor* and Tarbell's *Three Sisters*, was welcome in Boston, coinciding with and perhaps even helping to generate the city's interest in figurative Impressionism early in the twentieth century.

The Boston School's approach to subject matter was, like that of Hunt and Allston, prescriptive rather than descriptive, idealizing rather than realistic. This art was grounded, in other words, in an interest in a moral statement, in the presentation of an ideal that Bostonians like Henry James found to be lacking in Impressionism: ". . . the Impressionists . . . abjure virtue altogether, and declare that a subject which has been crudely chosen shall be loosely treated."[78] The ideal world that the Boston School painters were trying to represent had long been a preoccupation of the city's artists and their patrons. Inherent in Boston's support of her artists, from Allston to Paxton, is the Emersonian belief (a view, ironically, not far from Ruskin) that there is "an inextricable relation . . . between ethics and aesthetics" because "the only durable kind of beauty is spiritual or moral beauty, of which material beauty is but the exterior symbol."[79] Tarbell, Benson, and the others taught for many years at the School of the Museum of Fine Arts, transmitting their belief in an ideal art and in sound painting techniques to several generations of Boston painters, some of whom still continue to work in the Boston School manner today. In their continuing pursuit of an aesthetic that is cosmopolitan, moral, and outside the artistic mainstream defined by New York, these artists are the true inheritors of the Boston tradition.

1. "Boston Athenaeum Review," *Crayon* 1 (July 11, 1855), p. 24.
2. "Jarves's *Art Hints*," *North American Review* 81 (1855), p. 457.
3. Mesos, "The Athenaeum Exhibition," *Dwight's Journal of Music* 13 (June 5, 1858), p. 80.
4. Ernest W. Longfellow, *Random Memories* (Boston, 1922), p. 98.
5. Augustine Duganne, *Art's True Mission in America* (New York, 1853), p. 28.
6. William Howe Downes, "Boston Painters and Paintings I," *Atlantic Monthly* 62 (July 1888), pp. 90–91.
7. Jonathan Belcher to Jonathan Belcher, Jr., August 7, 1734, Jonathan Belcher Letterbooks, vol. 4 (January 23, 1734–April 31, 1735), Massachusetts Historical Society, Boston.
8. Byles's poem is quoted (in its entirety) in Henry Wilder Foote, *John Smibert, Painter* (Cambridge, Mass., 1950), pp. 54–55.
9. *Paul Revere's Boston* (Museum of Fine Arts, Boston, 1975), p. 27.
10. Feke had to travel to several cities to generate enough commissions to support himself, while Greenwood and Badger at times were forced to supplement their incomes derived from portrait painting with other kinds of work.
11. Copley to Benjamin West or Captain R. G. Bruce, 1767, *Letters and Papers of John Singleton Copley and Henry Pelham* (New York, 1970), pp. 65–66.
12. Downes describes this era as "a long period of almost entire vacuity in the history of Boston art," "Boston Painters and Paintings I," pp. 95–96.
13. Neil Harris, *The Artist in American Society: The Formative Years, 1790–1850* (New York, 1966), p. 33.
14. René Brimo, *L'Evolution du goût aux Etats-Unis* (Paris, 1938), p. 30. For Bowdoin's collection see also Marvin Sadik, "James Bowdoin III as Art Collector," *Colonial and Federal Portraits at Bowdoin College* (Brunswick, Maine, 1966), pp. 208–222.
15. "Historic Processions in Boston," *Publications of the Bostonian Society* 5 (1908), pp. 65–119.
16. Daniel Bowen, Broadside for Columbian Museum, Massachusetts Historical Society, Boston.
17. David Tatham, "D. C. Johnston's Satiric Views of Art in Boston, 1825–1850," *Art and Commerce* (Boston, 1978), p. 18.
18. Josiah Quincy, *History of the Boston Athenaeum* (Cambridge, Mass., 1851), p. 18.
19. Ibid., p. 28.
20. William Tudor, "An Institution for the Fine Arts," *North American Review* 11 (January 1816), p. 163.
21. Letter from William Tudor to Harrison Gray Otis, September 2, 1815, quoted in Samuel Eliot Morison, *The Life and Letters of Harrison Gray Otis* (Boston, 1913), pp. 246–248.
22. Thomas C. Carey, *Memoir of Thomas Handasyd Perkins: Containing Extracts from His Diaries and Letters* (Boston, 1856), p. 244. See also Tanya Boyett, "Thomas Handasyd Perkins: An Essay on Material Culture," *Old Time New England* 70 (1980), pp. 45–62.
23. Salmon's account book as reprinted in John Wilmerding, *Robert Salmon: Painter of Ship and Shore* (Boston, 1971), p. 92.
24. John Ward Dean, "Mr. Isaac P. Davis," *Memorial Biographies of the New England Historic Genealogical Society* 2 (Boston, 1881), p. 333.
25. Dana, as quoted in Mabel Munson Swan, *The Athenaeum Gallery 1827–1873* (Boston, 1940), pp. 53–54.
26. Benjamin Champney, *Sixty Years' Memory of Art and Artists* (Woburn, Mass., 1900), pp. 14–15.
27. Julia Ward Howe, quoted in E. P. Richardson, *Washington Allston: The Study of the Romantic Artist in America* (Chicago, 1948), p. 182.
28. Downes, "Boston Painters and Paintings II," *Atlantic Monthly* 62 (August 1888), pp. 258–259.
29. Walter K. Watkins, "The New England Museum and the Home of Art in Boston," *Publications of the Bostonian Society* 2 (second series; 1917); pp. 125–127.
30. In 1823, John Neal wrote in his novel *Randolph*: [Henry Sargent] ". . . has just painted a piece called the *Dinner Party*, after the manner of the *Capuchin Chapel*."
31. "Boston Exhibition of Pictures," *North American Review* 29 (July 1829), p. 259.
32. Frederic A. Sharf, "Art and Life in Boston, 1837 to 1850," unpublished senior honors thesis, Harvard University, 1956, p. 88.
33. *Boston Evening Transcript,* April 23, 1839.
34. "Constitution of the Boston Artists' Association," catalogue, "First Public Exhibition of Paintings at Harding's Gallery" (Boston, 1842), p. 3.
35. "Powers' Statue of the Greek Slave" (Boston, 1848), p. 4.
36. Letter from Horatio Greenough to Richard H. Dana, February 23, 1852, printed in *Catalogue of the Twenty-Sixth Exhibition of Paintings and Statuary at the Athenaeum Gallery* (Boston, 1853), p. 16.
37. "We have surpassed already the republic of Greece in our political institutions and I see no reason why we should not attempt to approach their excellence in the fine arts." Letter from Thomas Crawford to Charles Sumner, quoted in "Orpheus," *Democratic Review* 12 (May 1843), p. 451.
38. Story, quoted in Henry James, *William Wetmore Story and His Friends* I (Boston, 1903), p. 102.
39. William Wetmore Story, Phi Beta Kappa address, published in Story, *Nature and Art* (Boston, 1844), pp. 37–38.
40. Ralph Waldo Emerson, "The American Scholar," reprinted in *American Literature: The Makers and the Making* I, ed. Cleanth Brooks, R. W. B. Lewis, Robert Penn Warren (New York, 1973), p. 711.
41. Emerson, "Art," (1841), *Emerson's Essays,* ed. Irwin Edman (New York, 1951), pp. 248–253.
42. Nathaniel Hawthorne, *The Marble Faun* (1859) (New York, 1961), p. 246.
43. Elihu Vedder, in his *Digressions of V.* (Boston, 1910, p. 264) recounts his thoughts on this subject as expressed to Emerson: "I said, 'Mr. Emerson, I think there is a great difference between the literary man and the artist in regard to Europe. Nature is the same everywhere, but literature and art are Nature seen through other eyes, and a literary man in Patagonia without books to consult would be at a great disadvantage. Here he has all that is essential in the way of books: but to the artist, whose books are pictures, this land is Patagonia.'"
44. Helen M. Knowlton, *W. M. Hunt's Talks on Art* (Boston, 1875; 3d edition, 1881), p. 7.
45. Edward Wheelwright, "Personal Recollections of Jean-François Millet," *Atlantic Monthly* 38 (September 1876), pp. 257–276.
46. Arthur Dexter, "The Fine Arts in Boston," *Memorial History of Boston* 4, ed. Justin Winsor (Boston, 1881), p. 402.
47. Downes, "Boston Painters and Paintings III," *Atlantic Monthly* 62 (September 1888), p. 391.
48. Dexter, "The Fine Arts in Boston," p. 462.
49. Downes, "Boston Painters and Paintings III," *Atlantic Monthly* 62, (September 1888), p. 388.
50. Bostonians' admiration for Millet was expressed by Thomas Gold Appleton in his *Museum of Fine Arts: A Companion to the Catalogues* (Boston, 1877), pp. 52–53:
    Millet, born of country folk . . . has felt it his mission to express the light and shadow of the life of the *prolétaire*, or French peasant. This he has done with such fidelity to their humble pleasures and long unrelieved toil, and at the same time given such dignity and even grandeur to his homely figures, that at last after years of neglect he has succeeded in touching the world's heart. His ideas of art and truth were at the opposite pole from the fashionable frivolity of the empire."
51. Ibid.
52. These comments are quoted, with references cited, in Henry

Adams, "The Contradictions of William Morris Hunt," *William Morris Hunt: A Memorial Exhibition* (Museum of Fine Arts, Boston, 1979), p. 24.

53. Samuel L. Gerry, *Reminiscences of the Boston Art Club*, Boston (unpublished MS., ca. 1885; typescript in the MFA), pp. 1, 4.

54. [Henry James], "Hamerton's Contemporary French Painters," *North American Review* 106 (April 1868), p. 721.

55. Bicknell, letter to Vedder, May 8, 1866, quoted in Regina Soria, *Elihu Vedder. American Visionary Artist in Rome* (Rutherford, N.J., 1970), p. 48.

56. Downes, "Boston Painters and Paintings VI," *Atlantic Monthly* 62, (December 1888), p. 785.

57. Dexter, "The Fine Arts in Boston," p. 413.

58. "Art," *Atlantic Monthly* 35 (June 1875), pp. 751–752.

59. [Henry James], "Notes," *Nation* 20 (July 3, 1875), p. 376.

60. Josiah B. Millet, ed., *George Fuller, His Life and Works* (Boston, 1886), p. 51. I am grateful to Tanya Boyett for sharing with me her work on Fuller.

61. John La Farge, quoting the French romantic painter Eugène Fromentin in *Considerations on Paintings* (New York and London, 1895), p. 22.

62. [Henry James], "Art," *Atlantic Monthly* 29 (January, 1872), p. 117.

63. Elihu Vedder, *The Digressions of V.* (Boston 1910), pp. 259–260.

64. Walter Muir Whitehill, *Museum of Fine Arts, Boston, A Centennial History* (Cambridge, Mass., 1970), p. 10.

65. Calvin Tomkins, *Merchants and Masterpieces: The Story of the Metropolitan Museum of Art* (New York, 1970), pp. 23, 35.

66. [William Tudor], "Boston Athenaeum," *Monthly Anthology* 4 (May 1807), p. 2.

67. Dexter, "The Fine Arts in Boston," p. 407.

68. William Howe Downes, *The Life and Works of Winslow Homer* (Boston, 1911), p. 126.

69. In 1884, Catherine Lorillard Wolfe paid $2,500 for *The Life Line* (now in the Philadelphia Museum of Art). She subsequently sold it to Thomas B. Clarke. At the sale of Clarke's collection in 1899 it brought $4,500, a record price for a living American artist.

70. Constitution of the St. Botolph Club, January 1880, quoted in Talcott M. Banks, Jr., "The St. Botolph Club. Highlights from the First Forty Years," unpublished MS., St. Botolph Club, Boston.

71. Philip J. Hendy, *European and American Paintings in the Isabella Stewart Gardner Museum* (Boston, 1974), pp. 38–41, 178–180, 282–284.

72. No doubt this connection inspired the purchase of a Turner in 1899 and a Rossetti (*Love's Greeting*) some years before; more important was Mrs. Gardner's strong interest in the so-called Italian primitives (she would eventually own two Botticellis, a Piero della Francesca, and a Fra Angelico), righting Boston's wrong to Jarves.

73. René Brimo, *L'Evolution du goût aux Etats-Unis* (Paris, 1938), p. 86.

74. Frederick James Gregg, "Cubist and Futurist Pictures to be Exhibited in Boston by Copley Society," *Sunday Herald* (Boston, April 27, 1913), p. 28.

75. Charles Prendergast, note in the Prendergast sketchbooks, Museum of Fine Arts, as quoted in Amy Goldin, "The Brothers Prendergast," *Art in America* 64 (March–April 1976), p. 9.

76. Guy Pène du Bois, "The Boston Group of Painters: An Essay on Nationalism in Art," *Arts and Decoration* 5 (October 1915), p. 458.

77. John Rewald, *The History of Impressionism* (4th ed., New York, 1973).

78. Henry James, "Parisian Festivity," *New York Tribune* (May 13, 1876), as quoted in John L. Sweeney, ed., *The Painter's Eye* (Cambridge, Mass., 1956), p. 27.

79. William Howe Downes, "Training in Taste," *Atlantic Monthly* 93 (June 1904), p. 820.

CATALOGUE

JOHN SMIBERT (1688-1751)
active in Boston 1729–1751

1. *William Dudley*, 1729

Oil on canvas, 36⅛ x 28¼ in. (91.7 x 71.8 cm.)

Gift of Mrs. J. Brooks Fenno. 1979.768

PROVENANCE: Mrs. Arthur Bell, Boston, by 1950; Mrs. J. Brooks Fenno, Chestnut Hill, Mass.

BIBLIOGRAPHY: *Massachusetts Historical Society Proceedings,* January 1886, p. 197; Frederick W. Coburn, "John Smibert," *Art in America* 17 (June 1929), p. 177; Frank W. Bayley, *Five Colonial Artists* (Boston, 1929), p. 377 (as *Paul Dudley);* Henry Wilder Foote, *John Smibert, Painter* (Cambridge, Mass., 1950), p. 150; Sir David Evans, ed., *The Notebook of John Smibert* (Boston, 1969), pp. 21, 88, 105; Richard H. Saunders III, "John Smibert (1688-1751): Anglo-American Portrait Painter" (Ph.D. dissertation, Yale University, 1979), pp. 132-133.

Smibert had been in Boston only a few months when the Dudleys commissioned him to paint their portraits. Elizabeth Davenport Dudley (1704–1756) was the eldest daughter of Judge Addington Davenport of Boston. William Dudley (1686–1743) was the youngest son of Joseph Dudley, the former governor of Massachusetts, who had been called "the most hated man in New England"; despite his unpopularity he was an extremely wealthy man and a leader of society. William, who served as a member of the Governor's Council in the 1720s, shared his father's desire to live like an English gentleman; this ambition led him to seek out Smibert, who brought to Boston the latest fashions in London portraiture.

Despite their wealth, the Dudleys instructed Smibert to paint their portraits in the most economical format he offered, the kit-cat, which nonetheless allowed them to be shown over half-length and with a fanciful landscape behind them. The portrait of William Dudley is the more successful of the two: the figure is placed in the immediate foreground and so dominates the picture space; his striking red coat, though summarily painted, makes a forceful impression, as does his severe expression and the masterful gesture of the hand on the hip. Smibert rarely flattered his female sitters, and Mrs. Dudley is no exception: her face is quite plain, if well composed; her body is somewhat oddly proportioned, especially her overly long arms and broad, sloping shoulders; and the cape over her right arm is hastily rendered. Yet she, too, is an imposing personality. Her tilted head and half-smile are a coy complement to her husband's aggressive stare, while her gaze is forthright and directed at the viewer. As one would expect, these portraits are similar to Smibert's production during his last years in England, employing poses derived from Kneller and preserving the same balance between carefully delineated facial features and a generalized treatment of the remainder of the portrait.

44

2. *Mrs. William Dudley (Elizabeth Davenport)*, 1729

Oil on canvas, 35⅛ x 28⅛ in. (90.3 x 71.2 cm.)

Gift of Mrs. J. Brooks Fenno. 1979.769

PROVENANCE: Mrs. Arthur Bell, Boston, by 1950; Mrs. J. Brooks Fenno, Chestnut Hill, Mass.

EXHIBITIONS: "Loan Exhibition," Copley Society, Boston, 1922.

BIBLIOGRAPHY: *Massachusetts Historical Society Proceedings*, January 1886, p. 197; Henry Wilder Foote, *John Smibert, Painter* (Cambridge, Mass., 1950), pp. 150-151; Sir David Evans, ed., *The Notebook of John Smibert* (Boston, 1969), pp. 21, 88, 105; Richard H. Saunders III "John Smibert (1688-1751): Anglo-American Portrait Painter" (Ph.D. dissertation, Yale University, 1979), pp. 132-133.

3. *Daniel, Peter, and Andrew Oliver,* 1732

Oil on canvas, 39¼ x 57¾ (99.7 x 144.2 cm.)

Emily L. Ainsley Fund. 53.952

PROVENANCE: Andrew Oliver, Boston, 1732; Andrew Oliver, his son, Boston, 1774; descended in the family to Dr. Fitch Edward Oliver, Boston; Andrew, Edward, Lawrence, and Susan Oliver, his children, by 1930.

EXHIBITIONS: "One Hundred Colonial Portraits," Museum of Fine Arts, Boston, 1930; "John Smibert," Yale University Art Gallery, New Haven, 1949, no. 21; "The Olivers and Their Friends," Massachusetts Historical Society, Boston, 1960, no. 3.

BIBLIOGRAPHY: A. T. Perkins, "Blackburn and Smibert," *Massachusetts Historical Society Proceedings* 16 (1878), p. 397; F. W. Coburn, "John Smibert," *Art in America* 17 (1929), p. 178; Frank W. Bayley, *Five Colonial Artists* (Boston, 1929), p. 409; Henry Wilder Foote, *John Smibert, Painter* (Cambridge, Mass., 1950), pp. 176-177; Andrew Oliver, *Faces of a Family* (Cambridge, Mass., 1960), p. 4; Sir David Evans, ed., *The Notebook of John Smibert* (Boston, 1969), pp. 24, 91, 109; *American Paintings in the Museum of Fine Arts, Boston* (Boston, 1969), no. 888; Richard H. Saunders III, "John Smibert (1688–1751): Anglo-American Portrait Painter" (Ph.D. dissertation, Yale University, 1979), p. 156.

The Olivers were among Smibert's most loyal patrons in America. He painted at least eleven portraits of different members of the family between 1729 and about 1734, beginning with the patriarch, the Boston merchant Daniel Oliver, and his wife Elizabeth Belcher (both 1729; coll. Andrew Oliver, Brookline, Mass.). In 1732, Smibert painted their three sons, pictured here: Daniel Jr. (1704–1727), who had died of smallpox in England, but whose likeness here Smibert took from a miniature; Peter (1713–1791), who became chief justice of the Superior Court of Massachusetts; and Andrew (1706–1774), who served as the Loyalist lieutenant-governor of the Province of Massachusetts Bay during the 1770s.

It is not known whether Smibert resorted to any of the mezzotints he brought with him from England in 1729 for the composition of this portrait, but the device of grouping figures around a central table had been common in English portraiture since the sixteenth century,[1] and Smibert himself had used the motif in his famous portrait *The Bermuda Group: Dean George Berkeley and his Entourage* (Yale University Art Gallery, New Haven). Other than *The Bermuda Group,* this simple and direct composition is probably the first group portrait to be painted in America; its success stems from the immediacy and directness of Smibert's characterization.

All three brothers are pictured very close to the picture plane. Daniel, at left, sits stiffly erect, his face impassive and rather characterless, as one might expect from a likeness made at second hand. Peter is shown as the most casual of the brothers, his arm draped informally, if somewhat awkwardly, over the back of his chair. Andrew's thoughtful, serious expression is unusual for Smibert, whose sitters more often appear stern than sensitive; in none of Smibert's other portraits are a variety of personalities so convincingly portrayed.

1. Richard H. Saunders III, "John Smibert (1688–1751): Anglo-American Portrait Painter" (Ph.D. dissertation, Yale University, 1979), p. 149.

ROBERT FEKE (active before 1741 - after 1750)
active in Boston 1741 and 1748–1749

4. *Isaac Winslow*, ca. 1748

Oil on canvas, 50 x 40⅛ in. (127.0 x 101.8 cm.)

Gift in memory of the sitter's granddaughter (Mary Russell Winslow Bradford, 1793–1899), by her great-grandson, Russell Wiles. 42.424

PROVENANCE: Elizabeth Winslow Pickering, great-niece of the sitter; Arthur Pickering, her son, Roxbury, Mass., in 1873; Susan Howard Pickering, his daughter, Boston; Russell Wiles, Chicago, 1936.

EXHIBITIONS: "Robert Feke," Whitney Museum of American Art, New York, 1946, no. 30; "American Painting," Tate Gallery, London, 1946, no. 84; "Rediscoveries in American Art," Cincinnati Art Museum, 1955, no. 43.

BIBLIOGRAPHY: Augustus T. Perkins, *A Sketch in the Life . . . of John Singleton Copley* (Boston, 1873), supplement no. 2, p. 24 (as by Copley); Barbara N. Parker and Anne B. Wheeler, *John Singleton Copley* (Boston, 1938), p. 257; Barbara N. Parker, "A Member of the Winslow Family in Boston," *Bulletin of the Museum of Fine Arts* 40 (October 1942), pp. 147-148; James T. Flexner, "Robert Feke," *Magazine of Art* 40 (1947), p. 68; Henry Wilder Foote, "Robert Feke," *Art in America* 35 (1947), p. 68; Helen Comstock, "American Painting in the 18th Century," *Connoisseur* 134 (1955), p. 296; ————, "Feke and the Nelsons of Virginia," *Antiques* 75 (1959), p. 458; *American Paintings in the Museum of Fine Arts, Boston* (Boston, 1969), no. 398.

Although he succeeded John Smibert as the leading portraitist in New England, and was perhaps the finest painter in America before Copley, Robert Feke left behind little information about his life or the development of his career. Unlike Smibert, who practiced his trade almost exclusively in Boston, Feke was a peripatetic artist known to have painted in New York, Philadelphia, Newport, and Boston. He continued to translate the English portrait tradition into an American colonial idiom, as Smibert had; his sources were mezzotint engravings after the works of Kneller, Lely, and other seventeenth- and early eighteenth-century British portraitists, as well as the paintings of his predecessor in Boston.

Feke is known to have been in Boston in 1748. The most important portraits he completed that year were very similar three-quarter-length portraits of Boston's two leading merchants, James Bowdoin II (1726–1796) (Bowdoin College Museum of Art, Brunswick, Me.) and Isaac Winslow (1709–1777). Their deliberate pursuit of each of Boston's leading portraitists from Smibert and Badger to Copley, suggests friendly competition between the two men, who collaborated on several business ventures. Winslow, son of

the well-known Boston silversmith Edward Winslow, made his fortune as a shipper and land speculator; along with Bowdoin and other prominent Bostonians, he was a member of the Kennebunk Proprietorship, which was buying vast tracts of land in Maine in an effort to settle and develop that territory. Winslow commissioned Feke to paint this portrait and that of his wife, Lucy Waldo (Brooklyn Museum) in 1748, the year of their marriage.

For *Isaac Winslow*, Feke turned to a composition and pose that had been employed by John Smibert some ten years earlier. Smibert's last important commission, his portrait of Peter Faneuil (1739; Corcoran Gallery of Art, Washington), shows that sitter in a pose that Smibert had derived from Kneller and had been using for at least fifteen years. Like *Peter Faneuil*, in *Isaac Winslow* the figure is shown three-quarter length, his face turned toward the viewer, his right arm resting on a stone plinth and his left gesturing toward an open landscape. But Feke gave the well-worn formula new energy by an attention to details of color and texture of which Smibert was never capable. Most skillful is the contrast between Winslow's dull brown overcoat and the shining satin and sparkling embroidery of the waistcoat. Unlike the ashen sameness of the faces in Smibert's last portraits, Feke's likeness of Winslow is convincing; his expression and posture suggest a stateliness and dignity appropriate to his social position.

The delicately colored landscape in the background of *Isaac Winslow* was common in eighteenth-century portraiture. Feke seems to have appropriated some of the details of his landscape from *Peter Faneuil*, including the cloud patterns, the tiny ship in the far distance, and the horizon at the midpoint of the composition. He substituted for the large ship on the horizon in *Peter Faneuil* a tiny canoe just coming to shore, surely an allusion to the expeditions of discovery and settlement Winslow sponsored in Maine. This detail adds interest to the portrait and meaning to Winslow's gesture, and was in accord with contemporary treatises on portraiture, which advocated the inclusion of such "Historical Expressions" as "Robes, or other Marks of Dignity, or of a Profession, Employment or Amusement, a Book, a Ship, a favorite Dog" to illustrate the sitter's position in society.[1]

1. Jonathan Richardson, *An Essay on the Theory of Painting* (London, 1715), p. 99 as quoted in Richard H. Saunders III, "John Smibert (1688–1751): Anglo-American Painter" (Ph.D. dissertation, Yale University, 1979), p. 83.

JOHN GREENWOOD (1727-1792)
active in Boston 1742–1752

5. *Mrs. Henry Bromfield (Margaret Fayerweather)*, 1749-1750

Oil on canvas, 36 x 25¾ in. (91.5 x 65.4 cm.)

Emily L. Ainsley Fund. 62.173

PROVENANCE: Mrs. I. H. T. Blanchard (granddaughter of the sitter), Harvard, Mass., 1872; Miss Margaret Bromfield, Boston; Mrs. Henry E. Warner, South Lincoln, Mass., 1943; Mrs. Jean-Frédéric Wagnière (Margaret Warner), 1955.

BIBLIOGRAPHY: Barbara N. Parker and Anne B. Wheeler, *John Singleton Copley* (Boston, 1938), pp. 48-49; Alan Burroughs, *John Greenwood in America, 1745-52* (Andover, Mass., 1943), pp. 44-45, 63; Thomas N. Maytham, "Some Recent Accessions," *Museum of Fine Arts Bulletin* 60 (1962), pp. 140-141; *American Paintings in the Museum of Fine Arts, Boston* (Boston, 1969), no. 463; *American Art: 1750-1800. Towards Independence* (Yale University Art Gallery, New Haven, 1976), p. 71.

This modest, blunt portrait is one of a small number that can be attributed to Greenwood during his brief career in Boston. He is better known for his painting *Sea Captains Carousing in Surinam* (St. Louis Art Museum), based on a visit there in 1752, and for his career as an auctioneer and art dealer in London, where he settled ten years later. Once attributed to Copley,[1] this portrait of Mrs. Bromfield is characteristic of Greenwood's early work, for he imbued most of his sitters with the same features: high foreheads, long bulbous noses, wide almond-shaped eyes (which are, as here, occasionally noticeably different in size), and broad square shoulders, accented in his female sitters by a low U-shaped neckline.

Greenwood received his initial training from Thomas Johnston, a heraldic painter and engraver. Johnston no doubt introduced Greenwood to the British mezzotints that served most colonial portraitists as patterns for their images. For *Mrs. Bromfield*, Greenwood employed one of the most popular conventions of eighteenth-century female portraiture: the elegant gesture of lifting a flower from the lap and holding it at the breast. The antecedents of this gesture, and of the sitter's pose and the severe stone wall behind her, are to be found in prints such as *Princess Anne* (ca. 1683) by Isaac Beckett after Willem Wissing, *Princess Anne* (1692) by John Smith after Godfrey Kneller, or *Anne Oldfield* (ca. 1705–1710) by John Simon after Jonathan Richardson. But Greenwood seems to have found greater inspiration in the work of Robert Feke, from whose paintings he drew several compositional elements for *Mrs. Bromfield*.

Feke painted both Mrs. James Bowdoin II and Mrs. William Bowdoin (both Bowdoin College Museum of Art, Brunswick, Me.) in Boston. Greenwood may have based the pose of his sitter and the blue-brown color scheme on *Mrs. James Bowdoin*, while drawing from *Mrs. William Bowdoin* the devices of the stone pedestal and the stone wall placed immediately behind the sitter. Mrs. Bromfield's delicate gesture of raising a flower to her breast repeats Mrs. James Bowdoin's, and the two women wear virtually identical dresses and hairstyles—a fact attributable to the uniformity of fashions and possibly to the emulation of one sitter by another. It is natural that Greenwood would turn to Feke's work for inspiration, for Feke was the major painter in Boston at the time, John Smibert having ceased to paint and Joseph Badger working in his plain, uninspiring style in relative obscurity in Charlestown. Feke's work affected Greenwood's style as well as his composition, particularly in his emphasis on line; the hard, metallic surfaces in Greenwood's painting were an exaggeration of Feke's interest in satiny textures.

Margaret Fayerweather, born in 1732, was married at seventeen and had five children. This portrait was probably painted on the occasion of her marriage to Henry Bromfield, a prominent Boston merchant. She died of smallpox in 1762; shortly thereafter, Henry Bromfield remarried and moved his family to Harvard, Mass.[2]

1. Barbara N. Parker and Anne B. Wheeler, *John Singleton Copley* (Boston, 1938), pp. 48-49.
2. Daniel Denison Slade, "The Bromfield Family," *New England Historical and Genealogical Register* 26 (1872), pp. 37-39.

JOSEPH BADGER (1708-1765)

active in Boston after 1740–1765

6. *Mrs. John Edwards (Abigail Fowle),* ca. 1750-1760

Oil on canvas, 46⅜ x 35½ in. (117.7 x 90.2 cm.)

Gift of Dr. Charles Wendell Townsend. 24.421

PROVENANCE: Thomas Carter Smith (great-grandson of the sitter); Frances Barnard Townsend (his daughter); Dr. Charles Wendell Townsend, Boston (her son).

EXHIBITIONS: "Old and New England," Museum of Art, Rhode Island School of Design, Providence, 1945, no. 8; "From Colony to Nation," Art Institute of Chicago, 1949, n. 19; "Likeness of America 1680–1820," Fine Arts Center, Colorado Springs, 1949, no. 4; "Paintings in America, The Story of 450 Years," Detroit Institute of Arts, 1957, no. 21; "American Art 1750–1800: Towards Independence," Yale University Art Gallery, New Haven, 1976, no. 4.

BIBLIOGRAPHY: Lawrence Park, "An Account of Joseph Badger, and a Descriptive List of His Work," *Massachusetts Historical Society Proceedings* 51 (1918), p. 164; Frank W. Bayley, *Five Colonial Artists* (Boston, 1929), p. 21, repr. (misidentified as Mrs. Jonathan Edwards, née Sarah Pierepont [sic]); Cuthbert Lee, *Early American Portrait Painters* (New Haven, 1929), pp. 201, 204-205; Alan Burroughs, *Limmers and Likenesses* (Cambridge, Mass., 1936), fig. 41; Waldron Phoenix Belknap, Jr., *American Colonial Painting* (Cambridge, Mass., 1959), p. 290; *American Paintings in the Museum of Fine Arts, Boston* (Boston, 1969), no. 80.

Joseph Badger and Joseph Blackburn were contemporaries, both rising to prominence as portrait painters in Boston during the 1750s. They represent, nonetheless, opposite poles of the colonial portrait tradition: Blackburn, a highly skilled artist, was then the leading practitioner of the rococo in America, having brought with him from England a mastery of high-style portraiture acquired in the studios of Joseph Highmore and Thomas Hudson. Badger, on the other hand, was an unsophisticated painter, Boston-born and entirely self-taught. He began painting portraits after he was thirty years old, his only preparation for this profession being his work as a house painter and glazier.

Despite his lack of formal training, Badger, like Blackburn and their predecessors Robert Feke and John Smibert, drew upon English portraiture for compositional formulae and the poses of his sitters. The works of Lely, Kneller, Wissing, Vanderbank, and others were available to him through the mezzotint reproductions owned by John Smibert and Peter Pelham, which were circulated in the artistic community in Boston. Badger habitually adapted these rather complex models to his own plain style. For the portrait of Mrs. Edwards, he turned to an English type of three-quarter length, seated male portrait, such as *Sir Isaac Newton* by Vanderbank, which he knew through John Faber's engraving of 1726.[1] Badger made only minor changes from his model: Mrs. Edwards leans forward slightly in her chair, so she faces the viewer more squarely; the sitter's hands, which in the prototype rest casually on the arms of the chair, here are brought forward on the lap, and her left hand holds a book, presumably a prayer book, to which the other hand points, as though to draw attention to Mrs. Edwards's piety.

Badger used this model for several other portraits of both male and female sitters,[2] and in each case the subtle complications of pose and fluidity of line of the English portrait are converted to a more direct and elemental expression. Often the result is a rather crude portrait, lacking the rococo elegance that Blackburn was able to achieve working from similar models (see cat. no. 8). Badger's plain, awkward manner was best suited to the depiction of elderly sitters; *Mrs. Edwards* is a particularly successful example. About seventy years old when Badger painted her, she had by this time outlived two husbands, the first, William Smith, a prosperous shipmaster, and the second, John Edwards, a prominent Boston goldsmith. Although she was a wealthy woman at the time her portrait was painted, Badger included almost no indication of her prosperity: the large chair on which she sits lacks carved ornament or rich upholstery; the landscape behind her is generalized and without specific reference to the family's estate. Only the pearls on her neck suggest wealth, and they contrast incongruously with the plainness of her dress. In *Mrs. Edwards,* Badger created a particularly expressive image of puritanical severity: her pinched lips, stiff pose, and rather wooden manner were perfectly revealed by his awkward drawing, simplified forms, and rudimentary modeling; his pale colors, applied thinly over a very fine canvas, give Mrs. Edwards a wraith-like appearance that is at once haunting and forbidding.

1. Waldron Phoenix Belknap, Jr., *American Colonial Painting* (Cambridge, Mass., 1959), p. 290.
2. See *Mrs. Cornelius Waldo* (Worcester Art Museum) and *Thomas Cushing* (Essex Institute, Salem, Mass.), both mentioned in Belknap (see note 1).

JOSEPH BLACKBURN (active 1752-1774)
active in Boston 1753–1764

7. *Isaac Winslow and His Family*

Signed and dated lower left: *I. Blackburn Pinx 1755*

Oil on canvas, 54½ x 79½ in. (138.4 x 201.9 cm.)

Abraham Shuman Fund. 42.684

PROVENANCE: Isaac Winslow, Boston; Samuel Winslow, Roxbury, Mass., 1878, great-grandson of the sitter; Edward M. Winslow, Boston, 1902; George Scott Winslow, Boston, 1911; Anna W. Winslow, Newcastle, Me., 1942.

EXHIBITIONS: "Forty-seventh Exhibition of Paintings" Boston Athenaeum, 1871, no. 204; "One Hundred Colonial Portraits," Museum of Fine Arts, Boston, 1930, no. 99; "Life in America," Metropolitan Museum of Art, New York, 1939, no. 12; "New England Painting, 1700–1775," Worcester Art Museum, 1943 no. 28; "From Colony to Nation," Art Institute of Chicago, 1949, no. 23.

BIBLIOGRAPHY: Francis S. Drake, *34th Report of the Boston Records, the Town of Roxbury* (Boston, 1873), p. 257; Augustus T. Perkins, "Blackburn and Smibert," *Massachusetts Historical Society Proceedings* 16 (1878), p. 392; Waldo Lincoln, *Genealogy of the Waldo Family* (Worcester, Mass.), 1902), p. 188; Laurence Park, *Joseph Blackburn, a Colonial Portrait Painter* (Worcester, Mass., 1923), no. 88; Theodore Bolton and Harry S. Binsse, "An American Artist of Formula, Joseph Blackburn," *The Antiquarian* 15 (1930), p. 92; *American Paintings in the Museum of Fine Arts, Boston* (Boston, 1969), no. 144.

From the middle of the seventeenth century, members of the Winslow family were prominent in the political, commercial, and cultural life of the Plymouth Colony and later of Boston. They were also important patrons of the arts, and were painted by the Pollard Limner, John Smibert, Robert Feke, and John Singleton Copley, as well as by Blackburn. Isaac Winslow (1709–1777), who with his brother Joshua had established a profitable shipping business in Boston, was vitally interested in the arts, and had himself painted three times, first by Feke in 1748 (see cat. no. 4), here, with his family, eight years after his marriage to Lucy Waldo, and a third time by Copley with his second wife, Jemima Dubuke, in 1774 (Museum of Fine Arts, Boston).

It may well have been the popularity of Smibert's *Bermuda Group: Bishop Berkeley and his Entourage* (1729; Yale University Art Gallery, New Haven) that led Winslow to commission this elaborate portrait of himself and his family. Smibert's famous group portrait, which remained in the artist's Boston studio through the eighteenth century, had already inspired Feke's *Isaac Royall and His Family* 1741 Harvard University Law School, Cambridge) and John Greenwood's *The Greenwood-Lee Family* (ca. 1747; Mrs. George Shattuck, Boston). It is understandable that Winslow would choose to have himself and his family portrayed in such a fashion, and that he would choose Blackburn, who (after Feke's departure about 1750) had become the leading portraitist in Boston, to paint it.

Because he had been trained in England, Blackburn's knowledge of the conventions of group portraiture was not dependent on Smibert's *Bermuda Group* or on the mezzotints after British portraits in Smibert's studio, as Feke's and Greenwood's had been. Rather, the composition, the poses of the figures, and the light, delicate colors of *Isaac Winslow and his Family* were based on rococo portraits Blackburn knew in England before his departure for the colonies in 1752. In this portrait, he introduced to Boston a new formula for the depiction of a family group, in which the figures, rather than being posed around a table, are placed before a sylvan landscape. This convention had been known in England since the time of Charles I and had been used by Peter Lely and William Hogarth. The major practitioner of the out-of-door group portraits in England in the 1740s was Arthur Devis, whose charming conversation pieces were well known and, despite the somewhat wooden rendering of the figures, were often emulated. In the next decade, Devis's reputation was eclipsed by Thomas Hudson and John Zoffany, who placed more emphasis on the figures; Blackburn, too, was part of this movement, and brought the revised formula to America.

As in the remarkably similar *Thistlethwayte Family* (ca. 1757–1758; collection Mrs. D. L. Rowlands, Westminster, England) by Hudson, Blackburn arranged his sitters in a plane in the immediate foreground of the picture, and related them to one another by gesture while directing their gazes toward the viewer. The drape behind Winslow, the patriarch, and the view of a garden behind his children were traditional in English conversation pieces since Hogarth's time. The luxurious countryside, with a swan pond and the gates of a large estate visible in the background, were frequently represented features of many English country houses in the eighteenth century but unlikely in Boston; it may be that Blackburn drew these details from a print, although it has not been identified.

The poses of Blackburn's figures were popular in English portraiture of the preceding decade. The painting is, in fact, something of a pastiche, and may have been designed as a showcase to demonstrate the artist's familiarity with current modes of English high-style portraiture. Winslow's nonchalant stance was taken from Hudson's *Theodore Jacobsen* (1746; The Thomas Coram Foundation for Children, London); its suitability for depicting a man of means at ease with his family and for connecting the figure with others in the picture was recognized by Blackburn as well as by Hudson himself, for the latter used it again in several group portraits of the 1750s. This stiff, upright pose of Mrs. Winslow, holding her baby in her lap, was also used frequently by Hudson in the 1740s and '50s, for example in *Walter Radcliffe and His Family* (ca. 1742; private collection, Plymouth, England). For the figure of Lucy Waldo Winslow, who was six years old when this portrait was painted, Blackburn turned to an earlier source, the work of the seventeenth-century portraitist Peter Lely. Lely frequently portrayed his wealthy patrons' young daughters moving gracefully across the picture space, carrying garlands of flowers in their

aprons.[1] Blackburn altered his prototype somewhat by depicting Lucy Winslow carrying fruit, a hallmark of fertility usually reserved for young matrons, not small girls, who were more commonly portrayed as the virginal Diana. The fruit may have been intended to serve as an attribute of the mother, who bore eleven children, or of the family's prosperity generally; it also adds a pleasing note of color to the right side of the picture.

Despite the stylishness of this work, the convention of the out-of-doors group portrait was not developed in America, not even by Blackburn himself. In the next such paint- ing to be completed in Boston, Copley's image of Winslow and his wife of 1774, the artist reverted to the familiar device of arranging figures around a table. Nonetheless, Blackburn's attempt to introduce to the colonies an up-to-date formula was successful, if only for the remarkable complexity and innovation of this portrait.

1. See Lely's *Young Girl as a Shepherdess* and *Henrietta Boyle, Countess of Rochester* (both Devonshire Collection, Chatsworth) for examples of the figure type, which was derived from the painting of Rubens and Van Dyck.

8. *Susan Apthorp (Mrs. Thomas Bulfinch)*

Signed and dated center left: *I. Blackburn Pinxit 1757*

Oil on canvas, 50⅛ x 40⅛ in. (127.2 x 101.7 cm.)

Gift of Mr. and Mrs. J. Templeman Coolidge. 45.517

PROVENANCE: J. Templeman Coolidge, Jr., Boston, by 1895

EXHIBITIONS: "Portraits of Women," Copley Hall, Boston, 1895, no. 25; "Early American Portraits," Boston Art Club, 1911, no. 5; "Portraits by American Painters before the Revolution," Copley Society, Boston, 1922, no. 18; "One Hundred Colonial Portraits," Museum of Fine Arts, Boston, 1930, p. 7; "Likeness of America, 1680–1820," Fine Arts Center, Colorado Springs, 1949, no. 8; "American Art 1750–1800: Towards Independence," Yale University Art Gallery, New Haven, 1976, no. 5.

BIBLIOGRAPHY: A. T. Perkins, "Blackburn and Smibert," *Massachusetts Historical Society Proceedings* (1878), Vol. 16, p. 387; Lawrence Park, *Joseph Blackburn, a Colonial Portrait Painter* (Worcester, Mass., 1923), no. 5; C. A. Place, *Charles Bulfinch* (Boston and New York, 1923), p. 2; Frank W. Bayley, *Five Colonial Artists* (Boston, 1929), p. 61; Theodore Bolton and Harry L. Binsse, "An American Artist of Formula, Joseph Blackburn," *Antiquarian* 15 (1930), p. 88; *American Paintings in the Museum of Fine Arts, Boston* (Boston, 1969), no. 196.

Although little is known about Blackburn's life in England, it is surmised that he spent his early career as an assistant in the studio of an accomplished portrait painter of the period, perhaps Joseph Highmore or Thomas Hudson. His skill was not sufficient to allow him to compete successfully with those masters, so he left England about 1752, settling first in Bermuda and a year later in Boston, where he became the leading society portraitist of the 1750s. Catering to a clientele eager for portraiture in the latest style, Blackburn enabled them to show off their wealth and prosperity through his talent for painting luxurious fabrics, lace, and jewels.

Blackburn brought from England not only a facile painting technique but also a repertory of poses and compositional devices that his English masters had used to paint the British aristocracy. He customarily adopted these poses to create a flattering analogy between his sitters and their British counterparts. His portrait of Susan Apthorp repeats, with slight variations, the pose and design of Kneller's *Princess Anne* (ca. 1690; private collection, England), a famous image in its day, one that Blackburn had undoubtedly seen in England, if not in the original then in the mezzotint reproduction made in the 1690s.[1]

The pose is designed to reveal the grace and beauty of the sitter, to show her to be both dignified and appealing. Susan Apthorp, like Princess Anne, sits in an idyllic landscape painted in a manner ultimately derived from Salvator Rosa and Claude, a setting intended to allude to her wealth and her virginal beauty. The arrangement of her hands derives from Kneller's picture; there, they hold a flower, and in other paintings employing this pose a garland or a lapdog is pictured, but here they are empty, emphasizing the sitter's graceful fingers and tiny waist. Blackburn rearranged the figure slightly so that her elongated lower body is shifted to the right while her head is turned in the opposite direction. This further refines the complex elegance of Kneller's pose and better reveals the sitter's slender figure and long, graceful neck. Susan Apthorp's tilted head and half-smile became a trademark of Blackburn's, suggesting a personality both coy and reserved.

Susan Apthorp was twenty-five when Blackburn painted her; two years later she married Dr. Thomas Bulfinch of Boston. Their son was Charles Bulfinch, the great Boston architect. Also in 1757, and undoubtedly as part of the same commission, Blackburn painted Susan's parents, Charles and Grizel Eastwick Apthorp (private collection, Virginia); all three portraits are the same size (about 50 x 40 in.) and are three-quarter length. Mr. Apthorp's pose is a modification of the pose in Hudson's portrait of William Shirley (National Portrait Gallery; Washington, engraved by McArdell, ca. 1750); Mrs. Apthorp's pose, like her daughter's, derives from Kneller's *Princess Anne*.

Susan Apthorp is the most appealing and least contrived of the three pictures, and is one of the most successful of Blackburn's single-figure portraits. In general, Blackburn was more interested in rendering contrasting textures than in the faithful description of facial features, and here he skillfully articulated the satin of the dress with long, thin strokes of greenish-blue interspersed with strokes of rose; these colors harmonize with the tone of the landscape and contrast with the crisp white lace and finely drawn, rich, translucent pearls. At the same time, he achieved a convincing likeness and a sympathetic presentation of character, showing her to be, in the words of a contemporary, "a woman of marked intelligence and culturation."[2]

1. By John Smith, 1692, after Kneller.
2. Lawrence Park, *Joseph Blackburn, a Colonial Portrait Painter* (Worcester, Mass., 1923), p. 14.

JOHN SINGLETON COPLEY (1738-1815)
active in Boston 1753–1774

9. *Mrs. Samuel Quincy (Hannah Hill)*, ca. 1761

Oil on canvas, 35¾ x 28¼ in. (90.9 x 70.7 cm.)

Bequest of Miss Grace W. Treadwell. 1970.357

PROVENANCE: Quincy Phillips (great-grandson of the sitter), Cambridge, Mass., by 1873; Emily Treadwell Phillips (his wife); Grace W. Treadwell (her niece), Kittery Point, Maine.

EXHIBITIONS: "American Portraits by J. S. Copley," Hirschl & Adler Galleries, New York, 1975, no. 8; "Harvard Divided," Fogg Art Museum, Cambridge, 1976, no. 28; "Copleys from Boston," Philadelphia Museum of Art, 1980.

BIBLIOGRAPHY: Augustus T. Perkins, *A Sketch of the Life . . . of John Singleton Copley* (Boston, 1873), p. 97; Frank W. Bayley, *A Sketch of the Life . . . of John Singleton Copley* (Boston, 1910), p. 82; _____, *The Life and Works of John Singleton Copley* (Boston, 1915), p. 204; Theodore Bolton and Harry L. Binsse, "John Singleton Copley," *Antiquarian* 15 (December 1930), p. 118; Barbara N. Parker and Anne B. Wheeler, *John Singleton Copley* (Boston, 1938), p. 159; John Hill Morgan, *John Singleton Copley* (Windham, Conn., 1939), p. 14; Louisa Dresser, "Copley's Receipt for Payment for the Portraits of Mr. and Mrs. Samuel Phillips Savage, with a Note on Blackburn's Portrait of Hannah Babcock," *Worcester Art Museum Annual* 9 (1961), pp. 33-38; Jules Prown, *John Singleton Copley* (Cambridge, Mass., 1966), vol. I, pp. 34, 35, 36, 56; fig. 97; *American Paintings in the Museum of Fine Arts, Boston* (Boston, 1969), no. 255; Trevor Fairbrother, "Copley's Use of British Mezzotints for his American Portraits: A Reappraisal Prompted by New Discoveries," (Paintings Department files, Museum of Fine Arts, Boston).

Mrs. Samuel Quincy, born Hannah Hill, was about twenty-seven years old when Copley painted her portrait. Her parents, Thomas and Hannah Hill, owned a successful distillery business and considerable property in Boston. Her husband, a lawyer, was a member of the Quincy family that contributed so many public servants to Boston before and after the Revolution. However, Samuel Quincy's initial Whig sympathies turned into support for the Loyalist position, and in May 1775 he left Boston for England, leaving his family behind. Hannah Quincy and her children then moved into the Cambridge home of her brother, Henry Hill, a patriot. Although Quincy intended to return to Boston, the appearance of his name on the Banishment Act of 1778 made it impossible for him to do so. Letters from Quincy to his wife make clear the poignance of their separation but also their sharply divergent political views. Mrs. Quincy died in 1782 without seeing her husband again.[1]

Like so many of Copley's sitters, Mrs. Quincy was probably painted at the time of her marriage in 1761. Her husband was painted six or seven years later, but the event that occasioned his portrait (also in the Museum of Fine Arts, Boston) has not been recorded. Unlike his portraits of the John Amorys and other pairs in which husband and wife were painted several years apart, Copley did not attempt to make the painting of Samuel Quincy harmonize formally with that of his wife,[2] and as a result they are unsatisfying as pendants. Rather, *Mrs. Quincy* shares features with a small group of Copley's portraits of the early 1760s, such as *Dorothy Murray* (1759-1761; Fogg Art Museum, Cambridge), *Mrs. Daniel Rogers* (1762; private collection, Arlington, Va.), and *Mrs. Nathaniel Allan* (ca. 1763; Minneapolis Institute of Arts), in which young women are posed in elegant and somewhat fanciful costume.

Mrs. Quincy is the most striking and unusual of this group, for she is wearing not a contemporary dress but a seventeenth-century costume. Her pose was in fact derived from a portrait of Susanna Fourment by Rubens (Gulbenkian Museum, Lisbon), then believed to be a portrait of Rubens's wife by Van Dyck. That painting entered an English collection around 1730 and excited the imagination of a whole generation of British portraitists: for the next twenty years, many British ladies had their portraits painted dressed as "Rubens's wife."[3] Copley's portrait of Mrs. Quincy is a reflection of that vogue. He may have known one of the many engravings after the Rubens portrait, such as that by James McArdell of about 1746, but it is more likely that the pose and accessories he used in *Mrs. Quincy* were borrowed from a more demure rendering of the prototype: *Miss Hudson* by John Faber after Thomas Hudson, a print Joseph Blackburn had used as a model for his portrait of Hannah Babcock (Worcester Art Museum) two years earlier.[4]

Copley did not, as Blackburn had, experience firsthand the English craze for Van Dyck and for seventeenth-century costume, but he nonetheless came closer than Blackburn to the spirit of that vogue in his ambitious manipulation of his prototype. He retained from *Miss Hudson* the feather and fan hat, the turn of the head, and the arrangement of the hands (which hold a sprig of larkspur rather than a plume)—the elements that give the portrait its verve—changing only the direction of the larkspur so that feather, hat, and flowers create a sense of decorative closure on the picture surface appropriate to the immediacy of a half-length format. Copley eliminated the classicizing vase, the dog, and the parapet from his model, and employed instead a plain dark background in order to focus attention on the sitter. The dress Mrs. Quincy wears is a composite costume: the square bodice and satin stomacher were borrowed from *Miss Hudson;* the falling collar, the wide sleeve reaching to just below the elbow and pulled back with a gold chain, the sash imitating a high waist, and the colors of salmon-pink and blue were features of the "Van Dyck dress" revived in portraiture of the eighteenth century, such as James McArdell's *Mary Panton, Duchess of Ancaster,* after Hudson (ca. 1757), from which Copley drew the details of Mrs. Quincy's costume. And, as was common in British portraiture of the period as well as American, the lace and jewelry were most likely the sitter's own.[5]

Because this portrait is so beautiful and extraordinarily well painted, it is remarkable that the pose and costume do not recur in Copley's oeuvre. During this period, Copley was involved in a deliberate program of self-improvement

(continued on page 62)

and education. He was undoubtedly attracted to the sources he used for *Mrs. Quincy* because they afforded him the opportunity to acquaint himself with yet another old master pattern and, except for the response of his patrons, might have repeated this formula with variations in many other portraits, as he did with *Mrs. John Murray* (Worcester Art Museum), *Mrs. John Amory*, and *Mrs. Daniel Hubbard* (Art Institute of Chicago). But in fact, Copley must have realized that Mrs. Quincy looked somewhat incongruous in her seventeenth-century costume; beautiful though it is, her dress is not entirely suited to her retiring temperament and plain New England features. Furthermore, the absence of seventeenth-century costume from American portraiture of this period suggests that the fad for Van Dyck did not capture the fancy of colonial patrons as it did the English; it was undoubtedly too baroque, too exotic, and perhaps too Catholic for New England taste. And so Copley, who was a practical man above all else, put aside the formula

he used for *Mrs. Quincy* for ones more acceptable to his Boston patrons.

1. Barbara N. Parker and Anne B. Wheeler, *John Singleton Copley* (Boston, 1938), pp. 158-159. Additional biographical information is found in Linda Ayres, *Harvard Divided* (Fogg Art Museum, Cambridge, 1976), pp. 62-63.
2. Trevor Fairbrother, "Copley's Use of British Mezzotints for his American Portraits: A Reappraisal Prompted by New Discoveries," (Paintings Department files, Museum of Fine Arts, Boston).
3. Ellen G. Miles, *Thomas Hudson 1701–1779* (Greater London Council, London, 1979), no. 15.
4. Louisa Dresser, "Copley's Receipt for Payment for the Portraits of Mr. and Mrs. Samuel Phillips Savage with a Note on Blackburn's Portrait of Hannah Babcock," *Worcester Art Museum Annual* 9 (1961), pp. 36-38.
5. This information was graciously provided by Aileen Ribeiro, Head of the History of Dress Department, Courtauld Institute, London.

---

10. *Ezekiel Goldthwait,* 1771

Signed lower right: *JSC* (in monogram)

Oil on canvas, 50⅛ x 40 in. (127.3 x 101.5 cm.)

Bequest of John T. Bowen in memory of Eliza M. Bowen. 41.85

PROVENANCE: Mrs. William Alline (great-granddaughter of the sitter), Boston, by 1873; Dr. John T. Bowen (great-great-great-grandson), Boston, about 1900.

EXHIBITIONS: "Portraits by John Singleton Copley," Copley Hall, Boston, 1896, no. 67; "One Hundred Colonial Portraits," Museum of Fine Arts, Boston, 1930, no. 58; "Copleys from Boston," Philadelphia Museum of Art, 1980.

BIBLIOGRAPHY: Augustus T. Perkins, *A Sketch of the Life . . . of John Singleton Copley* (Boston, 1873), p. 57; C. Goldthwait, *Descendants of Thomas Goldthwait* (Hartford, 1899), p. 86; Frank W. Bayley, *A Sketch of the Life . . . of John Singleton Copley* (Boston, 1915), p. 120; Theodore Bolton and Harry L. Binsse, "John Singleton Copley," *Antiquarian* 15 (December 1930), no. 6, p. 116; Barbara N. Parker and Anne B. Wheeler, *John Singleton Copley* (Boston, 1938), pp. 84-85; Barbara N. Parker, "The Goldthwait Family," *Bulletin of the Museum of Fine Arts* 39 (June 1941), pp. 40-44; Jules Prown, *John Singleton Copley* (Cambridge, Mass., 1966), vol. 1, pp. 60, 75-76, 77, 82; *American Paintings in the Museum of Fine Arts, Boston* (Boston, 1969), no. 287.

Ezekiel (1710–1782) and Elizabeth Lewis Goldthwait (1715–1794) are among Copley's most prosperous-looking patrons; their aura of confidence and well-being accounts, in part, for the great popularity of these portraits. Ezekiel Goldthwait was born in Boston to a merchant family; he made his living as a public official, serving first as Town Clerk of Boston and later as Register of Deeds. Elizabeth Goldthwait, admired by her contemporaries for her elegant gardens, bore thirteen children, of whom five survived to adulthood. Copley used traditional eighteenth-century attributes to symbolize their

respective roles: Goldthwait holds a quill pen in one hand and a sheaf of papers in the other; his wife reaches toward a bowl piled high with apples, peaches, and other fruit, emblems of her fertility. The Goldthwaits' prosperity is indicated in these paintings by the quiet richness of their attire and their physical amplitude; their documented ability to pay Copley's high prices—over £58 for the pair of portraits and their frames—is a further measure of their material comfort.[1] As they are shown here, four years before the outbreak of the Revolution, the couple is middle-aged and in contemporary political terms would be characterized as middle-of-the-road: Goldthwait's original political position was moderate Whig, but as tensions increased in Boston, he moved to the right like so many of his upper-middle class peers, and became sympathetic to the Tory cause. Goldthwait was never particularly outspoken in his opposition to the rebellion, however, and when the hostilities began he was forced to flee not to England, as so many of his more active Tory brethren were, but only to the Boston suburb of Weston.

By 1771, when he painted the Goldthwaits, Copley completely dominated the portrait-painting market in Boston. He was also by this time in full command of his mature style: his work was no longer broadly and obviously experimental as it had been in the 1760s, rather, he was perfecting his technique within a narrower range of poses and decorative motifs. During this period, too, Copley was more interested in light than in brilliant rococo color schemes. Rather than using the strong red, blues, and greens of the portraits of the previous decade, Copley depicted Mrs. Goldthwait in muted tones—a warm brown dress ornamented only with black and white lace, and no colorful embroidery— and Mr. Goldthwait in a subdued reddish-brown coat and breeches. Both

(continued on page 64)

figures are illuminated by strong side lighting that anchors them firmly in space and draws our attention to their hands and faces; the brilliant light reveals the contrasting textures of satin and lace and dull broadcloth which Copley rendered so skillfully and convincingly.

Another feature of Copley's style during the late 1760s and early '70s is his increasing independence from English mezzotints as sources for poses and accessories. Mr. Goldthwait's desk, and Mrs. Goldthwait's chair and table, which appear in several portraits of this period, are American and undoubtedly part of the furnishings of Copley's studio.[2] The poses and gestures of these sitters seem to be his own invention as well. Copley depicted several of his patrons in similar positions, but with varying psychological emphasis. He used the informal pose in which Mr. Goldthwait is shown for several portraits of merchants, for example *Thomas Boylston II* (ca. 1767; Harvard University, Cambridge) and *John Erving* (ca. 1772; private collection, Santa Barbara, Calif.); however, Goldthwait lacks the intensity of the latter; being portrayed as a man of even-tempered, even bland seriousness. Mrs. Goldthwait, too, presents an image of self-satisfied prosperity; her complacent character is all the more evident when compared to the deeply thoughtful and sensitive *Mrs. Humphrey Devereux* (on loan to the National Art Gallery, Wellington, New Zealand, from the Greenwood family), a woman of Mrs. Goldthwait's age and social status, painted by Copley in the same year.

Mr. and Mrs. Ezekiel Goldthwait are part of a series of portraits of successful merchants and their wives that Copley painted between 1767 and 1771. They are the most vivid portraits of the group, appearing more natural and immediate than the rather vapid *Mr. and Mrs. Joseph Hooper* (1770–1771; private collection, Pikesville, Md.) and less self-consciously grand than *Mr. and Mrs. Jeremiah Lee* (1769; Wadsworth Atheneum, Hartford). The Goldthwait portraits most closely resemble *Mr. and Mrs. Isaac Smith* (1769; Yale University Art Gallery, New Haven), in which the same attributes (fruit, quill pen, and writing desk) appear. However, the Smiths exemplify the more ornate, rococo manner of portrait painting that Copley had for the most part abandoned by 1770; and in the portraits of the Goldthwaits, he reduced the number of ornamental details and concentrated instead on rendering a few material attributes in an extraordinarily lifelike manner. In contrast to the passive Isaac Smith, Ezekiel Goldthwait gives an impression of spontaneity: securely located in space, with every detail of his face and costume crisply delineated, he appears to be turning toward the viewer about to engage in conversation. As was common in portraits of women from this period, Mrs. Goldthwait is more richly attired than her husband and more formally posed, although her gesture of reaching toward the bowl of apples produces the effect of a specific movement in time. Her gesture also gave Copley the opportunity to demonstrate his virtuosity in painting the indicators of material comfort that most interested him in this painting: the lush globes of fruit, Mrs. Goldthwait's plump hands, the soft bands of lace falling back on her forearms, and–one of the most beautifully painted passages in all of Copley's works–the muted reflection of these things in the highly polished mahogany table.

1. Henry Pelham, acting as Copley's agent, billed the Goldthwaits for £58.12.0 on July 1, 1771. Prown estimated the Goldthwaits' annual income was between £500 and £1000, an extremely comfortable income for a colonial family; nevertheless, Copley's bill represents a not inconsiderable portion of that sum. Jules Prown, *John Singleton Copley* (Cambridge, Mass., 1966), vol. 1, pp. 75-76, 127, 134.

2. A chair similar to Mrs. Goldthwait's appears in the portraits *Mrs. Timothy Rogers* (1766–67; on loan to the Museum of Fine Arts, Boston), *Mrs. Isaac Smith* and *Mrs. James Russell* (1770–71; Museum of Fine Arts, Boston), although Copley changed the color in each case to compliment his color scheme.

---

11. *Mrs. Ezekiel Goldthwait (Elizabeth Lewis)*, 1771

Oil on canvas, 50⅜ x 40¼ in. (128.0 x 102.2 cm.)

Bequest of John T. Bowen in memory of Eliza M. Bowen. 41.84

PROVENANCE: Mrs. William Alline (great-granddaughter of the sitter), Boston, by 1873; Dr. John T. Bowen (great-great-great-grandson), Boston, about 1900.

EXHIBITIONS: "One Hundred Colonial Portraits," Museum of Fine Arts, Boston, 1930, no. 58; "American Paintings," Stedelijk Museum, Amsterdam, 1950, no. 3; "Amerikanische Malerei," Museum für Völkerkunde, Berlin, 1951, no. 2; "Two Hundred Years of American Painting," Vancouver Art Gallery, 1955, no. 5; "The American Muse," Corcoran Gallery, Washington, 1959, no. 1; "200 Years of American Painting," St. Louis City Art Museum,
1964, p. 2; "Copley," National Gallery of Art, Washington, 1965, no. 43; "Copleys from Boston," Philadelphia Museum of Art, 1980.

BIBLIOGRAPHY: Augustus T. Perkins, *A Sketch of the Life . . . of John Singleton Copley* (Boston, 1873), p. 57; Frank W. Bayley, *A Sketch of the Life . . . of John Singleton Copley* (Boston, 1910), p. 113; ———, *The Life and Works of John Singleton Copley* (Boston, 1915), p. 121; Theodore Bolton and Harry L. Binsse, "John Singleton Copley," *Antiquarian* 15 (December 1930), no. 6, p. 116; Barbara N. Parker and Anne B. Wheeler, *John Singleton Copley* (Boston, 1938), p. 85; Barbara N. Parker, "The Goldthwait Family," *Bulletin of the Museum of Fine Arts* 39 (June 1941), pp. 40–44; James T. Flexner, *John Singleton Copley* (Boston, 1948), p. 55; Virgil Barker, "Copley's American Portraits," *Magazine of Art* 43 (1950), p. 86; Jules Prown, *John Singleton Copley* (Cambridge, Mass., 1966), vol. 1, pp. 75-76; *American Paintings in the Museum of Fine Arts, Boston* (Boston, 1969), no. 288.

12. *The Copley Family*, 1780s

Oil on canvas, 20¾ x 26¼ in. (52.7 x 66.6 cm.)

Henry H. and Zoe Oliver Sherman Fund. 1977.775

PROVENANCE: Mrs. Gardiner Green (Elizabeth Copley), by 1803; Mrs. James Sullivan Amory, Brookline, Mass., by 1872; Martha Babcock Greene (Copley's granddaughter) by 1852; Ingersoll Amory, by 1938; Mrs. John McAndrews (Betty Amory Bartlett), by 1939; Robert and Daniel Amory (her nephews), by 1974.

RELATED WORKS: *The Copley Family*, 1776–1777, National Gallery of Art, Washington; Head of Mrs. Copley, John Jr., and Susannah, 1776, coll. JoAnn and Julian Ganz, Jr., Los Angeles; R. Thew, "The Copley Family," engraving after Copley, 1785.

EXHIBITIONS: "John Singleton Copley, 1738–1815," Museum of Fine Arts, Boston, 1938; "Four Boston Masters," Jewett Art Center, Wellesley College, Wellesley, Mass., 1959, no. 15; "John Singleton Copley," National Gallery of Art, Washington, 1965, no. 62; "Paul Revere's Boston," Museum of Fine Arts, Boston, 1975, no. 121; "Patriot Painters," Museum of Fine Arts, Boston, 1978; "Copleys from Boston," Philadelphia Museum of Art, 1980.

BIBLIOGRAPHY: Augustus T. Perkins, *A Sketch of the Life . . . of John Singleton Copley* (Boston, 1873), p. 48; Martha Amory, *The Domestic and Artistic Life of John Singleton Copley, R. A.* (Boston, 1882), pp. 79-80; Anna Wells Rutledge, "American Loyalists—A Drawing for a Noted Copley Group," *Art Quarterly* 20 (Summer 1957), pp. 195-203; Jules Prown, *John Singleton Copley* (Cambridge, Mass., 1966), vol. 2, pp. 262-263, 414-415.

Copley's decision to leave Boston for Europe in 1774 was a professional as well as a political one; the impending conflict and resulting decline in the number of his portrait commissions impelled him to act on a long-standing resolve to seek out Sir Joshua Reynolds and Benjamin West in London. After a tour of Paris and Florence and about a year in Rome, Copley settled in London in October 1775, and began *The Copley Family*, his first major work to be painted in England. *The Copley Family* records his attractive, prosperous-looking family: Richard Clarke, Copley's father-in-law, holding the infant Susanna at left; Elizabeth, the oldest child, standing at the center of the composition; Mrs. Copley, at right, holding John, Jr., while Mary leans on her mother's arm. Copley himself stands at left, behind his family, the drawings in his hand, like the painting as a whole, indicating his ambitions for his art.

Copley exhibited the first version of *The Copley Family* (National Gallery of Art, Washington) at the Royal Academy in 1777. The present painting in grisaille, long believed to be a sketch for the finished work, was in fact made later, in preparation for a print, as noted by Martha Amory: "It was engraved by R. Thew . . . the sketch made for the purpose, in sepia, showing, as well as the engraving, some difference from the picture, in which the artist introduced a heavy crimson curtain in place of the column that was in the original composition by which change the effect of the whole was much highlighted."[1] Thew's engraving is the same size as the grisaille and incorporates all of the changes Copley made from the Royal Academy version; the paint-

ing is in grisaille for the purpose of indicating dark/light relationships for the engraver (although Copley was unable to resist animating the picture by adding touches of blue at Susanna's waist and on his daughters' hats in the lower left corner). The differences in detail between the Washington and Boston versions also indicate that the grisaille is later, probably from the 1780s: Mrs. Copley now wears an up-to-date hairdo, comparable to that worn by Reynolds's or Gainsborough's ladies of the period, and her dress, more softly flowing and voluminous, also reflects the current fashion. A Hepplewhite settee has replaced the Chippendale sofa of the earlier version. More significantly, in the later work, the spatial relationship between the figures is clearer and the massive column and pedestal behind Copley, a motif he retained from the setting of *Mr. and Mrs. Ralph Izard* (1775; Museum of Fine Arts, Boston), is more clearly drawn and moved back in space.

The Copley Family is a remarkable testament to Copley's pictorial genius, demonstrating his thorough understanding of the neoclassical style, to which he was first exposed upon his arrival in Europe. It is, furthermore, the most complicated portrait he had attempted up to that time. The antecedents for his composition as a whole, as well as for the poses and gestures of individual figures, are not to be found in the famous group portraits by Smibert, Feke, and Blackburn which he had seen in his youth in Boston, but rather the developing neoclassical style, to which he had been exposed in Rome, and the elegant idealized portraits of his mentor, Sir Joshua Reynolds. In Copley's frieze-like composition the figures are spread across a shallow space and are related to one another by gesture. Each of the family members is clearly silhouetted, simply and nobly posed. Although the design retains the nervous animation and richly depicted detail of the rococo tradition rather than the grand gesture of neoclassicism, the shallow space and formally intertwined figures reflect the compositional designs of pioneer neoclassical painters such as George Romney (whose portrait of the Leigh family [1768; National Gallery of Victoria, Melbourne] was an important precedent for Copley's picture) and Gavin Hamilton, who had befriended Copley in Rome.

The Artist's Family by Benjamin West (1772; collection Mr. and Mrs. Paul Mellon, Upperville, Va.), may have inspired him to use the same subject in order to demonstrate to London society his abilities, but for the spirit of his portrait, as well as for the poses of individual figures, he turned to Sir Joshua Reynolds. In the 1770s, Reynolds painted family groups in an energetic, rather ebullient spirit, frequently showing an adoring mother whose children are clambering about her, as in *Augusta, Lady Cockburn and Her Children* (1774; National Gallery of Art, London). His group portraits dominated by men, such as *Hon. Henry Fane with his Guardians* (1766; Metropolitan Museum of Art, New York), are more restrained, and the figures are related to one another by gaze rather than by touch. Cop-

ley's portrait reflects both these modes, exhibiting a marked difference in mood between the two figure groups, which are linked by the central figure, Elizabeth. She looks directly at the viewer, and in her self-containment resembles *Miss Frances Crewe* (ca. 1775; Marquess of Crewe, London) and Reynolds's other portraits of children. The pose of Copley's wife and son, was adapted from Reynolds's *Mrs. Richard Hoare and Her Son* (1767–1768; Wallace Collection, London), although Copley was not as bold in his emphasis of the classical profile of his wife. Susanna, who playfully reaches up to embrace her grandfather, was also based on a pose from Reynolds *(Hon. Mrs. Edward Bouverie and her Son Edward,* 1770, Earl of Radnor, Longford Castle). Copley's own pose was one he had used previously, in his portrait of John Amory (1768; Museum of Fine Arts, Boston).[2]

The adaptation of motifs from several sources to create a harmonious composition was not a new practice for Cop-

ley; he had turned to mezzotints after British portraits for such details from the beginning of his career. But once in England, he had original works to consult and so was able to bridge the gap between styles available to him in Boston and artistic models current in Europe. *The Copley Family* was the first of a series of highly sophisticated, multifigured compositions that culminated in *Watson and the Shark* and *The Death of Major Pierson* and placed him in the forefront of neoclassical painting in England.

1. Martha Babcock Amory, *The Domestic and Artistic Life of John Singleton Copley* (Boston, 1882), p. 79. The engraving was published in unfinished state Nov. 25, 1789. The suggestion that the present painting was made in preparation for a print was made by Laura Luckey, Assistant Director, Museum of Art, Rhode Island School of Design.

2. Jules Prown, *John Singleton Copley* (Cambridge, Mass., 1966), I, pp. 60-61 and II, p. 262.

MATHER BROWN (1761-1831)
active in Boston 1777–1781

13. *Admiral Peter Rainier,* ca. 1786-1787

Oil on canvas, 30⅜ x 25¼ in. (77.1 x 64.1 cm.)

Mary Little Pierce Residuary Fund. 04.1757

PROVENANCE: Peter Rainier (nephew of the sitter), England; Hughes Stanton, England; with W. Scott and Sons, Montreal, by 1904.

EXHIBITIONS: "American Painting," M. H. deYoung Memorial Museum and California Palace of the Legion of Honor, San Francisco, 1935, no. 8 (as by Copley); "Seven Centuries of Painting," California Palace of the Legion of Honor, San Francisco, 1940, no. L-100 (as by Copley); "1776: The British Story of the American Revolution," National Maritime Museum, Greenwich, England, 1976, no. 497.

BIBLIOGRAPHY: George C. Mason, *Gilbert Stuart* (New York, 1879), p. 247; Lawrence Park, *Gilbert Stuart* (New York, 1926), II, no. 688; *American Paintings in the Museum of Fine Arts, Boston* (Boston, 1969), no. 182.

Like many young American artists of his generation, Boston-born Mather Brown found post-Revolutionary America a difficult place to find artistic training and patronage. After only the most rudimentary experience in New England as an itinerant portrait painter, he sailed for London and entered Benjamin West's studio in 1780. By 1782 he was exhibiting at the Royal Academy and by 1784 he moved into a studio in London's fashionable Cavendish Square, where he hoped his fortunes would keep pace with his developing skill. Like Copley, who had left Boston for London some six years before, Brown's ambition for his art caused him to seek a more sophisticated audience and supportive artistic community, but unlike Copley, who sought to gain recognition as a history painter, Brown's primary goal seems to have been financial success: "my great object is to get my Name established and to get Commissions from America, to paint their Friends and Relations here."[1]

Fame came slowly to Brown, and he first tried to advertise his skills by making portraits of prominent public figures based on prints and other likenesses. By about 1786, his reputation well established, he received numerous commissions, especially for portraits of naval officers in the East India Company. His greatest successes came two years later, when he was commissioned to paint Lord Heathfield, hero of the Siege of Gibraltar (ca. 1788–1792; Detroit Institute of Arts), and was appointed painter to the Duke of York.

Peter Rainier (1741–1808), whom Brown painted in London about 1786, had a long and illustrious naval career. In the 1750s and '60s he served on several ships in the Royal Navy, and in 1764 was employed by the East India Company. With the beginning of hostilities with the American colonies, Rainier returned to active naval duty as commander of the sloop Ostrich, which in 1778 captured a large American privateer. It is an indication of Brown's political sentiments (or perhaps his lack of any such feelings) that he did not hesitate to paint a man who had defeated his countrymen in military action. In the 1780s, when Brown painted his portrait, Rainier was serving in the East Indies, eventually rising to the rank of admiral and commander-in-chief of the East India Station.[2]

The Museum of Fine Arts acquired the portrait of Peter Rainier in 1904, when it was believed to be by Copley; subsequently the painting was attributed to Gilbert Stuart. In fact, *Peter Rainier* bears little resemblance to the work of either artist, but is characteristic of the paintings of several young artists in West's studio. The naval sitter and the resemblance to other signed portraits give credence to an attribution to Brown; the format of the portrait, the careful modeling of the sitter's face, and the contrast between the softly painted, cloud-filled background and the stolid figure rendered in bright, strong colors suggests that Brown's model was Joshua Reynolds's series of military portraits from the 1770s,[3] which were much in evidence in London when Brown was there.

1. Stuart P. Feld and Albert Ten Eyck Gardner, *American Paintings: A Catalogue of the Collection of the Metropolitan Museum of Art* (New York, 1965), p. 109.

2. "Rainier, Peter," *Dictionary of National Biography,* vol. 24 (London, 1909), pp. 622, 623.

3. For example, Reynolds's portraits of Honorable Augustus Hervey (1762; Town Hall, Bury St. Edmonds) and Admiral Sir Charles Saunders (1765–67; National Maritime Museum, Greenwich).

JOHN JOHNSTON (ca. 1753-1818)
active in Boston 1776–1818

14. *Man in a Gray Coat*, ca. 1788

Oil on canvas, 30 x 25 in. (76.1 x 63.5 cm.)

Gift of William Brewster. 29.893

PROVENANCE: ? J. Howith, Boston, 1844; William Brewster, Boston, by 1929.

BIBLIOGRAPHY: *American Paintings in the Museum of Fine Arts, Boston* (Boston, 1969), no. 67.

When John Singleton Copley left Boston for England in 1774, a great era of portraiture ended in Boston. The noted painters of colonial society—Smibert, Feke, Blackburn, Greenwood, and Badger—were dead or had long since departed; few young artists remained in Boston to fill the void. From the end of the Revolution to the turn of the century and the arrival of Gilbert Stuart there was relatively little artistic activity in Boston; replacing Copley were John Trumbull, who worked in Boston only until 1780, when he went to London to study; Christian Gullagher, who painted portraits in Boston from the 1790s; and several members of the Johnston family, of whom the youngest brother, John, was the most talented.

As with Copley, John Johnston's initial exposure to the fine arts came from an engraver: his father, Thomas Johnston, who also worked as a japanner and heraldic painter and who was also John Greenwood's first teacher. Following his father's death in 1767, John Johnston was apprenticed to John Gore, a coach and heraldic painter who ran a shop employing several young artists. At the same time, he had the opportunity to see many of the extraordinary portraits by Copley, for whose patrons he and his father and Gore were decorating furniture. Copley's work seems to have been the more critical influence for Johnston, even though he and his brother-in-law Daniel Rea inherited his father's very successful business and would labor for over ten years as Rea and Johnston, artisan-painters. Upon the dissolution of his partnership with Rea in 1787, Johnston chose to follow Copley's example and went into business for himself as a portrait painter.

This portrait of an unidentified sitter was probably painted by Johnston the following year, as is indicated by an old label on the back of the canvas: "This portrait was painted by J. Johnston, Boston, 1788, and restored by J. Howith, Boston, April 1844." *Man in a Gray Coat* is typical of Johnston's style, as documented in his signed work: he customarily endowed his figures with broad features and painted them in relatively plain costume according to the taste of the time; the simple half-length pose and sidelong glance is also characteristic.

Although a great deal plainer and somewhat more loosely painted than Copley's work, Johnston's portraits do develop the rococo portrait tradition that Copley mastered. Occasionally Johnston repeats Copley's compositional devices, as, for example, in *Mrs. Samuel Hill* (Friedsam Memorial Library, St. Bonaventure University, St. Bonaventure, New York) in which the sitter's chair (a studio prop) and the arrangement of her hands are a simplified version of those features in Copley's *Mrs. Isaac Smith* (1769; Yale University Art Gallery, New Haven). The present portrait owes a more significant debt to Copley, echoing a particularly interesting moment in that master's career. In the late 1760s and early '70s, Copley's interest in simple, straightforward poses and in the dramatic effects of directional lighting took precedence over rich colors and elaborate settings. Paintings such as *Samuel Verplanck* (1771; Metropolitan Museum of Art, New York) or the remarkable portrait of Samuel Adams (1770–1772; City of Boston, on deposit at the Museum of Fine Arts) illustrate this unusual phase of Copley's work. These were the paintings Johnston saw during his apprenticeship; no doubt he was impressed by the forcefulness of the Adams portrait and by the directness and simplicity of Copley's other paintings of this period, for he emulates that style in the muted colors, the strong side lighting, the careful attention to detail, and the intense self-assured gaze of *Man in a Gray Coat*.

CHRISTIAN GULLAGHER (1759-1826)
active in Newburyport, Mass., after 1783; in Boston, 1789–1797

15. *Major Benjamin Shaw,* ca. 1789

Oil on canvas, 35½ x 31½ in. (90 x 80 cm.)
Anonymous loan

Hailed in the Boston press in 1789 as one of "the two best portrait painters of this metropolis"[1] (John Johnston being the other), Danish-born Christian Gullagher emigrated to Massachusetts in the early 1780s, practicing his trade first in Newburyport and then in Boston. He and Johnston represented two different modes of portraiture in Boston between John Singleton Copley's departure for England in 1774 and Gilbert Stuart's arrival in Boston in 1805. Johnston's style was directly influenced by Copley and descended from the eighteenth-century British portrait tradition: he used a cool palette and formal poses, and occasionally was able to achieve characterizations almost as brilliant as Copley's. On the other hand, Gullagher's portraiture was more intimate and domestic, his palette brighter, and his sitters' features somewhat generalized. He developed this style at the Royal Academy of Fine Arts in Copenhagen, where he studied in the late 1770s. There the prevailing mode of portraiture was a more taciturn and restrained version of the brilliant rococo manner practiced by Nattier, Van Loo, Duplessis, and other French masters of the eighteenth century. The dashing brushwork, high-keyed color, and informality of their portraits were absorbed in a charming, if somewhat unsophisticated fashion, by Gullagher, who adapted the elegance of the French portraits to the plainer, middle-class circumstances of his American clients.

Major and Mrs. Shaw (and their son Tyler, probably painted at the same time; private collection, Boston) lived north of Boston and, as is suggested by their similarity to *Captain David Coats* and *Mehitable Coats* (St. Louis Art Museum), were probably painted toward the end of Gullagher's activity in Newburyport. Rather than depicting the Shaws in grand, formal poses, Gullagher showed them in the middle of domestic chores, as though the viewer had come upon them during a quiet evening at home (a conceit belied by the richness of their dress). Mehitable Shaw sits, half-turned in her green Windsor chair, with a thimble on her finger and some needlework in her lap. Benjamin Shaw's pose is casual, rakish; he turns to look suspiciously at the viewer who interrupts him as he stands at his writing desk, his sword, a reminder of his heroic activity during the Revolutionary War, by his side. Gullagher did not possess Copley's skill at characterization, and so the Shaws' features are somewhat rubbery and inexpressive. But he did take special pride in depicting costume, and has skillfully rendered the crisp, almost transparent lace at Mrs. Shaw's bodice and the Major's brilliant red coat and charming flowered vest.

1. *Massachusetts Centinel,* November 14, 1789 as quoted in Marvin Sadik, *Christian Gullagher. Portrait Painter to Federal America* (National Portrait Gallery, Washington, 1976), p. 11.

16. *Mehitable Shaw*, ca. 1789

Oil on canvas, 35½ x 31½ in. (90 x 80 cm.)
Anonymous loan

GILBERT STUART (1755-1828)
active in Boston 1805–1828

17. *Colonel James Swan, 1795*

Oil on canvas, 28¾ x 23¾ in. (73.0 x 60.2 cm.)

Swan Collection. Bequest of Elizabeth Howard Bartol. 27.538

PROVENANCE: Mrs. John Clarke Howard (the sitter's daughter), Boston, about 1830; Hepzibah Howard Wayland (her daughter), Providence, 1833; Howard Wayland (her son), Providence; Mrs. Charles Stafford (his widow), Providence; Miss Elizabeth Howard Bartol (the sitter's great-granddaughter), Boston, 1927.

EXHIBITIONS: "Exhibition of the Portraits of the Late Gilbert Stuart, Esq.," Boston Athenaeum, 1828, no. 191; "Exhibition of Portraits by Gilbert Stuart," Museum of Fine Arts, Boston, 1880, no. 222; "Loan Collection of Portraits," Copley Hall, Boston, 1896, no. 241; "Exhibition of American Painting," M. H. de Young Memorial Museum and California Palace of the Legion of Honor, San Francisco, 1935, no. 35; "Paul Revere's Boston," Museum of Fine Arts, Boston, 1975, no. 234; "Copley, Stuart, West," Museum of Fine Arts, Boston, 1976, no. 24; "Patriot Painters," Museum of Fine Arts, Boston, 1978.

BIBLIOGRAPHY: George C. Mason, *The Life and Works of Gilbert Stuart* (New York, 1879), p. 263; Lawrence Park, *Gilbert Stuart* (New York, 1926), vol. 2, no. 813; Howard C. Rice, "James Swan, Agent of the French Republic, 1794-1796," *New England Quarterly* 10 (September 1937), pp. 464-486; *American Paintings in the Museum of Fine Arts, Boston* (Boston, 1969), no. 906; Eleanor P. DeLorme, "James Swan's French Furniture," *Antiques* 107 (March 1975), pp. 452-461; —————, "The Swan Commissions: Four Portraits by Gilbert Stuart," *Winterthur Portfolio* 14 (Winter 1979), pp. 361-395.

James Swan was one of the most successful merchants in post-Revolutionary America, possessing a daring business sense and an easy morality, traits that enabled him to accumulate and squander great fortunes during his career. He was born in Scotland about 1754, came to America as a young man, became an apprentice in a Boston counting-house, and soon became involved in Revolutionary politics. His participation in the Boston Tea Party and the Battle of Bunker Hill won him public attention; his subsequent position as secretary of the Massachusetts War Board and his marriage to the wealthy Hepzibah Clarke provided him with the administrative experience, the opportunity, and the capital to make investments in real estate, especially in confiscated Loyalist property. He made—and subsequently lost—a fortune through such speculation, and finally had to flee to France to avoid his creditors.

Swan began commercial dealings with the French in 1788. He first furnished stores to the French navy; later, in 1794, he became an official agent of the French Republic, providing badly needed supplies for the war-torn country. To pay for these supplies, leaders of the Revolution authorized the confiscation and sale of the property of the deposed nobility. The furnishings from these estates found a ready market in America, and Swan made a second fortune implementing these sales. He himself also acquired a remarkable collection of French furniture (now in the Museum of Fine Arts, Boston).[1] During the 1790s Swan traveled between Europe and America, gaining a reputation for extravagant living. What is known about the rest of his life makes a romantic, if incredible story: in 1808, Swan was accused of owing a small debt to a German firm; as a point of honor he refused to settle the claim, but rather allowed himself to be imprisoned in Sante-Pélagie in Paris, where he remained, quite comfortably, until almost the end of his life.[2]

Swan commissioned Gilbert Stuart to paint his portrait in 1795. Swan was then in Philadelphia, the American headquarters of his firm Swan and Schweizer, as the agent of the French government to act in the negotiation of the liquidation of America's Revolutionary War debt to France. These negotiations took about a year, during which time Swan was also occupied with building a mansion for his family on land he owned in Dorchester, near Boston. The mansion was built to resemble a French pavilion; it housed Stuart's portrait and the furniture he had acquired from the French nobility. All of this property was left with his wife, who remained in America when Swan left for Europe in 1796, never to return.

In commissioning Stuart to paint this portrait, Swan chose the most skilled and most popular artist in America. By 1795, Stuart's reputation was growing rapidly: Washington sat for him in that year, and fashionable Philadelphians were flocking to his studio. Stuart was successful in Philadelphia (and in Washington and Boston, where he subsequently made his home) because of his great talent and because he brought the latest mode of English high-style portraiture to America. Stuart was in England from 1775 to 1787 studying with Benjamin West but learning more from the portraiture of Thomas Gainsborough and especially of George Romney, whose vibrant brushwork and clear color he equals. Here Swan's handsome features and dandified lifestyle are made vivid by the superb flesh tones for which Stuart was famous, and by the broadly yet delicately modeled planes of the face. Swan's costume is given secondary emphasis except for the cravat, in which the brush, loaded with pure white, defines contours and highlights with remarkable energy. The bold red, white, and blue color scheme sets off the more subtle tonalities of Swan's face, and the summarily painted background also acts as a foil for Swan's features, which were Stuart's main interest. Although Stuart used the bust-length format and the generalized background of drapery for many portraits during this decade, few rival the bravura performance of *Colonel James Swan*.

1. Swan's furniture collection is discussed in Eleanor P. DeLorme, "James Swan's French Furniture," *Antiques* 107 (March, 1975), pp. 452-461.
2. Swan's international career, and the story of his difficulties with the German firm are described in Howard C. Rice, "James Swan, Agent of the French Republic," *New England Quarterly* 10 (September, 1937), pp. 464-486.

18. Mrs. Thomas Dennie (Sarah Bryant), 1818

Oil on canvas, 30⅛ x 25⅛ in. (76.5 x 64.0 cm.)

Bequest of James Dennie. 05.296

PROVENANCE: James Dennie, Boston, grandson of the sitter.

EXHIBITIONS: "Portraits of Women," Copley Hall, Boston, 1895, no. 290; "American Painting," M. H. deYoung Memorial Museum and California Palace of the Legion of Honor, San Francisco, 1935, no. 26; "American Art," Brockton Art Center, Brockton, Mass., 1973; "Gilbert Stuart, Painter of Presidents," Everson Museum of Art, Syracuse, 1976.

BIBLIOGRAPHY: George C. Mason, *Life and Works of Gilbert Stuart* (New York, 1879), p. 173; Lawrence Park, *Gilbert Stuart* (New York, 1926), vol. 1, no. 235; Charles Merrill Mount, *Gilbert Stuart* (New York, 1964), p. 367; *American Paintings in the Museum of Fine Arts, Boston* (Boston, 1969), no. 939.

The shipmaster Thomas Dennie, whose portrait (also in the Museum of Fine Arts) is the companion to the present picture, was one of Boston's many merchants whom Stuart painted in the 1810s and '20s. He was the founder and principal partner of a successful shipping concern. In 1788 he married Sarah Bryant, daughter of James and Esther (Kidder) Bryant. When Stuart painted the Dennies they had been married for forty years; Dennie was sixty-two at the time and Mrs. Dennie was fifty-eight.

Stuart painted Mrs. Dennie as a stern, rather homely New England woman, illustrating the "good sense, and prudence, and judicious economy" by which she was known to her contemporaries.[1] Stuart chose to present her according to his usual formula for elderly women during those years:[2] she is shown half-length, seated in a Federal-styled chair with a blank background behind her and with no other props or attributes in the picture. This compositional type was derived from Sir Thomas Lawrence, whose works Stuart knew in England in the 1790s; Lawrence's sitters, however, prompted him to paint their faces with considerably more *brio* than Mrs. Dennie was able to inspire. Instead, Stuart reserved his painterly energy for her costume, which reveals the lively paint handling and vividness of color that marks his best works. Mrs. Dennie's coiffure and her attire are typical of that worn by wealthy American women during the Monroe era, and reflect, although in a restrained manner, the styles of the Napoleonic court: her hair in ringlets framing her face, her gown high-waisted and ornamented with an elaborate lace ruffle, a cap of tulle and lace, and a colorful Indian shawl, which was the height of fashion at the period.

1. Rev. John Lowell (minister of West Church, Boston), as quoted in *American Paintings in the Museum of Fine Arts, Boston* (Boston, 1969), p. 256.
2. See, for example *Mrs. Samuel Dunn* (ca. 1809–1815; Museum of Art, Rhode Island School of Design) or *Mrs. Paul Revere* (1813, Museum of Fine Arts, Boston).

19. Bishop Jean-Louis Lefebvre de Cheverus, 1823

Oil on canvas, 36¼ x 28⅜ in. (92.1 x 72.1 cm.)

Bequest of Mrs. Charlotte Gore Greenough Hervoches du Quilliou. 21.9

PROVENANCE: Mrs. John Gore (Mrs. Joseph Russell), Boston, 1823; Mrs. Horatio Greenough (her daughter), Boston, 1836; Mrs. Charlotte Hervoches du Quilliou (her daughter), La Tour de Peilz, Switzerland.

EXHIBITIONS: "First Exhibition of Paintings," Boston Athenaeum, 1827, no. 118; "Exhibition of the Portraits of the late Gilbert Stuart, Esq.," Boston Athenaeum, 1828, no. 109; "Fairmount Park Centennial," Philadelphia Museum of Art, 1876, no. 53c; "Exhibition of Portraits by Gilbert Stuart," Museum of Fine Arts, Boston, 1880, no. 251; "Memorial to Bishop Cheverus," Boston Athenaeum, 1951, pp. XII, XVIII (pl. I); "Gilbert Stuart, Portraitist to the Young Republic, 1755–1828," National Gallery of Art, Washington, 1967, no. 47; "Paul Revere's Boston," Museum of Fine Arts, Boston, 1976, no. 238; "Patriot Painters," Museum of Fine Arts, Boston, 1978; "Faces of 5000 Years," Museum of Fine Arts at Faneuil Hall, Boston, 1979.

BIBLIOGRAPHY: Henry T. Tuckerman, *Book of the Artists* (New York, 1870), p. 109; George C. Mason, *Life and Works of Gilbert Stuart* (New York, 1879), p. 158; Justin Winsor, *Memorial History of Boston* (Boston, 1881), vol. 3, p. 518; Lawrence Park, *Gilbert Stuart* (New York, 1926), vol. I, no. 155; Walter Muir Whitehill, *A Memorial to Bishop Cheverus* (Boston, 1951), plate I; Charles Merrill Mount, *Gilbert Stuart* (New York, 1964), pp. 365-366; *American Paintings in the Museum of Fine Arts, Boston* (Boston, 1969), no. 943.

In 1810, Jean-Louis Lefebvre Ann Madeleine de Cheverus was appointed the first Bishop of Boston. He came there in 1796, having served as a missionary to the Penobscot Indians in Maine; by personal example and by numerous contributions to the city's intellectual life, he helped to diminish the anti-Catholic sentiment in Boston and foster a spirit of religious toleration there. Cheverus was also responsible for expanding the activity and influence of the Catholic Church in Boston. In 1800, construction began on the Cathedral of the Holy Cross on Franklin Street, a building designed by Charles Bulfinch and funded by contributions from both Catholics and Protestants in Boston, including John Adams. The bishop was a personal friend of Adams's, of Harrison Gray Otis, Josiah Quincy, and other prominent citizens of Boston, and was active in several cultural organizations, including the Boston Athenaeum, to which he left his library. Cheverus served in Boston to increasing respect and acclaim until 1825, when he was recalled to France.[1]

Stuart's portrait of Cheverus was commissioned just prior to his departure by Mrs. John Gore of Boston. Stuart had painted Mrs. Gore several years earlier (ca. 1815, Museum of Fine Arts, Boston); her satisfaction with that portrait led her to commission the portrait of Cheverus and one of Dr. John Sylvester Gardiner, then rector of Trinity Church in Boston (present location unknown; formerly collection Robert H. Gardiner, Maine). The portraits are complementary: each cleric is shown half-length and dressed in ecclesiastical robes, holding a book from which he looks up to address the viewer. In the background is a classical column wrapped in fluttering drapery set against a cloudy sky.

The objects included in the portrait of Bishop Cheverus—the column, the drapery forming a canopy over the head of the sitter, the books—were standard elements of Stuart's portraiture, stemming from his days in England, where such devices appear in his portraits of Benjamin West (1780–1781; National Gallery, London), and Sir Joshua Reynolds (1784; National Gallery of Art, Washington). These props, especially the column, were components of neoclassical portraiture that were in abundance in London in the 1780s, and like his English colleagues, Stuart (who avoided painting detailed backgrounds whenever possible) used these formalized elements to allude to the dignity and erudition of his sitters. The composition of *Bishop Cheverus* is in fact quite similar to that of Stuart's portrait of *James Monroe* (1818–1820; Metropolitan Museum of Art, New York) and of *Archbishop John Carroll* (ca. 1804; Georgetown University, Washington). Not reserved solely for well-known sitters, these devices (drapery, the base of a classical column silhouetted against a cloudy sky, and hands marking the sitter's place in a book), are also found in Stuart's portraits of such unremarkable individuals as Mrs. Philip Nicker (ca. 1795; private collection) and John Shaw (1793; National Gallery of Ireland, Dublin).

In *Bishop Cheverus*, these objects have a specific formal function, as well as representing Cheverus as a man of letters. The device of one hand marking his place in a book while the other gestures toward the viewer in an attitude of benediction makes the portrait immediate and captures the attention of the viewer. The billowing drapery frames his head, and the sketchily painted curtain (the tassels at right have been left unfinished, so that the underpainting is still visible) makes a deliberate contrast with the tighter, more finished rendering of the facial features and clerical garb. The props also contribute to Stuart's carefully devised color scheme: the gold of the curtain echoes the gold of the bishop's cross and the edge of his book, and contrasts with the grays, whites, and reds of his costume, the same colors used in the painting of the hands and face.

1. Richard J. Purcell, "Cheverus, John Louis Ann, Magdalen Lefebvre de," *Dictionary of American Biography* (New York, 1930), vol. 4, pp. 61-62.

WASHINGTON ALLSTON (1779-1843)
active in Boston 1808–1811; 1818–1843

20. *Self Portrait*

Signed and dated center left: W. *Allston Romae 1805*

Oil on canvas, 35½ x 26½ in. (90.0 x 67.2 cm.)

Bequest of Miss Alice Hooper. 84.301

PROVENANCE: Mrs. Nathaniel Amory, Boston, 1839 (gift of the artist); Mrs. Wormely, Boston, 1865, her sister; John T. Johnston, New York, before 1876; Alice Hooper, Boston, 1876.

EXHIBITIONS: "Exhibition of Pictures, Painted by Washington Allston," Harding's Gallery, Boston, 1839, no. 23; "First Exhibition of Paintings," Westminster Hall, Newport, R.I., 1854, no. 130; "Exhibition of the Works of Washington Allston," Museum of Fine Arts, Boston, 1881, no. 229; "American Painting," M. H. deYoung Memorial Museum and California Palace of the Legion of Honor, San Francisco, 1935, no. 49; "American Painting—Inaugural Exhibition," Virginia Museum, Richmond, 1936, no. 16; "Tercentenary Exhibition," Harvard University, Cambridge, 1936, no. 4; "Washington Allston, 1779–1843," Detroit Institute of Arts, 1947, no. 1; "Great Americans," Museum of Fine Arts, Boston, 1954, no. 25; "The Face of America," Brooklyn Museum, 1957, no. 36; "American Painters of the South," Corcoran Gallery of Art, Washington, 1960, no. 57; "American Self Portraits," National Portrait Gallery, Washington, 1974, no. 15; "Portraits USA 1776-1976," Museum of Art, Pennsylvania State University, University Park, 1976, no. 15; " 'A Man of Genius': The Art of Washington Allston (1779-1843)," Museum of Fine Arts, Boston, 1979, no. 15.

BIBLIOGRAPHY: Moses F. Sweetser, *Allston* (Boston, 1879), pp. 111, 187; William Howe Downes, "Boston Painters and Paintings II: Allston and his Contemporaries," *Atlantic Monthly* 62 (August 1888), p. 260; Alan Burroughs, *Limners and Likenesses* (Cambridge, Mass., 1936), p. 129; Edgar P. Richardson, *Washington Allston* (Chicago, 1948), pp. 77, 190; *American Paintings in the Museum of Fine Arts, Boston* (Boston, 1969), no. 54.

Allston came to Rome in November of 1805, having spent the previous three years in Paris and at the Royal Academy in London. His years in Europe were dedicated to acquiring knowledge of artistic materials and techniques and, more important, to submerging himself in the works of the old masters, especially Raphael, Titian, and Claude. The *Self-Portrait,* one of Allston's first mature works, was painted in Rome shortly after his arrival. The image reflects the values held by the international colony of artists there; at the same time, it indicates Allston's understanding of his own character and his ambitions for his artistic career.

Allston had painted his own likeness several years before, while a student at Harvard (*Self-Portrait,* 1796–1800; Fogg Art Museum, Harvard University, Washington Allston Trust). Although his expression contains a hint of his romantic aspirations, the portrait as a whole resembles self-images painted by eighteenth-century artists. By showing himself in good clothing and in a grand setting, he emphasized his dignity and material well-being, as though to present himself as the equal of his classmates who sought careers in commerce or the law.[1] In the *Self-Portrait* of 1805, although Allston again characterized himself as a gentleman—his clothes are elegant and fashionable—and as an intellectual—his Phi Beta Kappa key hangs promi-

nently from his watch chain—his facial expression reveals a poetic consciousness. His pose is not conventional but easy and relaxed. His expression is meditative, his eyes dreamy; his gaze is directed toward the viewer yet does not really engage him. These features, the ambiguous architectural setting, and the cool, soft colors of the portrait create an air of detachment, of distance: Allston presented himself as a special consciousness, as a being who, because he is an artist, is somehow superior to the rest of mankind.

There is no parallel in America for Allston's portrait. But in Europe, especially in Rome, there were many young artists painting portraits that similarly departed from neoclassical conventions. The *Self-Portrait with Brown Collar* by the German artist Philip Otto Runge (1802; Kunsthalle, Hamburg) shares with Allston's image the thoughtful expression and studied informality of pose that were typical of the new romantic portrait style; Ingres's defiant *Self-Portrait* of 1804 (Musée Condé, Chantilly) painted shortly before the artist came to Rome, presents the idea of artistic superiority. In composition, Allston's work resembles J. M. W. Turner's *Self-Portrait* of about 1807 (Tate Gallery, London) and Ingres's portrait of the painter François-Marius Granet (ca. 1807; Museum, Aix-en-Provence), whom Allston knew in Rome, although Ingres's work postdates Allston's departure from Italy. These works indicate a deliberately designed image of the artistic personality. Their subjects—Allston, Turner, and Granet—are informally posed, their hair slightly tousled, their cravats loosely tied, their handsome features set off by a white collar. Their rather dandified clothes are casually worn; their expressions are intense and self-absorbed; they present themselves as men of intelligence and refinement, as "members of the republic of arts and letters."[2] This sense of detachment and superiority was at the base of the romantic conception of the artist, which differed markedly from the eighteenth-century view of the artist as gentleman, or the even earlier notion of the artist as craftsman. That Allston fully subscribed to this image of the artist is clear both from his own self-portrait, and from his contemporary portrait of Samuel Taylor Coleridge (1806 Fogg Art Museum, Harvard University, Washington Allston Trust), whom he depicted in the same way.

Characteristic of the artistic community in Rome of which Allston was a part was not only a determined independence from the norms and expectations of the prevailing neoclassical tradition but, paradoxically, a devotion to an artistic order that can only be described as classical and was founded in their admiration for Renaissance masters, in Allston's case particularly Titian and Raphael. A deliberate, if veiled, antiquarianism in Allston's portrait is indicated (as it is to an even greater degree in Ingres's portrait of Granet) by the architectural background, which alludes to both the Rome of the past and the Rome of his romantic imagination. The patchy, moldy wall behind Allston, the

(continued on page 84)

mingling of the artist's shadow with those indications of decay, and the spatial ambiguity suggest that the artist is at home in a past that is mysterious and poetic. Allston's technique, too, marks a desire to depart from the neoclassical tradition, and to emulate instead the Venetians' attention to pictorial surface. From Titian he learned to use muted colors and create softened contours through a complex system of glazing—a style virtually the opposite of the pure, strong colors and precise linearity of the preceding generation—to produce an evocative and enigmatic image. Such Renaissance portraits as Titian's *Man with a Glove* (1520–1523; Musée du Louvre, Paris), are the antecedents of Allston's image here, an image of cultivation and aristocratic

bearing combined with indications of special sensitivity, which for the rest of his career would define his view of his role as an artist. Allston's romantic *Self-Portrait* reflects his love and disciplined study of the old masters; he sought to achieve in it a classicism that was not ordered and rational but subjective and poetic.

1. The most noteworthy example of this type of self-portrait in American art, in which gentlemanly character and worldly success are advertised, is John Singleton Copley's *Portrait of the Copley Family* (1776–1777; National Gallery of Art, Washington).

2. Hugh Honour, *Romanticism* (New York, 1979), p. 249.

---

21. *Beatrice*, 1819

Oil on canvas, 30¼ x 25⅜ in. (76.9 x 64.5 cm.)

Anonymous gift. 59.778

PROVENANCE: Theodore Lyman, Boston, 1819; Samuel A. Eliot, Boston, 1839; Mrs. Samuel A. Eliot, Boston, 1879; Heirs of Mrs. Eliot, by 1881; Ellen T. Bullard, Boston, by 1946.

RELATED WORKS: *Beatrice (Dora Hay)* engraved by John Cheney, published in *The Token*, 1836 (reprinted in S. C. Atkinson, *Atkinson's Casket* [December 1837], p. 529).

EXHIBITIONS: "First Exhibition of Paintings," Boston Athenaeum, 1827, no. 37 (also "Thirtieth Exhibition," 1857, no. 211); "Exhibition of Pictures, Painted by Washington Allston," Harding's Gallery, Boston, 1839, no. 10; "First Exhibition of the Boston Artists' Association," Harding's Gallery, Boston, 1842, no. 70; "Sanitary Fair Exhibition," Boston, 1863; "Exhibition of the Works of Washington Allston," Museum of Fine Arts, Boston, 1881, no. 232; "Washington Allston, 1779–1843," Detroit Institute of Arts, 1947, no. 28; " 'A Man of Genius': The Art of Washington Allston (1779–1843)," Museum of Fine Arts, Boston, 1979, no. 53.

BIBLIOGRAPHY: J. Huntington, "The Allston Exhibition: A Letter to an American Artist Traveling Abroad," *Knickerbocker Magazine* 14 (1839), pp. 169, 171–173; William D. Ticknor, *Remarks on Mr. Allston's Paintings* (Boston, 1839), p. 28; Margaret Fuller, "A Record of Impressions Produced by the Exhibition of Mr. Allston's Pictures in the Summer of 1839," *Dial* 1 (1840), pp. 74, 79, 81; Oliver Wendell Holmes, "Exhibition of Pictures Painted by Washington Allston at Harding's Gallery, School Street," *North American Review* 50 (April 1840), pp. 375, 377–378; Anna Jameson, "Washington Allston," *Athenaeum* (London, Jan. 13, 1844), p. 41; Henry T. Tuckerman, *Book of the Artists* (New York, 1870), pp. 143, 147, 149; Moses F. Sweetser, *Allston* (Boston, 1879), pp. 111, 187; William Howe Downes, "Boston Painters and Paintings II: Allston and his Contemporaries," *Atlantic Monthly* 62 (August 1888), p. 260; Jared B. Flagg, *The Life and Letters of Washington Allston* (New York, 1892), p. 161; Edgar P. Richardson, *Washington Allston* (Chicago, 1948), pp. 139, 141, 148, 207; *American Paintings in the Museum of Fine Arts, Boston* (Boston, 1969), no. 64; Kenyon C. Bolton and Elizabeth Johns, *The Paintings of Washington Allston* (Lowe Art Museum, Coral Gables, Fla., 1975), pp. 9, 20; Elizabeth Johns, "Washington Allston: Method, Imagination, and Reality," *Winterthur Portfolio* 12 (1977), pp. 11, 12.

Allston frequently derived the subjects of his paintings from literature. Here he depicted Beatrice, the heroine of Dante's *Divine Comedy*, who was Dante's idealized love and who was invoked as the guardian spirit of the events described in the poem. It was Beatrice who sent Virgil to lead Dante through Hell and Purgatory; she then guided him through Paradise herself. Allston's interest in Dante was a part of the increasing enthusiasm for medieval art, architecture, and literature in the early nineteenth century. Whereas he did not incorporate aspects of Gothic style into this work, as many of his contemporaries would do, he did borrow extensively from an earlier style, and was one of many romantic artists to derive subjects from the writings of Dante.[1]

Beatrice is one of the first, and most beautiful, of Allston's many paintings of single figures in a mood of reverie. The roots of this subject are to be found in his early portraits of his first wife. *Ann Channing Allston* (1809–1811; coll. Henry Channing Rivers, Maine) is a quiet portrait of his wife reading. *The Valentine* (1809–1811; private collection, Boston), was probably based on that portrait, but is a more generalized image in which the anecdotal aspect is overshadowed by the mood of contemplation. Softly painted, richly but subtly colored, and suffused with a luminous atmosphere, *The Valentine* looks forward to the formal properties of *Beatrice*.

After these paintings, Allston experimented no further with this genre until about 1816, when he began work on *Beatrice* and painted *Contemplation* (Lord Egremont, Petworth, Sussex), which introduced a variant on the type: the contemplative figure set against a poetic landscape. Allston's return to these dreamy figures, now more idealized and less portrait-like than before, may have been occasioned by the death of his wife in February 1815, for she was the original inspiration. In the nearly dozen paintings of idealized female figures he would produce during the next two decades, Allston refrained from dramatizing any anecdote or inci-

(continued on page 86)

dent, encouraging the viewer instead to feel empathy with the subject, in this case a hauntingly beautiful woman who embodies grace and vaguely melancholy introspection.

For the forms and the spirit of his pictures, Allston drew upon memories of the Renaissance artists he admired, especially Titian and Raphael. These artists provided Allston with a precedent for using beautiful young women as the personification of ideals or virtues;[2] however, his figures embody a mood rather than being allegorical. Beatrice's pose and expression, as well as her gentle mood of reverie, also echo Raphael's characterization of female saints and the Madonna; many of these well-known compositions contain the dreamy expression, the gentle tilt of the head, and modest gesture that Allston would later use to suggest Beatrice's gentility and delicacy. Her gesture—her right hand at her breast, her left resting amid the folds of drapery in her lap—resembles the posture of Raphael's *Saint Catherine of Alexandria* (1507–1508; National Gallery, London). *Saint Catherine* seems to have been a special favorite of Allston's, for he used that figure as the basis for the pose of *Rosalie* (1835; Society for the Preservation of New England Antiquities, Boston), another meditative young woman.

Beatrice was greatly admired by Allston's contemporaries.[3] The painting was engraved in 1836 by John Cheney for the souvenir book *The Token* and, along with *Rosalie,* the *Spanish Girl,* and Allston's other paintings of reflective young women, inspired many artists of the next several generations to make paintings of this genre. William Morris Hunt, George Fuller, and G. W. Flagg all painted their own versions of *Beatrice,* occasionally with a literary connection but always alluding to a romantic, even melancholy state of mind. However, the Raphaelesque qualities that distinguish *Beatrice* seldom appear in these works and by mid-century, although such idealized figures continued to be painted in great numbers, their romantic traits were replaced by Victorian sentimentalism.

1. Blake's illustrations for the *Divine Comedy* (1824–1827, Tate Gallery, London), Delacroix's *Barque of Dante* (1822; Musée du Louvre, Paris) and his *Justice of Trajan* (1840; Musée des Beaux Arts, Rouen), and Ingres's *Paolo and Francesca* (1819; Musée des Beaux Arts, Angers) are among the best known of the numerous works based on Dante.

2. Well-known examples include: Titian's *Flora* (1520–1522; Uffizi, Florence) or his *Lavina with a Tray of Fruit* (1555; Staatliche Museen, Berlin-Dahlem), in which the artist's daughter represents fecundity. Allston drew upon a version of this picture for *The Sister* (ca. 1816–1817; Fogg Art Museum, Harvard University, Washington Allston Trust). See William Gerdts, "The Paintings of Washington Allston," " 'A Man of Genius': The Art of Washington Allston (1779–1843)" (Museum of Fine Arts, Boston, 1979), pp. 134-135.

3. The critical response to *Beatrice*—which became less favorable after Allston's death—as well as a discussion of the works it inspired, is found in Gerdts (ibid., p. 95).

22. *Moonlit Landscape*, 1819

Oil on canvas, 24¾ x 35¼ in. (63.0 x 89.5 cm.)

Gift of William Sturgis Bigelow. 21.1429

PROVENANCE: Possibly John Doggett, Boston, by 1829; J. H. Bigelow, Boston, by 1839; Mrs. Jacob Bigelow, Boston, by 1881; William Sturgis Bigelow, Boston.

EXHIBITIONS: "Third Exhibition of Paintings," Boston Athenaeum, 1829, no. 130 (also "Twenty-third Exhibition," 1850, no. 90, and "Thirtieth Exhibition," 1857, no. 222); "Exhibition of Pictures Painted by Washington Allston," Harding's Gallery, Boston, 1839, no. 24; "Exhibition of the Works of Washington Allston," Museum of Fine Arts, Boston, 1881, no. 215; "Night Scenes," Wadsworth Athenaeum, Hartford, 1940, no. 52; "Washington Allston 1779–1843," Detroit Institute of Arts, 1947, no. 26; "Painting in America, The Story of 450 Years," Detroit Institute of Arts, 1957, no. 67; "The American Vision," Wildenstein & Co., New York 1957, no. 7; "Four Boston Masters," Museum of Fine Arts, Boston, 1959, no. 22; "200 Years of American Painting," St. Louis City Art Museum, 1964, no. 9; "New England Art from New England Museums," Brockton Art Center, Brockton, Mass., 1969, no. 27; "19th-Century America, Paintings and Sculpture," Metropolitan Museum of Art, New York, 1970, no. 7; "To Look on Nature," Museum of Art, Rhode Island School of Design, Providence, 1972, no. 15; "200 Anni di Pittura Americana, 1776–1976," Galleria Nazionale d'Arte Moderna, Rome, 1976, no. 7; " 'A Man of Genius': The Art of Washington Allston (1779–1843)," Museum of Fine Arts, Boston, 1979, no. 54.

BIBLIOGRAPHY: Henry Pickering, *The Ruins of Paestum and Other Compositions in Verse* (Salem, Mass., 1822), pp. 91–94, 127; ———, "Moonlight, an Italian Scene," *Atlantic Souvenir* (Philadelphia, 1828), pp. 210–213; J. Huntington, "The Allston Exhibit; a Letter to an American Artist Travelling Abroad," *Knickerbocker* 14 (1839), p. 168; Moses F. Sweetser, *Allston* (Boston, 1879), pp. 115, 188; William Howe Downes, "Boston Painters and Paintings II: Allston and his Contemporaries," *Atlantic Monthly* 62 (August 1888), p. 260; James Thrall Soby and Dorothy C. Miller, *Romantic Painting in America* (Museum of Modern Art, New York, 1943), p. 13; Edgar P. Richardson, "Allston and the Development of Romantic Color," *Art Quarterly* 7 (1944), p. 54; ———, *Washington Allston* (Chicago, 1948), pp. 144–145, 202; Robert L. White, "Washington Allston: Banditti in Arcadia," *American Quarterly* 8 (1961), p. 395; William H. Gerdts, "Washington Allston and the German Romantic Classicists in Rome," *Art Quarterly* 32 (1969), p. 167; *American Paintings in the Museum of Fine Arts, Boston* (Boston, 1969), no. 65; Kenyon C. Bolton and Elizabeth Johns, *The Paintings of Washington Allston* (Lowe Art Museum, Coral Gables, Fla., 1975), pp. 7, 9; John Wilmerding, et. al., *American Light: The Luminist Movement* (National Gallery of Art, Washington, 1980), pp. 103, 104, 176, 184.

Moonlit Landscape was painted early in 1819, shortly after Allston returned to Boston from Europe, where he had lived for seven years. During that time Allston was occupied primarily with figure painting; this composition marks a return to the romantic landscape, a subject that first caught his interest in Italy many years before.

The painting, first shown to the public in 1829 at the annual exhibition of the Boston Athenaeum, was already well known to Allston's associates in Cambridgeport: its first documented owner was John Doggett, the renowned Boston framemaker; earlier it had inspired Allston's friend Henry Pickering to write several poems.[1] Allston himself took spe-

cial note of *Moonlit Landscape*, writing to William Collins that he had completed it during the first three months after his return from England. A poetic description of his arrival in Boston Harbor, sent to William Dunlap, has been associated with the picture:

> *The wind fell and left our ship almost stationary on a long low swell, as smooth as glass and undulating under one of our gorgeous autumnal skies like a prairie of amber. The moon looked down upon us like a living thing, as if to bid us welcome....*[2]

Whereas Pickering's poems interpret *Moonlit Landscape* as a eulogy for Italy, Allston's account of the scene in Boston Harbor suggests, on the other hand, that it dramatizes his arrival in America.

The sources for *Moonlit Landscape* are to be found in the work of the many artists whom Allston studied and admired in Italy and England. The painting is a romantic interpretation of the classical landscape tradition of Claude Lorrain, Salvator Rosa, and Gaspard Poussin, and also was influenced by the works of his English contemporaries. Of the seventeenth-century masters, Claude had the greatest effect on Allston, who emulated his well-balanced pictorial structure. He appropriated from Claude's landscapes a variety of motifs and devices, including the bridge set into the middle distance of the picture, the full moon casting a strong light on the water, and the *staffage* figures (which also resemble the banditti populating Salvator Rosa's landscapes), but adapted the Claudean formula to his nineteenth-century vision. Instead of the seemingly casually placed *coulisses* defining deliberate progression into space, he instituted a strict symmetry of pictorial elements; rather than the sense of closure and Arcadian isolation that results from the Claudean balance, Allston created infinitely extending space.

Among the modern masters, it was J. M. W. Turner, specifically his experiments with Claude's compositional structure, who had the greatest impact on Allston. Allston connected the two artists in his own mind, believing that "Turner was the greatest painter since the days of Claude."[3] Of Turner's many works that borrow from Claude, the engraving *The Bridge in the Middle Distance*, published in 1808, employs just those pictorial elements that Allston would use in *Moonlit Landscape*: the bridge, the low, hazy mountains at the horizon, and the shadowy architectural forms in the far distance. However, it is in the treatment of light that *Moonlit Landscape* comes closest to Turner's early works. In two of Turner's marine paintings, the *Mildmay Sea Piece* (1797; now lost; published in the *Liber Studiorum* in 1812) and *Fishermen at Sea* (1796; Tate Gallery, London; engraved by Turner for the *Liber*, but not published), swirling clouds are illuminated by a full moon, establishing a mood of drama and mystery: as in *Moonlit Landscape*, the backlighting, which silhouettes and generalizes the figures, imbues the painting with a universal meaning.[4]

Unlike many of Claude's and Turner's paintings, in which

(continued on page 88)

a topographical rendering is the point of departure for an idealized scene, Allston makes no attempt to represent a specific place, although his landscape is reminiscent of the Italian terrain he so loved. Nor is the painting allegorical; rather, as in *Beatrice* (cat. no. 22) and other works of this period, the sympathetic viewer was trusted to use his imagination to interpret the image. In this first work painted upon his return to America, Allston called upon the romantic imagery in which he had steeped himself in Europe, to create a poetic essay on transition and introspection, one that had autobiographical significance as well.

The bridge, given an almost iconic prominence by the symmetry and the attenuated perspective of the picture, serves both a formal and a metaphoric function. It connects the right and left halves of the picture; it also symbolizes movement and transition. In aesthetic theory of this period, the bridge was often seen as a heroic form, one that, by indicating progression, implied hope.[5] Allston underscored this connotation by showing the moonlight—used to establish a contemplative mood—streaming under the arches of the bridge and leading to the pilgrim-like figures on shore. The image suggests both arrival and departure and, as such, may reflect Allston's own experiences: his sighting of Boston Harbor and his memories of Italy and its great artis-

tic tradition of which he felt himself to be a part. The somber, introspective mood mirrors Allston's sorrow at leaving that rich culture; the images of transition and transcendence may have expressed his hope of bringing the tradition to America.

1. The provenance of this picture, and its connections with Pickering's poetry, are discussed by Marcia Wallace, "Washington Allston's *Moonlit Landscape*," (unpublished MS., Paintings Department Files, Museum of Fine Arts, Boston). See also William Gerdts, "The Paintings of Washington Allston," " *'A Man of Genius': The Art of Washington Allston (1779–1843)"* (Museum of Fine Arts, Boston, 1979), pp. 144-145.

2. William Dunlap, *History of the Rise and Progress of the Arts of Design in the United States,* 1834 (reprint New York, 1969, vol. 2), p. 183.

3. Reported by C. R. Leslie and quoted in Gerdts, "The Paintings of Washington Allston," p. 98.

4. These comparisons were noted by Wallace (see note 1), who also observes parallels between Allston's works and the moonlit landscapes of Wright of Derby and Caspar David Friedrich.

5. Adele Holcomb, "The Bridge in the Middle Distance: Symbolic Elements in Romantic Landscape," *Art Quarterly* 36 (Spring 1974), pp. 49-53. Holcomb quotes Uvedale Price (*An Essay on the Picturesque, as Compared to the Sublime and the Beautiful* [London, 1796], vol. 2, p. 334) who asserts that bridges unite "perhaps in a higher degree than any other building, beauty, grandeur, utility, and real as well as apparent difficulty."

ROBERT PECKHAM (1785-1877)
active in Westminster, Mass., 1809–1850

23. *The Peckham-Sawyer Family,* ca. 1817

(Evidence of signature lower left)

Oil on canvas, 26¾ x 32½ in. (68.0 x 82.4 cm.)

Charles Henry Hayden Fund. 1979.394

PROVENANCE: George Peckham, Winchester, Mass. (great-great-grandson of the artist).

During the first decades of the nineteenth century, painting in Boston was dominated by Gilbert Stuart, and later by Chester Harding. At the same time, there were several painters, for the most part self-trained, working in quite different styles in the rural areas of New England. Robert Peckham is one of a few such artists known to have worked near Boston. He was born in Petersham, Massachusetts, in 1785, is said to have earned a Master of Arts degree from Harvard, and married Ruth Sawyer of Bolton in 1813. An influential member of his church, Peckham was appointed a deacon in 1828, and used that position to express his radical views on temperance and abolition of slavery. He was painting by 1809, and during the next two decades produced many portraits in the north central Massachusetts towns of Bolton, Billerica, Holden, and Royalston, each less than fifty miles from his home in Westminster. Best known are Peckham's stylized, severely outlined portraits of children, painted in bright colors and often including their favorite toys.[1]

The Peckham-Sawyer Family is the most complex and ambititous composition known by Peckham. It shows four generations of his wife's family with the artist second from right, seated around a table at the end of a family dinner. The occasion was clearly not a joyous one, and it has been suggested that the family's solemn expressions reflect their sorrow at the loss of young Elizabeth, standing fourth from left, who died in 1817.[2] Family tradition and the ages of his sitters indicate that Peckham painted this portrait in that year. However, *The Peckham-Sawyer Family* is surprisingly more sophisticated and competent in academic terms than were Peckham's portraits of the next decade. Those works demonstrate the stylistic traits commonly associated with "folk" or "provincial" paintings: strong emphasis on line; flat, bright colors; and a distortion of perspective and anatomical proportions, which in Peckham's work results in bizarre, hydrocephalic figures. Nor does *The Peckham-Sawyer Family* resemble the large-scale family portraits of the period by Erastus Salisbury Field or Ralph Earl, although like those works it is a revealing document of daily middle-class life in the early nineteenth century. Rather, *The Peckham-Sawyer Family* derives from the prevailing academic style in New York and New England and, despite Peckham's provincial origins, in the organization of pictorial elements is a distant echo of the precepts of the neoclassical tradition.

It is possible that Peckham was exposed to neoclassical compositions during his stay at Harvard. His picture is unusually small for a subject of such detail and complexity, and it may be that a print after an English or French group portrait, readily obtainable in Boston, may have guided him in the poses and arrangement of his figures. Peckham also may have been introduced to the neoclassical style through contact with artists such as Ezra Ames (active in the Worcester area in the 1790s) who were attempting to work in that manner. But whatever the source of his exposure, the current high style clearly affected Peckham's composition of his portrait: his figures, though fully three-dimensional, are spread out across a shallow space in a frieze-like arrangement; the light entering the composition through the window at left sharply outlines the forms and accentuates the profiles of the three figures in the center of the composition. The figures are organized into carefully balanced groups, a symmetry echoed in the extraordinary still life on the table in the foreground, whose simplicity and geometry are reminiscent of the compositions of Raphaelle Peale.

Five years later, Peckham adopted the eccentric, "primitive" style for which he is best known, a style that belies his earlier sophistication. This odd progression from academic to folk is characteristic of several other provincial painters, without apparent cause.[3] One can only guess that the curious evolution of Peckham's art was another reflection of the personal eccentricity that led him to so radically espouse political causes that he was eventually excommunicated from his church.

1. For biographical information, see Dale T. Johnson, "Deacon Robert Peckham: Delineator of the 'Human Face Divine'," *American Art Journal* 11 (January 1979), pp. 27-36.
2. I am grateful to Laura Luckey, Assistant Director, Museum of Art, Rhode Island School of Design, for this suggestion.
3. Erastus Salisbury Field studied for a brief period with S. F. B. Morse in New York before evolving his idiosyncratic style. An equally eccentric figure, Ammi Phillips, painted in several different manners during his long career; his work is sometimes nearly academic and at others quintessentially primitive.

HENRY SARGENT (1770-1845)

active in Boston 1790–1793; 1799–1845

24. *The Dinner Party*, ca. 1820-1821

Oil on canvas, 61⅝ x 49⅝ in. (156.5 x 126.1 cm.)

Gift of Mrs. Horatio A. Lamb in memory of Mr. and Mrs. Winthrop Sargent. 19.13

PROVENANCE: David L. Brown, Boston, 1821; Henry Sargent (the artist), Boston, by 1842; Winthrop Henry Sargent (the artist's grandson), Boston; Mrs. Winthrop Sargent, Boston; Mrs. Horatio A. Lamb (her sister), Milton, Mass.

EXHIBITIONS: "First Public Exhibition of the Boston Artists' Association," Harding's Gallery, Boston, 1842, no. 58; "American Genre Painting," Whitney Museum of American Art, New York, 1925, no. 91; "American Life," Rochester Memorial Art Gallery, 1935, no. 31; "Survey of American Painting," Carnegie Institute, Pittsburgh, 1940, no. 108; "American Processional," Corcoran Gallery of Art, Washington, 1950, no. 120; "American Painting in the Nineteenth Century," American Federation of Arts, New York, 1953, no. 81; "Painting in America: The Story of 450 Years," Detroit Institute of Arts, 1957, no. 59; "The American Muse," Corcoran Gallery of Art, Washington, 1959, no. 103; "Boston Painters: 1720–1940," Boston University School of Fine and Applied Arts, 1968, no. 75; "The Arts of the Young Republic: The Age of William Dunlap," William Hayes Ackland Art Center, University of North Carolina, Chapel Hill, 1968, no. 119; "19th-Century America: Paintings and Sculpture," Metropolitan Museum of Art, New York, 1970, no. 27.

BIBLIOGRAPHY: William Dunlap, *History of the Rise and Progress of the Arts of Design in the United States* (New York, 1834), vol. 2, p. 63; Julia DeWolf Addison, "Henry Sargent, a Boston Painter," *Art in America* 17 (1929), pp. 280-284; Alan Burroughs, *Limners and Likenesses* (Cambridge, Mass., 1936), p. 116; R. Ralston, "19th-Century New York Interiors," *Antiques* 43 (1943), p. 266; M. B. Cowdrey, "Paintings as Documents," *Antiques* 58 (1950), p. 373; Harold Kicker, *The Architecture of Charles Bulfinch* (Cambridge, Mass., 1969), p. 55; *American Paintings in the Museum of Fine Arts, Boston* (Boston, 1969), no. 851.

Well known as an illustration of manners and architectural fashions in Federal Boston, Henry Sargent's *Dinner Party* also documents the artistic life and taste of that city in the early nineteenth century. The painting (which Sargent, primarily a portraitist, described to John Trumbull as "my first attempt at a work of this kind,"[1]) was bought in 1821 by the Boston drawing master David L. Brown, and sent on tour to New York, Philadelphia, and other cities, where it elicited much critical attention. William Dunlap praised the picture for its "extraordinary powers of light and shade," and for the "spirit and exactness" of the portraits.[2] John Neal described *The Dinner Party* in his 1823 novel *Randolph* as being painted "after the manner of the 'Capuchin Chapel,'" a reference to a much-admired composition by the French artist François Marius Granet, shown in Boston a few years before.[3] In the catalogue of the first exhibition of the Boston Artists' Association (of which Sargent was vice-president), held at Harding's Gallery in 1842, *The Dinner Party* was compared with Granet's work, and was praised for its "close imitation of nature—correct perspective . . . and remarkable clearness of its atmosphere."[4]

The connection with Granet's picture, which so many of Sargent's admirers found noteworthy, reveals Boston's eagerness for an association with contemporary trends in European painting. Exhibited in Boston only a few years after its completion in 1815, *The Choir of the Capuchin Church in Rome* introduced a new romantic style of painting practiced in Europe at the turn of the century. The mysterious atmosphere of Granet's painting, created by the medieval setting and the back lighting, by the massive architecture, and by organizing the figures along the lines of perspective, were artistic features new to Boston; the enthusiasm with which the painting was received there led Sargent, one of the city's most popular painters, to borrow Granet's design for his own composition.

Sargent's adaptation of romanticism was cautious, and retained many attributes of the neoclassical style. While using the exaggerated perspective and dramatic chiaroscuro of *The Choir of the Capuchins,* he eliminated the mystery of the French work and converted the monastic ceremony into a domestic one. *The Dinner Party* depicts Sargent's own dining room at 10 Franklin Place, Boston (a building designed by Charles Bulfinch in 1793), which is shown through an arched doorway leading from the parlor. The painting is believed to document a meeting of the Wednesday Evening Club, a social organization which gathered to exchange political news and opinions over a supper given at the home of one of the members. While most of the participants are not specifically identifiable, the third figure seated at right resembles a Sargent self-portrait of about 1795 (Museum of Fine Arts, Boston). The servants have removed the tablecloth, and the gentlemen are engaged in genial conversations over the final course of wine, nuts, and fruit. Sargent's careful description of these and other domestic details—the Greek-key chair rail and dentilled cornice, the small neoclassical bust over the doorway and glass-domed clock over the delicately carved mantel, and the many paintings hung in the room—advertises his social position as a man of wealth and taste.

The use of strong dark-light contrasts and the emphasis on silhouetted figures lit from behind are even more evident in the companion to this picture, *The Tea Party* (Museum of Fine Arts, Boston), which Sargent painted a few years later. That painting, too, documents a social event, and is set in a fashionable parlor of a Boston house, perhaps Sargent's own. Ever sensitive to changing styles, Sargent in that picture documented the new vogue for the French-inspired empire gowns, hairstyles, and furnishings that swept Boston in the 1820s.

1. Letter from Henry Sargent to John Trumbull, Boston, September 17, 1821 (Archives of American Art).
2. William Dunlap, *History of the Rise and Progress of the Arts of Design in the United States* (New York, 1834), vol. 2, p. 63.
3. John Neal, as quoted in *19th-Century America: Paintings and Sculpture* (Metropolitan Museum of Art, New York, 1970), no. 27.
4. *The Constitution of the Boston Artists' Association, with a Catalogue of the First Public Exhibition of Paintings at Harding's Gallery* (Boston, 1842), no. 38.

ALVAN FISHER (1792-1863)
active in Boston and Dedham, Mass., 1810–1821; 1826–1863

25. *Sugar Loaf Mountain*

Signed and dated lower right: *A. Fisher 1821*

Oil on canvas, 25⅝ x 33 in. (65.0 x 83.8 cm.)

M. and M. Karolik Collection. 47.1154

PROVENANCE: Goodspeed's Book Shop, Boston, 1939; Leroy Ireland, New York; with Victor Spark, New York, 1944; with Macbeth Gallery, New York, 1945; Maxim Karolik, Newport, R.I.

EXHIBITIONS: "American Landscape: A Changing Frontier," National Collection of Fine Arts, Washington, 1966; "Hudson River School," State University College, Genesco, N.Y., 1968; "Artists of the Hudson River School," R. W. Norton Gallery, Shreveport, La., 1973, no. 4.

BIBLIOGRAPHY: *Month at Goodspeed's* (April 1939), p. 245; Alan Burroughs, "A Letter from Alvan Fisher," *Art in America* 32 (July 1944), p. 123; *M. and M. Karolik Collection of American Paintings, 1815–1865* (Cambridge, Mass., 1949), no. 115; Virgil Barker, *American Painting* (New York, 1950), p. 300; Mabel M. Swan, "The Unpublished Notebooks of Alvan Fisher," *Antiques* (August 1955), p. 127; *American Paintings in the Museum of Fine Arts, Boston* (Boston, 1969), no. 404.

With Thomas Doughty, who became his close friend and sketching companion, and Joshua Shaw in Philadelphia, Alvan Fisher was one of the first American artists to specialize in landscape painting. Like the British painters of the picturesque who were their models, these men attempted to reveal the ideal, poetic aspect of natural scenery; their art was a modest prelude to the paintings of the Hudson River School, to both the heroic compositions of Cole and Church, and the quieter panoramas of Kensett and Lane.

In the 1820s Fisher traveled through Vermont, western Massachusetts and upstate New York, recording his observations of American wilderness scenery in his notebook.

The present painting, based on pencil and watercolor sketches made at the site, depicts Sugar Loaf Mountain, near Deerfield, Massachusetts; as was his custom, Fisher combined and rearranged observed details to conform to the conventions of picturesque landscape. His composition, carefully balanced yet asymmetrical, contains the "water, rising ground, and woody banks," prescribed by the eighteenth-century landscape theorist William Gilpin as ingredients of the picturesque; in place of the castle, a requisite ingredient of grander European landscapes,[1] is the mountain with a tiny settlement (indicated by the rising smoke) at its base: a typically American adaptation of the formula.[2]

Using a compositional device popular with British landscape painters from Gainsborough to Constable, one ultimately traceable—as with so many conventions of romantic landscape painting—to Claude, Fisher placed his foreground in shadow and joined it to the sunny middle ground by means of a winding stream. The hunters, whose red jackets provide a cheerful coloristic accent, are observers of the gentle wilderness and, as such, are surrogates for the artist himself. However, Fisher's technique lagged behind his aesthetic ambition: the middle ground lacks definition, and the composition is conventional, lacking a sense of specific place. At the same time, Fisher's palette of soft greens, yellows, and grays, and his feathery brushwork are successful in creating a mood of sylvan intimacy that is clearly deeply felt.

1. William Gilpin, *Observations on Several Parts of England (Cambridge, Norfolk, Suffolk, and Essex)* (third edition, London, 1809), p. 120.

2. See, for example, Frederic E. Church's *Mount Ktaadn* (1853; Yale University Art Gallery, New Haven) for a later illustration of this type.

JOHN NEAGLE (1796-1860)
active in Boston 1825

26. *Gilbert Stuart*

Signed and dated upper left: *J. Neagle 1825*

Oil on canvas, 27 x 22⅛ in. (66.5 x 56.0 cm.)

Robert J. Edwards Fund. 1975.807

PROVENANCE: Isaac P. Davis, Boston, ca. 1825–1827; Boston Athenaeum, 1853; on deposit at the Museum of Fine Arts, Boston, 1876–1975.

RELATED WORKS: *Gilbert Stuart,* Historical Society of Pennsylvania, Philadelphia; *Gilbert Stuart,* Museum of Art, Rhode Island School of Design, Providence.

EXHIBITIONS: Annual Exhibitions, Boston Athenaeum, between 1853 and 1876 (excepting 1857 and 1858); "Contemporary Art," Museum of Fine Arts, Boston, 1879, no. 98; "Early American Portraits," Boston Art Club, Boston, 1911, no. 30; "Life in America," Metropolitan Museum of Art, New York, 1939, no. 76; "Makers of History in Washington, 1800–1950," National Gallery of Art, Washington, 1950, p. 19; "The Arts of the Young Republic: The Age of William Dunlap," William Hayes Ackland Art Center, University of North Carolina, Chapel Hill, 1968, no. 82; "Portraits USA 1776–1976," Museum of Art, Pennsylvania State University, University Park, 1976; "The Patriot Painters," Museum of Fine Arts, Boston, 1978.

BIBLIOGRAPHY: William Dunlap, *History of the Rise and Progress of the Arts of Design* (New York, 1834), vol. 1, pp. 254-255; Henry T. Tuckerman, *Book of the Artists* (New York, 1870), pp. 111, 627; Justin Winsor, *Memorial History of Boston* (Boston, 1881), vol. 4, p. 390; Jane Stuart, "Anecdotes of Gilbert Stuart," *Scribner's Monthly* 14 (July 1877), p. 379; Clara Erskine Clement and Lawrence Hutton, *Artists of the Nineteenth Century and Their Works* (Boston, 1884; reprinted St. Louis, 1969), p. 194; Virgil Barker, "Neagle," *The Arts* 8 (1925), p. 7; *Portraits by Neagle,* Pennsylvania Academy of the Fine Arts (Philadelphia, 1925), pp. 7-9; Lawrence Park, *Gilbert Stuart* (New York, 1926), vol. 1, p. 57; William Sawitzky, "The Posthumous Career of Old Pat," *Antiques* 25 (March 1934), p. 93; John Hill Morgan, *Gilbert Stuart and his Pupils* (New York, 1939) pp. 68-69; Mabel M. Swan, *The Athenaeum Gallery* (Boston, 1940), p. 129; Marguerite Lynch, "John Neagle's 'Diary'," *Art in America* 37 (April 1949), p. 83; Charles Merrill Mount, *Gilbert Stuart, A Biography* (New York, 1964), p. 324.

Gilbert Stuart's influence on American art was widespread. He was best known in Boston, where he painted the aristocracy and the politically powerful; in addition, his work was admired in New York, Philadelphia, and Washington, where he spent the early years of his career. His effect on younger artists was also significant. Although he took no pupils for regular instruction, he encouraged many local painters, such as James Frothingham, Gilbert Stuart Newton, and Chester Harding. The inspiration of Stuart's works was felt in other centers as well: John Vanderlyn and Samuel F. B. Morse, both of whom worked in New York, sought Stuart's advice, as did Thomas Sully of Philadelphia. In 1825, John Neagle, an artist of developing reputation in Philadelphia and Sully's protégé, traveled to Boston to receive instruction from Stuart and to paint his portrait.

Neagle's reactions to his meeting with Stuart were recorded by William Dunlap, who noted Neagle's astonishment and gratitude for being allowed to paint Stuart when several others, including Stuart's favorite pupil, James

Frothingham, had been denied the privilege: "That he should have honored me, an humble artist and a stranger, by not only sitting for one portrait entire, but by sitting for the completion of a copy, is singular. My portrait is the last ever painted of this distinguished artist."[1]

Although this painting and the replica now in Philadelphia are both inscribed with the date 1825, Neagle continued to work on the likeness for the next two years, keeping it in his studio to serve as a model for later portraits. Surprisingly, although Neagle's portraits of the 1830s would reflect Stuart's technique, little of his influence is apparent here. Rather, Neagle used a compositional formula that he had found successful for male portraits: Stuart is shown bust length (rather than half length, which was Stuart's favorite pose) and turned three-quarters toward the viewer. His head and shoulders fill the picture. By using a neutral background and suppressing all incidental detail, Neagle was able to concentrate upon Stuart's facial features and his wistful expression. The loose, free brushwork in the portrait—the cravat is particularly well painted—and the relatively heavy impasto, especially in highlighted areas, may be the legacy of Thomas Sully. The success of this portrait, and the sensitivity with which Neagle depicted his sitter, is especially apparent in comparison with the copy in Philadelphia. There Stuart's features are generalized and bland; because Neagle emphasized the aristocratic and reserved side of Stuart's character, the second version seems less warm and personal.

Although Neagle's image of Stuart is now revered as the most telling likeness of the artist, it was not appreciated by his family. Jane Stuart, the youngest of Stuart's children, wrote of the painting:

This portrait, so stupid to the last degree, I should think would put to flight the theory of physiognomy, that the features are an indication of the character. . . . It is curious that he should have transmitted to posterity the portraits of the distinguished men of his day, giving each great man his particular attribute, and that his own portrait should pass down to posterity utterly devoid of intellectual expression—in fact the representation of a driveller.[2]

Other critics, both of her time and the present day, would disagree with Jane Stuart's evaluation of the picture, describing it as "the best portrait of him which exists."[3] Today it is appreciated as a dignified and sympathetic likeness of one of America's most distinguished painters.

1. John Neagle, as quoted in William Dunlap, *A History of the Rise and Progress of the Arts of Design in the United States* (New York, 1834; 1919 edition, vol. 1), p. 254.
2. Jane Stuart, "Anecdotes of Gilbert Stuart," *Scribner's Monthly* 14 (July 1887), p. 379.
3. Samuel Isham, *The History of American Painting* (New York, 1936), p. 179. See also Clara Erskine Clement and Lawrence Hutton, *Artists of the Nineteenth Century and their Works* (Boston, 1884; reprinted St. Louis, 1969), and Mabel M. Swan, *The Athenaeum Gallery* (Boston, 1940), p. 129.

97

THOMAS DOUGHTY (1793-1856)
active in Boston 1829–1830; 1832–1837; 1843

27. *New Hampshire Lake,* ca. 1832

Signed lower left: *T. Doughty*

Oil on canvas, 26 x 36¼ in. (66.2 x 92.0 cm.)

Bequest of Maxim Karolik. 64.425

PROVENANCE: With Victor Spark, New York; Maxim Karolik, Newport, R.I., 1950.

EXHIBITIONS: "19th-Century Paintings from the Private Collection of Maxim Karolik," Worcester Art Museum, 1952, no. 14; "19th-Century American Paintings," Smithsonian Institution (traveling exhibition) 1954, no. 17; "Two Centuries of Art in New Hampshire," New Hampshire Historical Society, Concord, 1966; "Painting in the White Mountains," Tarmworth, N.H., 1966.

BIBLIOGRAPHY: Thomas N. Maytham, "A Trove of Doughtys" *Antiques* 88 (November 1965), pp. 681-682; *American Paintings in the Museum of Fine Arts, Boston* (Boston, 1969), no. 345.

Thomas Doughty, the son of a Philadelphia ship carpenter, came to Boston in 1829 to learn the lithographic trade, for which the city was famous, and again in the 1830s, when he became a part of Boston's artistic community, exhibiting at the Athenaeum and at Harding's Gallery, and associating with Chester Harding, Francis Alexander, Alvan Fisher, and other prominent painters. With Fisher, a fellow landscape painter, he made sketching tours through Maine, western Massachusetts, and the White Mountains in New Hampshire; the present painting is probably based on sketches Doughty made during the early years of his residence in Boston.

Although the exact site Doughty represented here has not been identified (it has been associated with New Hampshire by tradition) the rolling hills opening onto a tiny, tree-ringed pasture and then to a broad lake are typical features of New England scenery. Viewed from an elevated perspective, the landscape spreads panoramically before the viewer; the path, curving through the shadowy foreground toward the sunlit meadow in the middle distance, provides an entrance to the bucolic scene. Doughty especially favored the combination of pastoral and wilderness elements. The winding road, majestic trees, grazing cows and the farm boy walking toward them would become standard features of his compositions in later years; here the rendering of warm summer light and the precise calligraphic brushstrokes defining the plants, leaves, tree trunks, and branches raise this image above the formula.

JEREMIAH PEARSON HARDY (1800-1887)
active in Boston ca. 1821

28. *Catherine Wheeler Hardy and her Daughter*, ca. 1842

Oil on canvas, 29⅛ x 36 in. (73.9 x 91.6 cm.)

M. and M. Karolik Collection. 47.1146

PROVENANCE: Charlotte W. Hardy, Brewer, Me. (great-niece of the artist); with Victor Spark, New York, 1944; Maxim Karolik, Newport, R.I., 1944.

EXHIBITIONS: "American Paintings, 1815–1865," Museum of Fine Arts, Boston, 1957, no. 74; "Art in Maine," Colby College Art Museum, Waterville, Me., 1963, no. 51; "Jeremiah Pearson Hardy, Maine Portraitist," Colby College Art Museum, Waterville, Me., 1966; "The American Vision," Knoedler Galleries, New York, 1968, no. 15; "19th-Century America," Metropolitan Museum of Art, New York, 1970, no. 67; "Windows and Doors," The Heckscher Museum, Huntington, L.I., 1972; "The American Portrait: from the Death of Stuart to the Rise of Sargent," Worcester Art Museum, 1973, no. 22; "Selections from the M. and M. Karolik Collection of American Paintings, 1815–1865," Museum of Fine Arts, Boston, 1975, no. 22; "Versatility—Yankee Style," William A. Farnsworth Library and Art Museum, Rockland, Maine, 1977; "Nineteenth-Century American Paintings from the Storerooms," Museum of Fine Arts, Boston, 1979.

BIBLIOGRAPHY: F. H. Eckstorm, "Jeremiah P. Hardy," *Old-Time New England*, 30 (October 1939), pp. 44-45; *M. and M. Karolik Collection of American Paintings 1815–1865* (Cambridge, Mass., 1949), no. 127; *American Paintings in the Museum of Fine Arts, Boston* (Boston, 1969), no. 487; Rosamund Olmstead Humm, *Children in America* (High Museum of Art, Atlanta, 1979), pp. 18-19.

In this portrait, Hardy depicts his wife and daughter in the parlor of their home in Bangor, Maine. The Penobscot River is visible through the window behind them. Catherine Hardy, here shown in her mid-thirties, was descended from the Sears family, who were prominent in Boston during the Revolutionary War era; their daughter, Anne Eliza, was Hardy's constant companion in his studio and later became an accomplished painter of flower and fruit still lifes. Hardy was well known in Maine for his portraiture, having brought to the Bangor area a knowledge of academic painting techniques acquired during the 1820s, when he studied with the drawing master David L. Brown in Boston, and then in New York with Samuel F. B. Morse. Despite this training, however, his work retains a provincial character; this painting, like most of his works from the 1840s and '50s, is a mixture of an unsophisticated drawing style and a knowledgeable adaptation of academic compositional sources.

Hardy's image of his wife and daughter was shaped by two facets of romantic painting that were current in Europe, and to a lesser degree, in America, in the early nineteenth century. The grand romantic portrait tradition dominated by Sir Thomas Lawrence in England from the turn of the century (and practiced in America by Sully and Neagle in Philadelphia and by Chester Harding in Boston in the 1840s) provided Hardy with the compositional formula for this picture. Lawrence popularized the device of plac-

ing his sitters on a plush chair or sofa, with drapery drawn up behind them to reveal an open window; of his many portraits so composed, perhaps the closest to Hardy's painting is *Lady Dover with her Son Henry* (1828; Captain Charles Hepburn, Glasgow), which Hardy undoubtedly knew from engravings made in 1831.[1] In the 1840s, Hardy used this compositional mode several times, but his versions were always more modest than Lawrence's: in *Catherine Wheeler Hardy and her Daughter*, the mother is plainly dressed, the couch suggests solid, middle-class comfort rather than aristocratic elegance, and a simple paneled window frame has replaced the majestic column frequently found in Lawrence's work.

The pensive mood of this picture distinguishes it from most works based on Lawrence's innovations, as does the pronounced emphasis on the open window. These devices connect Hardy with a group of early nineteenth-century German artists whose works he undoubtedly never saw but whose spirit this painting shares. Artists such as Casper David Friedrich, Martin Drölling, and Friedrich Wilhelm von Schadow frequently painted portraits and domestic genre scenes featuring a figure or figures (usually women), in an attitude of quiet absorption and meditation, before an open window. For these artists, the open window came to represent a threshold beyond which the lure of nature was felt. Despite the realistic manner in which the pictures were painted, they were not meant to be merely descriptive, but rather to express the conflict felt by these romantic artists between the active life and the security of domesticity.[2]

Despite his relative isolation in Maine, Hardy remarkably turned to the same imagery as did the German artists to express the conflict between security and adventure. His wife and daughter are posed in attitudes quite distinct from those of Lawrence's sitters, for they address neither the viewer nor each other, and wear expressions which are strangely passive and contemplative. The heavy curtains, parted to frame their heads, also direct the viewer's attention to the view through the window, and so to the river which winds into the distance. The contrast between the interior, and its associations of familiarity and security, and the landscape vista, which for the romantic mind meant the unknowable and infinite, is underscored by the differences in paint handling and palette in the two areas of the picture. The details of the furnishings and the costumes, and the facial features of the women are sharply drawn and somewhat flat, while the background is luminous and atmospheric; strong, dark primary colors predominate in the interior, while the landscape is painted in soft, pastel tones.

Anne Eliza and Mrs. Hardy are thus shown as belonging neither to the world of nature nor entirely to the world of domestic comfort. Mrs. Hardy has interrupted her daughter's drawing lesson to pursue some private fantasy, and even Anne Eliza's features seem ethereal because the light coming in from the window outlines her face from behind.

The poetic, evocative mood makes *Catherine Wheeler Hardy and her Daughter* Hardy's richest and most personal portrait, for in it he has gone beyond academic conventions and created an image which suggests not only the character of the sitters but his own romantic sensibility.

1. The painting was reproduced in mezzotint by S. Cousins in 1831, and was also used as the frontispiece for *Literary Souvenir* (1831) in the form of a line engraving by J. C. Armytage. See Kenneth Garlick, "A Catalogue of the Paintings, Drawings and Pastels of Sir Thomas Lawrence," *Walpole Society, 39,* 1964, p. 70. Hardy's admiration for Lawrence's work stemmed from his student days in Boston. One of his earliest known works is a copy of Lawrence's *John Philip Kemble as Hamlet* (1801; National Gallery, London; Hardy's copy, Colby College Art Museum).

2. These paintings are discussed by Lorenz Eitner, "The Open Window and the Storm-Tossed Boat: An Essay in the Iconography of Romanticism," *Art Bulletin* 37 (Dec. 1955), pp. 281-290, and J. A. Schmoll gen. Eisenwerth, "Fensterbilder: Motivketten in der europäischen Malerei," *Beiträge zur Motivkunde des 19. Jahrhunderts,* ed. Ludwig Grote (Munich, 1970), pp. 13-166.

FRANCIS ALEXANDER (1800-1880)
active in Boton 1827–1831; 1833–1853

29. *Charles Dickens*, 1842

Oil on canvas, 44¼ x 36 in. (112.4 x 91.5 cm.)

Gift of the estate of Mrs. James T. Fields. 24.18

PROVENANCE: Francis Alexander, Boston, to 1872; Mr. and Mrs. James T. Fields, Boston; Fields estate, to 1924.

EXHIBITIONS: "Seventeenth Exhibition of Paintings," Boston Athenaeum, 1843, no. 77 (also "Forty-seventh Exhibition," 1871, no. 239, and "Forty-eighth Exhibition," 1872, no. 215); "Loan Collection of Portraits," Copley Hall, Boston, 1896, no. 6; "Eighty Eminent Painters of New England," Lyman Allen Museum, New London, 1947, no. 55.

BIBLIOGRAPHY: F. G. Kilton, "Charles Dickens and His Less Familiar Portraits," *Magazine of Art* 11 (London, 1888), p. 287; ———, *Dickens by Pen and Pencil* (London, 1890) vol. 1, facing p. 41; M. A. DeWolf Howe, "The Story of the Dickens Portrait," *Brentano's Book Chat* (midwinter 1923), pp. 22-25; Edward F. Payne, *Dickens' Days in Boston* (Boston, 1927), pp. 4, 13; Alan Burroughs, *Limners and Likenesses* (Cambridge, Mass., 1936), p. 127; Catherine W. Pierce, "Francis Alexander," *Old-Time New England* 44, (Oct.–Dec. 1953), pp. 41, 44; *American Paintings in the Museum of Fine Arts, Boston* (Boston, 1969), no. 48; Richard Ormond, *Early Victorian Portraits* (London, 1973), vol. 1, p. 143; Philip Collins, "Charles Dickens," *Abroad in America: Visitors to the New Nation, 1766–1914* (National Portrait Gallery, Washington, 1976), p. 82; Arnold Whitredge, "Dickens and Thackeray in America," *New York Historical Quarterly* 62 (July 1978), p. 218.

Alexander painted this portrait of Dickens in 1842, during the writer's first visit to America. An atypical work for Alexander, who usually favored the half-length format popularized by Gilbert Stuart, the painting shows a three-quarter view of the sitter and includes a narrative aspect seldom present in his portraits. In these features he may have been influenced by Daniel Maclise, whose portrait of Dickens, painted in 1839 (Tate Gallery, London) was the best-known image of the writer; it was engraved for the serialized publication of *Nicholas Nickelby* and appeared as the frontispiece of the collected edition of 1840.[1] Maclise's portrait, like Alexander's, shows Dickens at his writing desk, his head raised, his expression thoughtful. The two portraits are quite dissimilar in spirit, however, and may reflect the differences between England's and America's images of Dickens. Maclise characterizes Dickens as a romantic genius: he looks up from his writing in a moment of poetic inspiration, and is clearly occupied with lofty thoughts. The light that bathes his face shows idealized and noble features. Alexander, on the other hand, places Dickens in a setting as plain as Maclise's is ornate (possibly the author's room at the Tremont House in Boston, while Maclise painted him in his luxurious study); the author is shown not communing with his muse but rather confronting the viewer who has interrupted him, wearing an expression that is solemn, direct, and rather curious. Compared to other portraits and photographs of Dickens from the period, Alexander accurately depicted Dickens's features, yet the author seems quite young and somewhat effeminate-looking. The rendering is intimate where Maclise's is grand; the familiarity of the por-

trait suggests that in America Dickens was seen as more of a popular hero than as a moral paragon.

The controversial circumstances surrounding Alexander's portrait were a portent of Dickens's changing attitude about America. Dickens arrived in Boston, the first stop on a twenty-week tour of the United States, on January 22, 1842. He had great expectations about America, which he hoped would be progressive and truly democratic as England was not; Americans, for their part, were equally eager for his visit. In Boston, people lined the streets to see him; he was honored as "The Literary Guest of the Nation" and was regarded as a kindred spirit because of the concern for social evils and sympathy for the common man expressed in his novels. The initial days of Dickens's visit, spent in Boston, went reasonably well, and neither party was prepared for the disillusionment that followed.

The privilege of making the first portraits of Dickens in America was extended to Alexander and to Henry Dexter, a local sculptor who specialized in marble portrait busts. Dexter's portrait was a great success, and copies of the marble bust were displayed in several cities Dickens visited on his tour. Alexander, a Connecticut-born artist who, with James Frothingham and Chester Harding, was among the leading portraitists in Boston after the death of Gilbert Stuart, was also a logical choice for the honor; however, the rumor that he obtained permission to paint Dickens by approaching him on board his ship while it was still quarantined in Boston Harbor sullied his reputation: the local press called Alexander an "art jockey" and Longfellow, sharing their disdain, used the term "Alexandered," to mean badgered.[2] In fact, Alexander had been enterprising, but not improperly so, for he wrote to Dickens before his arrival in Boston and was granted permission in advance to make the portrait.

After the painting was finished, a further misunderstanding arose that vitiated the friendship between Dickens and Alexander. Alexander intended to circulate his image of Dickens by having a large engraving made. In order to raise money for the plate, Alexander placed the portrait on exhibition in Boston and charged admission. This angered Dickens, who felt that Alexander was attempting to capitalize on their friendship and to use the portrait in a greedy scheme. Dickens's irritation with Alexander was one of several episodes in his gradual disillusionment with America. Although he would continue to speak highly of Boston ("Boston is what I would have the whole United States to be"),[3] his contempt for America's citizens and institutions was great, as his *American Notes* and his bitterly satiric novel *Martin Chuzzlewit* make clear. And he would never again allow an American artist to paint his portrait.

1. Richard Ormond, *Early Victorian Portraits* (London, 1973), vol. I, p. 139.
2. Catherine W. Pierce, "Francis Alexander," *Old-Time New England* 44 (October-December 1953), p. 41.
3. Dickens, as quoted in Philip Collins, "Charles Dickens," *Abroad in America: Visitors to the New Nation 1776-1914* (Washington, 1976), p. 86.

WILLIAM MATTHEW PRIOR (1806-1873)
active in Boston 1848–1873

30. *William Allen*

Inscribed on back: *W. Allen/By Wm. M. Prior/1843*

Oil on canvas, 32¼ x 40⅛ in. (81.8 x 101.9 cm.)

M. and M. Karolik Collection. 44.466

PROVENANCE: Samuel Parker Allen, Cambridge[port], Mass., 1843; James Morse Allen, Cambridge, Mass. (his son); Greta Allen, Dorchester, Mass. (daughter of James Allen) with Bessie Howard, Boston, 1946; Maxim Karolik, Newport, R.I., 1946.

EXHIBITIONS: "Children and Flowers," Winnipeg Art Gallery, Manitoba, 1958; "Art in Maine," Colby College Art Museum, Waterville, Me., 1963, no. 101; "M. and M. Karolik Memorial Exhibition," Museum of Fine Arts, Boston, 1964; "American Primitive Painting," Copley Society, Boston, 1969; "Nineteenth-Century American Paintings from the Storerooms," Museum of Fine Arts, Boston, 1979.

BIBLIOGRAPHY: Jean Lipman and Alice Winchester, *Primitive Painters in America, 1750–1950* (New York, 1950), p. 87; *American Paintings in the Museum of Fine Arts, Boston* (Boston, 1969), no. 820.

By 1841, after a decade of traveling in Massachusetts and Maine, William Matthew Prior had settled in Boston. With his wife Rosamund and her brothers Joseph, Nathaniel, and Sturtevant Hamblen, he established "the Painting Garret," a studio at 36 Trenton Street, East Boston, and painted portraits of local citizens.[1] Prior's brother-in-law worked in a style very similar to his, and even may have contributed to portraits bearing Prior's signature. Usually, however, Prior signed and dated his paintings on the back of the canvas, as is the case here; the others inscribed their works "Painted in Prior's Garret."

Prior painted this picture of the two-year-old William Allen in 1843. The Allens were a prominent Cambridge family whose wealth came from the manufacture of iron; their home stood on Massachusetts Avenue in Cambridge, on the site of the present City Hall. The greyhounds shown with young Master Allen were family pets and were depicted on the family crest.[2] The landscape background, though inspired by the family's spacious grounds, was probably imaginary.

Although Prior was self-taught as a painter, his device of depicting a child in a grove of trees in the heart of a lush woods recalls a popular convention of eighteenth-century British portraiture. Engravings after Reynolds's and Gainsborough's paintings were widely circulated in America by the early nineteenth century, and Prior was undoubtedly familiar with them. One picture by Reynolds has particular relevance for Prior's portrait of Allen: *Master Henry Hoare —The Young Gardener* (1788; Toledo Museum of Art),

which was reproduced in an engraving in 1789 and also in mezzotint about that time,[3] contains elements so similar to those in Prior's painting—a straw hat, prominently placed in the lower right corner, a dog with a thick, elaborate collar, brightly colored flowers, and of course the woodland setting—that it may have been the inspiration for it. The landscape background in *William Allen* and the aristocratic greyhounds were meant to allude to the wealth and social position of the family; as in similar English portraits of children, this setting also implied an association between the innocence of childhood and the purity of nature.

Prior's portrait of William Allen is an exceptional work in the history of nineteenth-century American folk art. Most so-called primitive artists pictured their sitters against plain backgrounds or in interiors. Landscape settings were quite rare, and the soft, atmospheric tones with which the trees and sky are painted also differ from the flat, bright colors typical of folk painting. Prior used similar romantic landscapes as backgrounds for a few other portraits, such as *Miss Jones* (1846; coll. Peter Tillou, Litchfield, Conn.), and the same style, though with a more specific treatment of the foliage, is found in the few landscapes known by Prior.[4] The figure of William Allen bears features characteristic of Prior's portraits: the sloping shoulders and stubby, elephantine legs, the high forehead, broadly set eyes, and small, round chin. However, this picture is unusually lyrical, for it was painted with sweeping curvilinear strokes that model the figure and the bodies of the dogs as well as creating an elegant decorative pattern on the surface of the picture.

Prior produced many different kinds of portraits, from the standard flat and wooden folk image to this sophisticated composition. These variations reflect not a development in the artist's style but apparently indicate instead the price the sitter paid for the portrait, as shown by an advertisement Prior placed in the *Maine Inquirer* in 1831: "Persons wishing for a flat picture can have a likeness without shadow or shade for one-quarter the price."[5]

1. Nina Fletcher Little, "William Matthew Prior," *Primitive Painters in America,* Jean Lipman and Alice Winchester, eds. (New York, 1950), p. 86.
2. Letter from Greta Allen to Maxim Karolik, December 6, 1945, Paintings Department files, Museum of Fine Arts, Boston.
3. *Toledo Museum of Art: European Paintings* (Toledo, 1973), p. 138.
4. E.g. *View off Mattapoissett,* Mass., coll. Nina Fletcher Little. Reproduced in Nina Fletcher Little, "William Matthew Prior, Traveling Artist," *Antiques* 53 (January 1948), p. 47.
5. Advertisement in the *Maine Inquirer* (April 5, 1831), as quoted in ibid, p. 45.

GEORGE LORING BROWN (1814-1889)
active in Boston 1832, 1834–1839, 1863–1889

31. *Castello dell'Ovo, Bay of Naples*

Inscribed on back: *View of the Castello dell'Ovo, Bay of Naples. G. L. Brown. 1844. Naples Ital. Painted for Geo. Tiffany Esq. Baltimore*

Oil on canvas, 31 x 39 in. (78.8 x 99.0 cm.)

M. and M. Karolik Collection. 47.1196.

PROVENANCE: Geo. Tiffany, Baltimore; with Victor Spark, New York; Maxim Karolik, Newport, R.I., by 1944.

EXHIBITIONS: "George Loring Brown: Landscapes of Europe and America 1834–1880," Robert Hull Fleming Museum, Burlington, Vt., 1973, no. 2.

BIBLIOGRAPHY: *M. and M. Karolik Collection of American Paintings 1815 to 1865* (Cambridge, Mass., 1943), no. 73; *American Paintings in the Museum of Fine Arts, Boston* (Boston, 1969), no. 169.

Hailed by a nineteenth-century critic as "the American Claude, the Yankee Turner, and the Bostonian Rubens,"[1] George Loring Brown belonged to the same artistic generation as the Boston sculptors Thomas Crawford and Horatio Greenough, and, like them, he spent his formative years in Rome. Boston-born and trained there as an illustrator, he was befriended early in his career by the prominent collectors Isaac P. Davis and John P. Cushing, who sponsored his first trip to Europe in the early 1830s.[2] There he studied with the French landscapist Eugène Isabey; another important aspect of his training was making copies of paintings in the Louvre (particularly those by Ruysdael, Constable, and Claude), which were eagerly bought up in Boston. Brown's second sojourn in Europe (1840–1859) was financed by commissions for more copies, especially of works by Claude; his original compositions were also eagerly sought by the many American tourists traveling through Italy in the 1840s and '50s. Even after he returned to America in 1859 Brown continued to paint Italian scenes, but his popularity waned as Boston was caught up in enthusiasm for a younger, francophilic generation of American painters dominated by William Morris Hunt.

From the mid-eighteenth century, Naples had rivaled Rome as an artistic attraction; Brown first went there in the summer of 1844. He chose for the subject of this painting, not the recently active volcano Mt. Vesuvius, which so many artists of recent generations had made the subject of cataclysmic scenes,[3] but rather the more quietly picturesque Castello dell'Ovo, a sixteenth-century fortress built on a small rocky island in the Bay of Naples. The fortress derived its name from the oval shape of the rock on which it was built, and from an ancient legend that discusses its creation by the sorcerer Virgil, who anchored it to an egg in the sea. Brown did not allude to this myth in his picture, but rather showed the island as the site of bustling marine and possibly military activity, and populated by a multitude of tiny figures dressed in colorful seventeenth-century costume.

These figures were derived from the *banditti* in paintings by Claude—the artist Brown most admired—but the composition is related only indirectly to Claude's harbor scenes. The prominent, massive central motif flanked by a boat in the left foreground and the volcano in the right far distance is a heavy-handed rendition of Claude's subtle compositional balances, and the sharply receding road is distinctly un-Claudian (although that device was used by several early nineteenth-century landscapists, including J. M. W. Turner). Brown's particularized brushwork and crusty impasto is also unlike Claude's softly painted surfaces; rather, his technique reflects that of his tutor, Isabey, who worked with a cooler, less acid palette than Brown but who used similar short, precise brushstrokes to build up a textured surface. The naïveté of design in Brown's painting is compensated by his bright, daring palette and his energetic rendition of forms; the picture's anecdotal content—the swelling waves, the rocking boats and the ant-like activity in the foreground—cleverly balances the solid, monumental structure dominating the composition.

1. *The New York Times* (June 7, 1885), p. 7 as quoted in Thomas W. Leavitt, *George Loring Brown: Landscapes of Europe and America 1834–1880* (Robert Hull Fleming Museum, Burlington, Vt., 1973), p. 11.
2. William David Barry, "George Loring Brown: Patrons and Patronage," ibid., p. 51.
3. For a discussion of late eighteenth- and early nineteenth-century images of this site, see Alexandra R. Murphy, *Visions of Vesuvius* (Museum of Fine Arts, Boston, 1978).

CHESTER HARDING (1792-1866)
active in Boston 1822–1823; 1826–1866

32. *Mrs. Abbott Lawrence,* ca. 1855

Oil on canvas, 27½ x 22¼ in. (69.2 x 56.5 cm.)

Gift of the Misses Aimée and Rosamond Lamb. 61.240

PROVENANCE: Mrs. Abbott Lawrence, Boston, 1855–1860; Mrs. Augustus Lowell, Boston; A. [bbott] Lawrence Lowell, Boston; Mrs. Horatio A. Lamb, Milton, Mass.; Aimée and Rosamond Lamb,' 1959.

EXHIBITIONS: "19th-Century America," Metropolitan Museum of Art, New York, 1970, no. 38; "The Gothic Revival Style in America," Museum of Fine Arts, Houston, 1976, no. 172.

BIBLIOGRAPHY: *American Paintings in the Museum of Fine Arts, Boston* (Boston, 1969). no. 479.

Harding's portrait of Katherine Bigelow Lawrence is a curious mixture of the elegant and the prosaic. Borrowing a compositional mode from Sir Thomas Lawrence, whose works were very much in vogue when Harding visited England some thirty years before, he showed Mrs. Lawrence seated in her best chair, an elaborate example of the newly fashionable Gothic Revival style. As in many of Lawrence's portraits, the chair is placed before a heavy curtain that opens onto an airy landscape.[1] However, Harding made no attempt to appropriate Lawrence's fluid brushwork and his dramatic use of light and shadow. His tight, rather dry style is better suited to the other elements of the portrait: Mrs. Lawrence's homely features and stringy hair, her plain, black gown, her knitting basket (perhaps the most felicitously painted portion of the painting), and the long red scarf on which she is working.

Harding probably painted Mrs. Lawrence shortly after 1855, the year of her husband's death. Mrs. Lawrence is depicted as a widow, dressed in black with a thin veil over her head, and with a cross at her neck. On her arm is a mourning bracelet containing a portrait of a man, presumably her husband; the ring on her right hand may be a mourning ring. Her late husband, Abbott Lawrence, had been a prominent businessman in Boston, the senior partner in a family firm that sold textiles imported from England and later those made in New England mills. Lawrence's

longstanding connection with England, culminating with his ambassadorship between 1849–1852, and his family's frequent visits there, explains Mrs. Lawrence's willingness to be painted in a format that she undoubtedly remembered from those journeys.

Harding's knowledge of British portraiture stemmed from his two visits to England, made between 1823 and 1826, when he was in his early thirties, and again in 1846 and 1847. However, even his initial exposure to Lawrence, Romney, and others did not shake his extreme confidence in his own plain manner, for he made his first trip to England after a meteoric rise to prominence in Boston.

Born in New Hampshire to an impoverished family, Harding moved to Boston in 1822, and was encouraged and sent his first commissions by Gilbert Stuart. From that point, "Harding fever" swept Boston, and the vogue for portraits by Harding grew with every trip he made abroad. Perhaps because he was reluctant to alter a successful formula, he at first incorporated little of what he saw in England into his portrait style: through the 1820s and '30s he continued to use the half-length format popularized by Stuart and, like him, to show his sitters against a plain or draped background. About the time of his second trip to England, aspects of British portraiture began to appear in Harding's work (although the influence was not great enough to cause him to loosen his rather simple, linear brushwork); the portrait of Abbott Lawrence (Museum of Fine Arts, Boston), painted about five years before that of his wife, and of Abbott's brother Amos (ca. 1845; National Gallery of Art, Washington), all reflect this influence.[2]

1. See, for example, Lawrence's portrait of Queen Charlotte (1790; Her Majesty the Queen, Windsor Castle).

2. Abbott Lawrence is shown standing beside a table, his right leg slightly forward, his right hand holding a book on the table, his head turned to the right. This pose was popularized by Sir Thomas Lawrence, who used it for many male portraits, such as *George IV* (1821; Her Majesty the Queen, St. James's Palace). Harding used this format earlier for his life-size portrait of Chief Justice John Marshall (ca. 1830; Boston Athenaeum).

WILLIAM SHARP (1803-1875)
active in Boston 1840–1875

33. *Fruit and Flower Piece,* 1848

Oil on canvas, 36 x 29 in. (91.4 x 73.6 cm.)

Bequest of Maxim Karolik. 64.449

PROVENANCE: Mrs. Lottie J. Whitney, Jamaica Plain, Mass.; Mrs. Robert W. Swift, Jr., Milton, Mass. (her granddaughter), by 1948; with Gustav Klimann, Boston, 1959; Maxim Karolik, Newport, R.I.

EXHIBITIONS: "American Paintings, 1815–1865," Parrish Art Museum, Southampton, L.I., 1961, no. 34; "Centennial Celebration," Brockton Public Library, Brockton, Mass., 1967; "William Sharp," Massachusetts Historical Society, Boston, 1973; "Exhibition of the Works of William, William C., and James C. Sharp," Boston Athenaeum, 1978.

BIBLIOGRAPHY: *American Paintings in the Museum of Fine Arts, Boston* (Boston, 1969), no. 875.

William Sharp was primarily a lithographer; the few paintings known by him today all reflect the aesthetic of his printmaking trade. He was born in England and worked there as a lithographer in the 1830s, making prints after portraits by John Hayter and other artists popular at that time. After emigrating to America in 1838 or 1839, he settled in Boston, where by 1840 he was active in the lithographic firm of Sharp and Michelin. This association was one of several partnerships Sharp formed in the early 1840s; in 1845, he started his own lithographic firm, which specialized in the designing and printing of illustrations for sheet music.

Sharp soon became involved in projects that better suited his talents and training. His finest and best-known works were botanical prints, which appeared as illustrations in C. H. Hovey's *Fruits of America* (Boston, 1852–1856) and John Fisk Allen's *Victoria Regia, or the Great Water Lily of America* (Boston, 1854). These prints, made at the same time that Sharp was painting *Fruit and Flower Piece,* marked the culmination of twenty years' experimentation with the technique of color lithography.[1] They indicate Sharp's range and versatility as an artist, for the fruits are simply drawn botanical specimens in the tradition of sixteenth-century herbals, while the lilies are startling, sensuous close-up views of the flowers floating in water, anticipating Pre-Raphaelite compositions.

The aesthetic governing Sharp's botanical prints was carried over into *Fruit and Flower Piece.* The flowers and fruits are drawn with a sharpness, elegance, and rhythm that is more characteristic of a linear than a painterly mode; the bright, flat colors used here are also typical of his prints. Sharp constructed his composition in an additive manner: the major specimens do not overlap, and there is little modeling. Evidently, he was more concerned with the illustration of each individual blossom than with the plastic character of the bouquet as a whole.

The antecedents of Sharp's composition are the fruit and flower paintings of Dutch and Flemish artists of the seventeenth century. In particular, *Fruit and Flower Piece* derives from the works of Rachael Ruysch, Jan van Huysum, and other artists working at the end of the century who abandoned the strict symmetry of earlier compositions for the kind of informally balanced arrangement Sharp used here, and who, rather than placing their bouquet in a niche or against a plain background, combined precisely delineated flowers with a more broadly rendered landscape, creating a painterly tour-de-force. Sharp used this device for his composition, cleverly paralleling the rather generalized landscape in the far distance with a more tightly painted illusionistic view of a river and mountains in the cartouche of the vase.

Sharp's interest in Dutch still-life painting was probably kindled in England, where as a reproductive printmaker he would have had ample opportunity to consider a variety of models for his work, and where several minor artists were working in this manner early in the century.[2] There were some parallels in America—although not in Boston—for this kind of still-life painting: Severin Roesen, a German-born painter who worked in Pennsylvania and New York in the 1850s, also painted fruit and flower pieces modeled after Dutch still lifes, although for him the intermediary was nineteenth-century German, rather than English, painting.[3] Sharp's compositions are on the whole more linear than Roesen's and have a brighter, less naturalistic palette, creating an impression of decorative artificiality rather than of abundance and prosperity. Despite the popularity of his prints, Sharp's patternistic approach to still-life painting found few adherents in Boston, and with the exception of a few compositions in the same style painted by his son James C. Sharp, by the 1860s still-life painting in Boston was dominated by the intimate, lyrical style of John LaFarge.

1. Bettina A. Norton, "William Sharp: Accomplished Lithographer," *Art and Commerce: American Prints of the Nineteenth Century* (Boston, 1978), pp. 50-75, especially pp. 57-58.
2. Among British artists working in the tradition of the seventeenth-century Dutch still-life painting were William Etty, Peter De Wint, George Lance, Edward Coleman, and William Duffield. See Dennis Farr, *William Etty* (London, 1958), p. 87.
3. Roesen's major source was probably the work of Johann Wilhelm Preyer, who was active in Düsseldorf in the 1830s and '40s. See *Die Düsseldorfer Malerschule* (Düsseldorf, 1979), pp. 422-425, and William H. Gerdts and Russell Burke, *American Still-Life Painting* (New York, 1971), p. 61.

III

FITZ HUGH LANE (1804-1865)
active in Boston 1832–1848, and in Gloucester, Mass., 1848–1865

34. *Ships in Ice Off Ten-Pound Island, Gloucester,* 1850s

Oil on canvas, 12 x 19⅝ in. (30.6 x 50.0 cm.)

M. and M. Karolik Collection. 48.447

PROVENANCE: Mrs. John LeFavour Stanley, Gloucester, Mass.; Mrs. Louise S. Campbell, Montclair, N.J.; with Charles D. Childs, Boston, 1943; Maxim Karolik, Newport, R.I., 1944.

EXHIBITIONS: "Exhibition of Marine Painting," Colby College Art Museum, Waterville, Me., 1944, no. 1; "Commemorative Exhibition: Paintings by M. J. Heade and F. H. Lane. . . .," M. Knoedler and Co., New York, 1954, no. 7; "American Painting from 1830," Everson Museum of Art, Syracuse, 1965; "Fitz Hugh Lane," DeCordova Museum, Lincoln, Mass., 1966, no. 22; "The Painter and the New World," Museum of Fine Arts, Montreal, 1967, no. 238; "The Artist and the Sea," Miami Art Center, 1969, no. 22; "Fitz Hugh Lane," William A. Farnsworth Library and Art Museum, Rockland, Me., 1974; "Near Looking," Northern Illinois University, DeKalb, 1974; "Seascape and the American Imagination," Whitney Museum of American Art, New York, 1975, no. 69; "Marine Painting," Museum of Fine Arts, St. Petersburg, Fla., 1976; "Nineteenth-Century American Paintings from the Storerooms," Museum of Fine Arts, Boston, 1979.

BIBLIOGRAPHY: *M. and M. Karolik Collection of American Paintings, 1815–1865* (Cambridge, Mass., 1949), no. 183; John Wilmerding, *Fitz Hugh Lane, 1804–1865, American Marine Painter* (Salem, Mass., 1964), p. 40, fig. 15; "A Selection of Marine Paintings by Fitz Hugh Lane," *The American Neptune Pictorial Supplement VII* (Salem, Mass., 1965), no. 36; *American Paintings in the Museum of Fine Arts, Boston* (Boston, 1969), no. 709; John Wilmerding, *Fitz Hugh Lane* (New York, 1971), p. 63; ———, "Fitz Hugh Lane: Imitations and Attributions," *American Art Journal* 3 (Fall 1971), pp. 35-36.

Ships in Ice Off Ten-Pound Island, Gloucester is Lane's only known winter scene. Like most of his mature paintings it combines topographical precision—Ten-Pound Island, so named because it was purchased from a local Indian tribe for that sum, is visible on the horizon at left—and a magical sense of luminosity and infinite space. Lane evoked the bar-

ren atmosphere of a New England winter by using a cool palette and subtle modulations of tone; despite the small size of his canvas, he achieved the effect of monumentality and spaciousness by means of a low horizon and disparity in scale between the ships and the tiny figures that surround them.

Lane's picture may have been suggested by an actual incident, for the icing over of Gloucester Harbor was an unusual occurrence, and one that he, a constant observer of the Gloucester shoreline, is likely to have found noteworthy. Both his subject and winter scenes generally were relatively rare, having few precedents in the tradition of topographical marine painting from which his style developed. Occasionally, books of travel and exploration would depict such a scene, and Lane may have known an image such as *The Ships of Lord Mulgrave's Expeditions Embedded in Ice in the Polar Regions* by the British marine painter John Clevely, which was published in 1774 in Captain Phipps's (later Lord Mulgrave) *Voyage toward the North Pole,* and which represents a similar subject: seamen trying to free an icebound ship. John S. Blunt, a little-known Boston artist working some twenty years before Lane, also explored the theme of ships locked in ice in *Boston Harbor* (1835; Museum of Fine Arts, Boston). Like these two works, Lane's picture is characterized by a simplicity of composition, a fidelity to natural detail, and a precision of drawing that suggests an underlying documentary intention. But at the same time, Lane's manipulation of scale and the effect of light and atmosphere in the painting distinguishes it from its topographical prototypes, and create a parable of man's relationship with his environment worthy of Turner's great romantic seascapes: the men Lane shows working to free their ice-bound ship are tiny; they seem ineffectual next to the mammoth ship and broad expanse of frozen sea and blue-gray sky. The overwhelming impression is of action stopped, locked in, by the powerful forces of nature.

35. *Fresh Water Cove from Dolliver's Neck, Gloucester,* early 1850s

Oil on canvas, 24⅛ x 36 in. (61.3 x 91.5 cm.)

M. and M. Karolik Collection. 48.445

PROVENANCE: Leo Landry, Lynn, Mass.; with Harvey F. Additon, Boston, 1946; Maxim Karolik, Newport, R.I., 1946.

RELATED WORKS: *Fresh Water Cove,* pencil drawing, Cape Ann Historical Association, Gloucester.

EXHIBITIONS: "Commemorative Exhibition: Paintings by M. J. Heade and F. H. Lane...," M. Knoedler and Co., New York, 1954, no. 3; "American Realists," Art Gallery of Hamilton, Ontario, 1961, no 41; "Maxim Karolik Memorial Exhibition," Museum of Fine Arts, Boston, 1964; "Fitz Hugh Lane," DeCordova Museum, Lincoln, Mass., 1966, no. 8.

BIBLIOGRAPHY: *M. and M. Karolik Collection of American Paintings, 1815–1865* (Cambridge, Mass., 1949), no. 181; John Wilmerding, *Fitz Hugh Lane 1804–1865, American Marine Painter* (Salem, Mass., 1964), p. 55, no. 17; *American Paintings in the Museum of Fine Arts, Boston* (Boston, 1969), no. 707; John Wilmerding, *Fitz Hugh Lane* (New York, 1971), p. 66.

So named because Champlain landed there in 1607 in search of drinkable water, Fresh Water Cove was first painted by Lane in the early 1850s, a few years after he gave up his position at J. W. A. Scott's lithography shop in Boston, and moved permanently to Gloucester. With its several harbors, coves, and inlets, Gloucester provided Lane with subject matter for his paintings and lithographs for the rest of his life. Especially during the 1850s, his work in the two media was closely related: in the lithograph *View of Gloucester* (1855; Cape Ann Historical Association, Gloucester), Lane employed a very similar composition. Two strips of land, the foreground empty and the distant shore populated, on either side of a body of water create a panoramic view in which over half of the composition is given over to sky. In another picture of the same period, *Looking Up Squam River from "Done Fudging"* (mid 1850s; Cape Ann Historical Association, Gloucester), Lane again employed a horizontal format to suggest the expanse of the site; as in *Fresh Water Cove,* he also used a gentle diagonal, a line of rocks instead of a fence, as counterpoint to the dominant

horizontals, and to lead the eye into the picture space. At the same time that he was working on these modest views, Lane was also developing a more ambitious theme, his series of harbor views, beginning with *New York Harbor* in 1850, then in 1852 *Salem Harbor* (roughly contemporary with *Fresh Water Cove*), and finally *Boston Harbor* (cat. no. 36) at the end of the decade (all in the Museum of Fine Arts, Boston). The harbor views are monumental works, dramatically conceived and brilliantly painted, and were for Lane a complement to the quieter, more picturesque views painted in Gloucester.

Fresh Water Cove is closely dependent on a pencil drawing Lane made of the site (Cape Ann Historical Association). It is a quick sketch, intended to record the topographical features of the site, with neither the crystalline precision nor the delicate rendering of foreground detail of the painting. Showing the continuation of the water beyond the edge of the island, the drawing is, in fact, more panoramic and frieze-like than the painting, exhibiting the sense of frozen motion prevalent in the latter but without emphasis on any particular motif or topographical feature. In the painting, Lane diminished the size of the houses on the far shore and added the sailboats—three under sail and one with its sails being furled—for narrative interest and compositional focus.

In 1857, Lane painted Dolliver's Neck again (*Dolliver's Neck and the Western Shore from Field Beach;* Cape Ann Historical Association), but from a different viewpoint and in a different mood. There the beached boat and the bleak rocky shore create the impression of anxiety and loneliness, a theme Lane would develop more fully in his mystical Brace's Rock series, painted in the Civil War years. In *Fresh Water Cove,* however, Dolliver's Neck is depicted as a setting for prosperity and general well-being. The colorful late-summer foliage in the foreground, delineated with Pre-Raphaelite precision, the snug houses comfortably nestled in the trees on the opposite shore, the clean white boats sailing peacefully toward shore, and the billowing clouds as delicate as Ruysdael's, define an optimistic and secure vision, an image of uninterrupted harmony between man and nature.

36. *Boston Harbor*, ca. 1858

Oil on canvas, 26⅛ x 42 in. (66.4 x 106.6 cm.)

M. and M. Karolik Collection, by exchange. 66.339

PROVENANCE: (?) Mrs. Charles M. Pierce, New Bedford, Mass.; Mrs. Willis E. Lounge, New Bedford (her daughter); Mrs. Grace H. Sargent, New Bedford (her daughter); Mrs. Thomas W. Farnsworth, Jr., New Bedford, about 1960 (her daughter).

EXHIBITIONS: "Thirty-second Exhibition of Paintings," Boston Athenaeum, 1858, no. 232; "200 Anni di Pittura Americana (1776–1976)," Galleria Nazionale d'Arte Moderna, Rome, 1976, no. 19; "American Light: The Luminist Movement," National Gallery of Art, Washington, 1980, no. 238.

BIBLIOGRAPHY: John Wilmerding, *A History of American Marine Painting* (Salem, Mass., 1968), pp. 132-133, 162, plate 13; *American Paintings in the Museum of Fine Arts, Boston* (Boston, 1969), no. 712; John Wilmerding, *Robert Salmon, Painter of Ship and Shore* (Salem, Mass., 1971), p. 82; —————, *Fitz Hugh Lane* (New York, 1971), pp. 75-76.

The present painting, the last of Lane's many views of Boston Harbor, is one of the most ambitious compositions he ever painted. It is probably the *Boston Harbor* he exhibited at the Boston Athenaeum in 1858, at the end of his association with that institution. *Boston Harbor* was the culmination of Lane's pictorial aspirations; in it he combined a faithful observation of nature with a grander pictorial scheme.

The origins of Lane's subject are found in the late-eighteenth-century tradition of British marine painting, especially in the works of Robert Salmon, who brought that tradition to Boston and who was Lane's neighbor at Pendleton's lithographic shop in Boston in 1834. Salmon's crisp, precise brushwork, his gray-green palette, and several of his compositional designs influenced Lane's early paintings, and even as late as 1858, Lane continued to be affected by Salmon's style. *Boston Harbor* closely resembles Salmon's *Boston Harbor from Constitution Wharf* (ca. 1842; United States Naval Academy Museum, Annapolis)[1] in the near symmetry of the composition; the emphasis on two large ships, one viewed from the stern, the other turned at an angle to the picture plane; the accuracy with which the boat's rigging is rendered; and the topographical detail along the horizon. But the calm, poetic mood of *Boston Harbor* and Lane's interest in light and atmosphere distinguish it from Salmon's work and from the topographical marine tradition; these qualities are in accord with the romantic sensibilities of the day.

To achieve his poetic vision, Lane altered his palette from the grays, greens, and blues of his early work to the pale yet brilliant colors of the sunset sky. He minimized the signs of human activity that abound in Salmon's paintings for the sake of greater concentration on the two monumental ships, silhouetted against the richly colored sky. The small boat being rowed to shore, a motif that was standard in eighteenth- and nineteenth-century marine compositions and that was used there to generate a sense of scale and human context for the scene, becomes a central element in Lane's picture; it is further emphasized by the ribbon of reflected sunlight next to the boat. Here the figures take on the role of the poetic observer in a romantic vista; they help to establish the overlarge scale of the boats and exaggerated expanse of the water. Lane painted this view of Boston Harbor from a hill in East Boston (a vantage point popular with artists who made views of the city and the bay) and rendered topographical details accurately—for example, the State House and the Old South Church are visible on the shoreline—but by lowering the horizon and distorting the scale, Lane made the harbor seem as wide as the ocean.

The awesome quietness of *Boston Harbor* reflects the romantic view of nature introduced to Boston by Washington Allston and Thomas Cole, whose grand panoramic visions Lane coupled with the less melancholy, Ruskin-inspired naturalism that dominated mid-century American painting. His pantheistic image is not without an element of nostalgia and foreboding similar to that which governed Coles' gloomier world view—the steamboat at right, tiny but vividly white and representing the new, mechanized direction of shipping, invades the world of the more beautiful and beloved sailing ships—but the prevailing mood of the picture is of harmony and calm. By balancing a faithful rendition of the observed scene with a romantic interpretation of that natural truth, Lane created in *Boston Harbor* an Edenic vision of man in nature.

1. John Wilmerding, *A History of American Marine Painting* (Salem, Mass., 1968), pp. 132-133.

BENJAMIN CHAMPNEY (1817-1907)
active in Boston and New Hampshire ca. 1834–1907

37. *Mount Chocorua, New Hampshire*

Signed and dated lower left: *B. Champney 1858*

Oil on canvas, 12 x 17⅞ in. (30.4 x 45.4 cm.)

Bequest of Maxim Karolik. 64.423

PROVENANCE: Mr. Stearns, by 1859; with Childs Gallery, Boston; Maxim Karolik, Newport, R.I., 1944.

RELATED WORKS: *Mount Chocorua*, chromolithograph drawn by Charles Armstrong, printed by Louis Prang & Company, Boston, 1870.

EXHIBITIONS: "Thirty-fourth Exhibition of Paintings," Boston Athenaeum, 1859, no. 85.

BIBLIOGRAPHY: *American Paintings in the Museum of Fine Arts, Boston* (Boston, 1969), no. 202.

Beginning in 1849, it was Champney's custom to spend summers sketching in the White Mountains of New Hampshire, and in the following winters "to paint pictures from my summer studies,"[1] first in his studio in Tremont Temple in Boston where Fitz Hugh Lane, Joseph Ames, and John Pope were also working, and later in his North Conway home. Born in New Hampshire, Champney received his first artistic training in Boston with the lithographer Thomas F. Moore, who also employed Lane, William Rimmer, and William Sharp. He also began sketching on his own, and as did many young artists in Boston in the 1830s, Champney sought encouragement for his developing talent from Washington Allston, then the most admired artist in the city. Allston praised his work, and advised him to go to Europe to study. In 1841 Champney made the first of several trips abroad, spending most of his time in Paris and Italy, but also visiting the flourishing artistic community in Düsseldorf. Thus by the 1850s Champney had the benefit of long exposure to European painting and to current artistic trends in Europe, had received advice from America's foremost "old master," and had the opportunity to exchange ideas with many young American artists (among them John F. Kensett, John W. Casilear, Asher B. Durand, William Morris Hunt, William Babcock, and W. A. Gay) whom he met during his European travels.

Mount Chocorua is an imposing single peak in north-central New Hampshire, just south of the more famous Presidential Range. At mid-century, the White Mountains attracted many artists, especially from New York, who made sketching tours of Chocorua, Kearsarge, the Presidential Range and the bucolic North Conway Valley. Champney here showed Mount Chocorua from the north from a vantage point on the Swift River, paying careful attention to topographical detail: in his composition he emphasized the mountain's majestic profile, but also carefully rendered the ridges and valleys on its face.

Although he spent almost all of his artistic life in and around Boston, Champney's mature style does not reflect the modes of landscape painting associated with the city: neither the romanticism of Allston's late landscapes and the warm-toned, hazy panoramas of Fisher and Doughty nor the loosely painted, brown-toned Barbizon style that would dominate Boston painting from the 1860s to the end of the century is visible here. Rather, he used the tight, smoothly painted technique and the neat monochrome palette characteristic of the Hudson River School at mid-century. *Mount Chocorua* is painted with tiny, almost invisible brushstrokes and a muted palette. Gray tones predominate, and the yellow flowers in the lower left foreground and the greenish-ocher of the middle distance provide the main coloristic accents. Unlike the best of the Hudson River School paintings from this period, there is little sense of directed light or palpable atmosphere in *Mount Chocorua*, and the rendering of the reflection of the trees in the water is hesitant. On the other hand, the terrain of the mountainside, the slight bending of the trees to suggest a gentle breeze, and the ripples breaking over the rocks in the water are well painted, and give the impression of nature freshly observed. Champney's style was undoubtedly affected by the New York artists, particularly his close friend Kensett, with whom he painted every summer; it represents a brief moment of the Hudson River School style in Boston before that city was swept by Barbizon.

1. Benjamin Champney, *Sixty Years' Memories of Art and Artists* (Boston, 1899), p. 99.

38. *Meditation by the Sea,* ca. 1860-1865

Oil on canvas, 13½ x 19⅝ in. (34.6 x 49.8 cm.)

M. and M. Karolik Collection. 45.892

PROVENANCE: With J. B. Neumann, New York, 1943; Maxim Karolik, Newport, R.I., 1943.

EXHIBITIONS: "Romantic Painting in America," Museum of Modern Art, New York, 1943, no. 213; "American Painting," Tate Gallery, London, 1946, no. 4; "American Paintings, 1815-1865," Museum of Fine Arts, Boston, 1957, no. 13; "42 Karolik Paintings," Wadsworth Atheneum, Hartford, 1963; M. and M. Karolik Memorial Exhibition," Museum of Fine Arts, Boston, 1964; "American Landscape: A Changing Frontier," National Collection of Fine Arts, Washington, 1966; "The Painter and the New World," Montreal Museum of Fine Arts, 1967, no. 217; "Collector's Choice," Museum of Early American Folk Art, New York, 1969; "The Flowering of American Folk Art, 1776-1876," Whitney Museum of American Art, New York, 1974, no. 96; "Seascape and the American Imagination," Whitney Museum of American Art, New York, 1975, no. 104; "Selections from the M. and M. Karolik Collection of American Paintings, 1815-1865," Museum of Fine Arts, Boston, 1975, no. 37; "American Marine Painting," Virginia Museum of Fine Arts, Richmond, 1976, no. 23; "The Second Greatest Show on Earth. The Making of a Museum," Museum of Fine Arts, Boston, 1977, no. 26; "American Light: The Luminist Movement," National Gallery of Art, Washington, 1980, no. 150.

BIBLIOGRAPHY: *M. and M. Karolik Collection of American Paintings, 1815-1865* (Cambridge, Mass., 1949), no. 25; *American Paintings in the Museum of Fine Arts, Boston* (Boston, 1969), no. 27; John Wilmerding, *American Art* (New York, 1976), p. 103.

A source for this well-known folk image has recently come to light, providing new evidence for the dating of the picture and suggesting the identity of the site represented. In the September 1860 issue of *Harper's New Monthly Magazine* an article appeared by D. H. Strother entitled "A Summer in New England," with illustrations by Porte Crayon.[1] Porte Crayon was Strother himself, a Virginia-born artist and illustrator who was a frequent contributor to *Harper's*.[2] In the article, he recounted his travels through Cape Cod and the islands to the south; he focused particularly on the community of Gay Head on Martha's Vineyard, describing its beach as follows: "It is an earthy cliff, about 130 feet in height, its base washed by the Atlantic waves, its top covered with green-sward to the very brink." His account of an early morning visit to the "long stretch of sand and pebble beach," was accompanied by an illustration titled "The Ocean Surf." This wood engraving was the model and the text a source of information for the artist who painted *Meditation by the Sea.*

The painter deviated from his model in several ways, and so transformed a topographical sketch into an eerie imaginary scene. He elongated the composition, rendering more dramatic the high horizon line and vast stretch of beach. He added the high, steep cliff described by Strother as characteristic of Gay Head, and brought the figure closer to the foreground, exaggerating—in fact, making almost surreal—the difference in scale between the figure and the natural elements. The artist also seems to have restructured Strother's picture so that the base and top of the cliff, and the shoreline recede dramatically to a point on the horizon at left. This application of single-point perspective indicates that the artist had some formal training, but perhaps not enough to master the expressive effect of the device. While creating a sense of vast distance, the perspective pulls the viewer's eye past the figure and into the background, where the artist, misinterpreting the profile of the buildings on the horizon in Strother's picture, has placed a group of mammoth, cone-shaped rocks.

The man in *Meditation by the Sea* wears what appears to be a Civil War uniform, which suggests that the painting was done in the 1860s, or shortly after the wood engraving appeared. The figure's pensive attitude, and the somewhat surreal, pessimistic tone of the composition may reflect something of the nation's mood during the Civil War, a mood not present in the wood engraving or in the article it accompanies.

There is still no clue to the identity of the artist who painted this picture. It was clearly not Strother, who was a more conventional draftsman and less well attuned to current artistic trends. For despite his naïveté, the painter of *Meditation by the Sea* had seen and absorbed the lessons of contemporary academic painting in America. He was particularly aware of Luminist painting, whose characteristic attributes—an oblong format, long, uninterrupted horizon line, a tendency to a monochrome palette, and a special concern for light and atmosphere—he imitated here. In addition, he has been compared to Fitz Hugh Lane in his attitude toward nature and in his technical approach,[3] and many other artists active in the 1860s and '70s, including John F. Kensett, T. Worthington Whittredge, and Martin J. Heade, painted a similar subject. The compositions of these and other painters explain the changes this anonymous artist made from his model; they were his standard and his inspiration in designing this picture.

1. David H. Strother, "A Summer in New England," *Harper's New Monthly Magazine* (September 21, 1860), pp. 442-461. I am grateful to Dr. Walter Mann of Boston, who discovered the illustration on which *Meditation by the Sea* was based and generously shared his findings with the Paintings Department.

2. G. C. Groce and D. H. Wallace, *The New-York Historical Society's Dictionary of Artists in America, 1564-1860* (New Haven, 1957), p. 611.

3. John Wilmerding, *American Art* (New York, 1976), p. 103.

MARTIN JOHNSON HEADE (1819-1904)

active in Boston 1861; in Newburyport, Mass., 1860s

39. *Approaching Storm: Beach Near Newport,* ca. 1860

Oil on canvas, 28 x 58¼ in. (71.2 x 148.0 cm.)

M. and M. Karolik Collection. 45.889

PROVENANCE: Henry Goddard Pickering, Boston, by 1925; Mrs. Richard Y. Fitzgerald, Boston (his niece), after 1926; with Harvey F. Additon, Boston, 1940; With Castagno Galleries, Boston, 1943; with Charles D. Childs, Boston, 1943; with Newhouse Galleries and A. F. Mondschein, New York, 1944; with Macbeth Gallery, New York, 1944; Stephen C. Clark, New York, 1944; with Macbeth Gallery, New York, 1945; Maxim Karolik, Newport, R.I., 1945.

EXHIBITIONS: "The American Scene," Newhouse Galleries, New York, 1944, no. 2; "Commemorative Exhibition: Paintings of M. J. Heade and F. H. Lane," Knoedler and Co., New York, 1954, no. 13; "The American Muse," Corcoran Gallery of Art, Washington, 1959; "42 Karolik Paintings," Wadsworth Atheneum, Hartford, 1963; "Four Centuries of American Masterpieces," Gallery of Better Living Center, World's Fair, Flushing Meadow, N.Y., 1964; "The Seashore in American Painting," Carnegie Institute, Pittsburgh, 1965, no. 36; "American Landscape: A Changing Frontier," National Collection of Fine Arts, Washington, 1966; "The Painter and the New World," Montreal Museum of Fine Arts, 1967, no. 221; "Martin Johnson Heade," University of Maryland Art Gallery, College Park, 1969, no. 22; "New England Art from New England Museums," Brockton Art Center, Brockton, Mass., 1969; "Drama of the Sea," Heckscher Museum, Huntington, N.Y., 1975; "Marine Painting in America," Virginia Museum, Richmond, 1976, no. 30; "American Light: The Luminist Movement," National Gallery of Art, Washington, 1980, no. 79.

BIBLIOGRAPHY: Robert G. McIntyre, *Martin Johnson Heade* (New York, 1948), pl. 6; *M. and M. Karolik Collection of American Paintings, 1815-1865* (Cambridge, Mass., 1949), no. 137; John Wilmerding, *A History of American Marine Painting* (Boston, 1968), pp. 184, 187; *American Paintings in the Museum of Fine Arts, Boston* (Boston, 1969), no. 511; John Wilmerding, *Fitz Hugh Lane* (New York, 1971), fig. 81; Theodore E. Stebbins, Jr., *The Life and Works of Martin Johnson Heade* (New Haven, 1975), pp. 76-77, no. 111; John Wilmerding, *American Art* (New York, 1976), pp. 96-97.

Although it is only one of many depictions of the Newport beach painted in the 1860s and '70s, Heade's *Approaching Storm* remains a special vision, one of the most compelling and enigmatic images in American art. Many interpretations have been suggested for the picture: Heade's biographer has called it a culmination of Heade's series of shoreline pictures, a precursor of the apocalyptic vision in his *Thunderstorm over Narragansett Bay* (1868; Amon Carter Museum, Fort Worth), and an image of nature at her most terrible.[1] The painting has also been held to express the psychic shock caused by the Civil War, giving "unknowing voice to the end of Eden in a nation now at war with itself."[2] *Approaching Storm* is a late, idiosyncratic, example of romantic landscape painting in America. In it, Heade was concerned with the representation of the sublime, but rather than showing the forces of nature to be spectacularly dra-

matic, as Frederic Church did in *Cotopaxi* (1862; Detroit Institute of Arts), or extraordinarily terrible and violent, as in Thomas Cole's *Course of Empire: Destruction* (1836; New-York Historical Society), his vision of the sublime in nature is eerie, ominous, and deadly calm.

Several artists, among them John F. Kensett and Alfred T. Bricher, painted the same stretch of Newport Beach that Heade depicted here, but they emphasized the calm and not the horror, faithfully rendering the carefully observed facts of nature. Like their works, Heade's picture tells no story (the human figures on the nearest sailboat are barely visible), relying on formal elements to create the mood. Instead of realistic representation, however, Heade exaggerated his forms—the long, drawn-out shoreline, the odd, lava-like rocks, and the startling contrast between the light-colored beach, the black sea, and the brilliant white of the tiny, isolated sailboats—to arrive at a troubling, surreal vision.

Heade had experimented with his theme several years earlier. In *The Coming Storm* (1859; Metropolitan Museum of Art, New York) the mood of brooding terror is created by brilliant unearthly light, which throws into stark contrast the black water and the white strips of land surrounding it. The use of black water, perhaps the most startling and powerful motif in these compositions, was not Heade's invention but can be traced to Washington Allston, whose *Rising of a Thunderstorm at Sea* (1804; Museum of Fine Arts, Boston) was a more conventional representation of the sublime in terms of a dramatic storm at sea. But Allston's work and the paintings by J. M. W. Turner that may have inspired it are full of action and are exhilarating, not threatening, in the contest depicted between man and nature. A closer parallel to Heade's vision is found in the work of John Martin, whose paintings Heade could well have seen while in Europe between 1847 and 1850; he undoubtedly knew Martin's prints, whose effective use of inky blackness to render apocalyptic events (for example, "The Opening of the Seventh Seal," *Illustrations of the New Testament*, London, 1836) may have suggested to Heade the use of black in the evocation of the sublime.

It is not only the blackness but the deliberate distortion of forms and the suppressed painterliness (so antithetical to the romantic exuberance of his British predecessors) that give *Approaching Storm* a primitive and totemic appearance. These features suggest a frozen world, a world gone wrong: Heade's grim view of Newport Beach may have been prompted by the horrible events of the Civil War, but it also has a more universal meaning. It is, in fact, the negation of the romantic sublime: in *Approaching Storm*, nature's grandeur has an undercurrent of preternatural evil.

1. Thedore E. Stebbins, Jr., *The Life and Works of Martin Johnson Heade* (New Haven, 1975), p. 77.

2. John Wilmerding, *American Art* (New York, 1976), p. 97.

40. *Salt Marshes*, ca. 1865-1870

Oil on canvas, 15½ x 30⅜ in. (39.3 x 77.0 cm.)

M. and M. Karolik Collection. 47.1152

PROVENANCE: Mrs. Bailey Fraser, Newton, Mass.; with A. F. Mondschein, New York, 1945; Maxim Karolik, Newport, R.I., 1945.

EXHIBITIONS: "Martin Johnson Heade, Fitz Hugh Lane," M. Knoedler and Co., New York, 1954, no. 19; "American Paintings from the Museum of Fine Arts," Brockton Art Center, Brockton, Mass., 1974; "In this Academy," Pennsylvania Academy of the Fine Arts, Philadelphia, 1976, no. 171; "Kaleidoscope of American Painting," William Rockhill Nelson Gallery, Kansas City, 1978, no. 56.

BIBLIOGRAPHY: *M. and M. Karolik Collection of American Paintings, 1815–1865* (Cambridge, Mass., 1949), no. 142; *American Paintings in the Museum of Fine Arts, Boston* (Boston, 1969), no. 519; Peter Bermingham, *American Art in the Barbizon Mood* (National Collection of Fine Arts, Washington, 1975), p. 51; Theodore E. Stebbins, Jr., *The Life and Works of Martin Johnson Heade* (New Haven, 1975), no. 117.

The salt marshes along the eastern seaboard, which Heade first painted in 1859, became his signature subject in the following decades, as the Newport shoreline was J. F. Kensett's and the Gloucester coast Fitz Hugh Lane's. Although Heade, a constant traveler, would paint the flat marshlands in Rhode Island, New Jersey and, late in his life, in Florida (his last marsh scene is dated 1904, the year of his death), the series of marsh scenes begun at Newburyport, Massachusetts at the close of the Civil War remain the most successful of these works. Here, Heade's growing command of a Luminist style coincided with his romantic preoccupation with changing weather as a metaphor for the transitoriness and endurance of nature, and with the marsh in particular as the setting for an ideal relationship between man and nature. The present painting, although previously believed to represent the marshes at Newport, Rhode Island, is, in fact, part of this series, which includes *Newburyport Marshes, Passing Storm* (Bowdoin College Museum of Art, Brunswick, Me.), *Summer Showers* (Brooklyn Museum) and *Sudden Showers, Newburyport Marshes* (private collection, Brookline, Mass.), all quite similar in size, composition, and detail to the present picture; only the weather conditions vary.

Although they have been called "his wilderness, his Niagara"[1] (allusions to the favorite subjects of Thomas Cole and Frederic Church), Heade's marsh scenes were not in fact part of the tradition of monumental and dramatic landscape paintings, of the "operatic sublime."[2] Rather, these modest landscapes are an understated depiction of the transcendental vision of harmony, even a merging, between man and his natural environment. Heade's marshes represent an ideal world, one that is neither wilderness nor civilization, neither destructive of man nor likely to be destroyed by him. Heade's farmers harvest the wild marsh grass but cannot cultivate it; they reap nature's bounty without harming her.

The quiet grandeur of Heade's vision of the marshlands is expressed through the attenuated shape of the canvas (nearly twice as broad as it is high), the lowered viewpoint, and the scale, which, despite the small size of the picture plane, create a panoramic expanse. The river snakes through alternating planes of sunlight and shadow through endless marshes toward the horizon; the haystacks rapidly decrease in size. The tiny cows in the middle ground (and the tinier figures near the horizon) contribute to the sense of vast distances; they also enliven the landscape by adding narrative interest and provide a point of identification for the viewer. Unlike Church's landscapes, where the figures are shown as awed observers standing at the edge of nature's grandeur, man is located firmly within the landscape in Heade's paintings and, like the haystacks he has erected, is an integral (if temporary) part of it.

Heade balances the infinite space and timeless serenity of his marsh compositions with dramatic changes in light and atmosphere. Here menacing gray clouds indicate a gathering storm; the shadows of these clouds cover most of the meadowlands. Only a few patches of sun remain, and these, we sense from Heade's subtle evocations of motion within his aura of endless stillness, will disappear in a moment, as the storm breaks overhead.

1. Theodore E. Stebbins, Jr., *The Life and Works of Martin Johnson Heade* (New Haven, 1975), p. 42.
2. See Barbara Novak, "Grand Opera and the Small Still Voice," *Art in America* 59 (March-April 1971), pp. 64-73.

WILLIAM MORRIS HUNT (1824-1879)
active in Boston 1855–1879

41. *The Fortune Teller*

Signed and dated lower left: *W. M. Hunt/1852*

Oil on canvas, 55¼ x 51 in. (140.3 x 129.5 cm.)

Bequest of Elizabeth Howes. 07.136

PROVENANCE: Frank B. Brooks, Boston, 1852; James R. Gregerson, Boston, after 1857; Miss Elizabeth Howes.

RELATED WORKS: Study for "The Fortune Teller" (ca. 1852, Museum of Fine Arts, Boston, Bequest of Maxim Karolik); study for the head of the mother, ca. 1852 (formerly collection of Mrs. Horatio N. Slater; current location unknown); study for the head of the child (location unknown).

EXHIBITIONS: "Exposition Universelle," Paris, 1852; "Twenty-sixth Exhibition of Paintings," Boston Athenaeum, 1853, no. 134 (also "Twenty-seventh Exhibition," 1854, no. 133, "Twenty-eighth Exhibition," 1855, no. 90, "Twenty-ninth Exhibition," 1856, no. 64, and "Thirtieth Exhibition," 1857, no. 120); Annual exhibition, National Academy of Design, New York, 1856, no. 30; "Exhibition of the Works of William Morris Hunt," Museum of Fine Arts, Boston, 1879, no. 83; "Memorial Exhibition of the Works of William Morris Hunt," Museum of Fine Arts, Boston, 1924, no. 96; "William Morris Hunt: A Memorial Exhibition," Museum of Fine Arts, Boston, 1979, no. 21.

BIBLIOGRAPHY: "Exhibition of the National Academy," *Crayon* 3 (May 1856), p. 147; Henry C. Angell, *Records of William M. Hunt* (Boston, 1881), vii; Susan Hale, ed., *Life and Letters of Thomas Gold Appleton* (New York, 1885), p. 280; Helen M. Knowlton, *The Art Life of William Morris Hunt* (Boston, 1899), p. 27; Julia DeWolf Addison, *The Boston Museum of Fine Arts* (Boston, 1910), p. 33; Martha Shannon, *Boston Days of William Morris Hunt* (Boston, 1923), pp. 36, 41, 158; Mahonri Sharp Young, "William Morris Hunt: A Proper Bostonian," *Apollo* 85 (January 1966), p. 24; *American Paintings in the Museum of Fine Arts, Boston* (Boston, 1969), no. 584.

In 1846, after traveling in Europe for three years, Hunt entered the Paris studio of Thomas Couture. At that time, Couture was becoming increasingly well known: he had won a medal for a painting exhibited in the Salon of 1844 and would receive even greater acclaim in 1847 for *The Romans of the Decadence*. Hunt thus chose for his teacher one of the most celebrated artists in Paris, a master who was at odds with the French Academy (an attitude that no doubt appealed to Hunt's rebellious spirit) but who would nonetheless become one of the most revered teachers of art in the nineteenth century, numbering among his pupils Puvis de Chavannes and Edouard Manet. Hunt was one of Couture's first pupils and became a lifelong disciple, claiming: "I owe a great deal to Thomas Couture; more . . . than I do anyone else."[1]

Of the many lessons Hunt learned from Couture, the most important for the technique of *The Fortune Teller* was the procedure of developing the finished work directly from a sketch, without resorting to intermediate studies as was standard academic practice. Couture advocated that the underdrawing, reflecting the artist's spontaneous impression of the subject, be allowed to show through subsequent layers of paint to create a sense of depth and luminosity.[2] Hunt used this technique in *The Fortune Teller*: the grainy surface texture, so similar to that of many of Couture's paintings, results from thin layers of paint having been applied over a charcoal underdrawing on a coarsely woven canvas. The contours of the figures drawn not on the surface but defined by the outlines of the sketch beneath, are thus more convincingly depicted.

Although painted several years after Hunt left Couture's studio, *The Fortune Teller* is still a student's work; its composition and subject indicate Hunt's thoughtful application of his master's methods. The old hag at the right of Hunt's image was undoubtedly based on the figure of the money lender in Couture's *Love of Gold* (Musée de Toulouse), the painting for which Couture won a medal in the Salon of 1844.[3] The arrangement of the figure group was not drawn directly from any known work by Couture; however, it, too, reflects Couture's teachings. He urged his students to emulate the old masters, especially the artists of the Renaissance, and from time to time he took his students to the Louvre, where he directed their attention particularly to the works of Correggio and the Venetians.[4] Hunt clearly followed Couture's advice, for the influence of these masters is apparent in the softened contours and the rich colors of *The Fortune Teller*; furthermore, the facial types and compositional arrangement Hunt used here closely follows works by Correggio such as *The Madonna and Child with the Infant St. John and St. Elizabeth* (John G. Johnson Collection, Philadelphia Museum of Art) and especially *The Marriage of St. Catherine* (Galleria Nazionale, Naples).

1. Helen M. Knowlton, ed., *W. M. Hunt: Talks on Art*, 2nd series (Boston, 1882), pp. 74-75.
2. Albert Boime, *The Academy and French Painting in the Nineteenth Century* (London, 1971), pp. 72-73.
3. That Couture was in the habit, at least in later years, of teaching from *The Love of Gold* is documented by Ernest W. Longfellow, who studied with Couture in 1876 and 1877. Part of his training with Couture was to copy studies made for *The Love of Gold*. Ernest W. Longfellow, "Reminiscences of Thomas Couture," *Atlantic Monthly* 52 (August, 1883), p. 240.
4. Boime, *The Academy and French Painting*, p. 71.

42. *Mrs. Robert C. Winthrop, Jr. (Frances Pickering Adams)*

Signed and dated lower right: *WM Hunt/1861*

Oil on canvas, 46¼ x 35¼ in. (117.5 x 89.5 cm.)

Gift through Miss Clara Bowdoin Winthrop. 24.339

PROVENANCE: Clara Bowdoin Winthrop, Boston, by 1924.

EXHIBITIONS: Thomas Crane Public Library, Quincy, Mass., 1955; "The American Portrait: from the Death of Stuart to the Rise of Sargent," Worcester Art Museum, 1973, no. 33; "William Morris Hunt: A Memorial Exhibition," Museum of Fine Arts, Boston, 1979, no. 7.

BIBLIOGRAPHY: Helen M. Knowlton, *The Art Life of William Morris Hunt* (Boston, 1899), p. 48; *American Paintings in the Museum of Fine Arts, Boston* (Boston, 1969), no. 597; Martha J. Hoppin, "William Morris Hunt: Portraits from Photographs," *American Art Journal* 11 (April 1979), pp. 55-56.

In 1861 Hunt was living in Newport, and was busy with portrait commissions from socially prominent Bostonians. *Mrs. Robert C. Winthrop, Jr.* was painted at the same time as Hunt's other great portraits of women—such as that of Susan Brimmer Inches (ca. 1862; private collection) and of Mrs. Jefferson Randolph Coolidge (1861; private collection)—and like them is a dazzling display of brilliant color. Unlike those portraits, however, the present painting was not made from life but was based on a photograph, for Mrs. Winthrop died of tuberculosis the year before, while traveling in Europe, and her husband commissioned the portrait as a memorial to her.

Hunt painted many portraits from photographs during his career.[1] This one of Mrs. Winthrop differs markedly from the others, for Hunt has placed the figure before a dark interior background rather than a light, generalized one, and emphasized costume and incidental detail rather than

delineating facial features with precision. The Winthrop family complained about this, claiming that the portrait was not a good likeness.[2] The blurred features that make this portrait so unusual may simply reflect Hunt's difficulty in working from a photograph; more likely, however, the style in which the picture was painted indicates that Hunt was still, six years after his return to America, deeply stimulated by French art.

The manner of Thomas Couture, Hunt's first teacher in Paris, is clearly evident in this portrait. The softened contours, the bravura brushwork, the emphasis on silhouette, and especially the idealization of the figure, are characteristic of Couture's portraits and especially his figure paintings. Hunt was also influenced by painters such as Franz-Xavier Winterhalter and other society portraitists of the Second Empire who emphasized costume, setting, and material detail, and painted in vibrant colors.[3] But unlike those somewhat vapid and brittle likenesses, the portrait of Mrs. Winthrop possesses a soulfulness and melancholy, an ethereal quality that was rare in French portraiture since the time of Ingres, and was unique in America.

1. These were usually of men of some political prominence (such as *Judge Lemuel Shaw*, 1859, Essex County Bar Association, Salem, Mass.), men who presumably had little time or patience for lengthy sittings. In Mrs. Winthrop's case, the nature of the commission made the use of a photograph necessary; Hunt probably used a *carte de visite*, made in Europe, showing a full-length or three-quarter figure. See Martha J. Hoppin, "William Morris Hunt: Portraits from Photographs," *American Art Journal* 11 (April 1979), p. 56.

2. Letter of September 18, 1924 from Edward Everett, nephew of the sitter, to the Curator, Museum of Fine Arts, Boston (Paintings Department files).

3. The best known of these portraits is Winterhalter's *Empress Eugénie Surrounded by her Ladies-in-Waiting* (1855; Musée National du Château, Compiègne).

43. *Self-Portrait*

Signed and dated center right: *WMH/1866 (initials in monogram)*

Oil on canvas, 30⅜ x 25½ in. (77.1 x 64.8 cm.)

William Wilkins Warren Fund. 97.63

PROVENANCE: Mrs. Eleanor Hunt Diederich, before 1897.

EXHIBITIONS: "Loan Collection of Paintings by the Late William Morris Hunt," Metropolitan Museum of Art, New York, 1880, no. 22; "Memorial Exhibition of the Works of William Morris Hunt," Museum of Fine Arts, Boston, 1924, no. 17; "Centennial Exhibition of Paintings by William Morris Hunt," Albright Art Gallery, Buffalo, 1924, no. 2; "American Art," Lawrence Art Gallery, Williamstown, Mass., 1960, p. 3; "William Morris Hunt: A Memorial Exhibition," Museum of Fine Arts, Boston, 1979, no. 11.

BIBLIOGRAPHY: Julia DeWolf Addison, *The Boston Museum of Fine Arts* (Boston, 1910), p. 32; Martha Shannon, *The Boston Days of William Morris Hunt* (Boston, 1923), frontispiece; Alan Burroughs, *Limners and Likenesses* (Cambridge, Mass., 1936), p. 172; *American Paintings in the Museum of Fine Arts, Boston* (Boston, 1969), no. 610.

This brooding, romantic image is Hunt's most impressive portrait. In it he was able to combine his artistic self-image with his attitude toward the community that patronized him. Hunt was disdainful of the Boston aristocracy into which he was born and married: he deliberately challenged Boston's propriety by his eccentric behavior, and he ridiculed his contemporaries for their provincialism and for their inability to understand the new revolutionary art to which he introduced them.[1] He was Boston's first artistic bohemian, yet in the same image that his odd, crossed-arm pose and unfashionably long beard proclaim his bohemianism, his intense, moody gaze and shadowed face reveal a measure of disappointment and self-doubt.

Ironically, Hunt's belief that Boston did not appreciate his art or that of the French painters he championed was for the most part imagined. In 1866, when he painted this picture, he was the most successful portrait painter in Boston; he had turned Boston's taste away from the nearly exhausted tradition of British-inspired portraiture that had been practiced by artists such as Chester Harding and Francis Alexander in the 1840s and '50s and had introduced a brilliant continental manner that linked Boston's patrons to the contemporary high-style portraiture in France.[2] Furthermore, based on his example, several Bostonians, among them Ernest W. Longfellow, son of the poet, and Edward Wheelwright, an important art critic in the 1870s, traveled to France to seek out Hunt's masters, Thomas Couture and Jean-François Millet. Because of his enthusiasm for Couture, Millet, and painters of the Barbizon school, Hunt's contemporaries eagerly began to collect their works, and Hunt's own paintings inspired by these artists were increas-

ingly well received. In short, Boston's espousal of French culture in the period following the Civil War, and its receptivity to American painters influenced by French art, was due largely to the efforts of William Morris Hunt.

This image, the most successful and revealing of Hunt's four self-portraits,[3] was painted in a manner with which Hunt had been experimenting since the late 1850s, and which was a significant departure from the prevailing mode of the day. The device of silhouetting a figure against a light ground, which he first used in his portrait of Judge Lemuel Shaw in 1850, was derived from Couture, who exploited it, as Hunt did here, to monumentalize the figure. The heavy impasto and the animated brushwork in this painting were also learned from Couture; these features, too, emphasize the figure's sculptural presence. The brightness of the image and the iconic quality of the figure distinguish Hunt's picture from portraits by artists such as Joseph Ames, Moses Wight, and G. P. A. Healy, his leading competitors in Boston. The astounding expressiveness of this portrait surpasses most American portraiture of the period and rivals the best work of Couture.

During the Civil War years, Hunt was occupied with many commissioned portraits, works today regarded as his most successful but least rewarding for him; at the same time, he was experimenting with ideas and techniques gleaned from Couture and Millet. By the mid-'60s, Hunt was beginning to seek a new direction for his art, one less involved with portrait painting and more independent of his French masters. However, it was not until he began painting landscapes in the late 1870s that he found an appropriately expressive vehicle for his artistic ideas. The self-portrait of 1866 was painted at this turning point in Hunt's career. In it he revealed not only the romantic temperament of the artist's genius but also his restlessness and concern for the future direction of his art.

1. Hunt was extremely disdainful of the snobbish antiquarianism and lack of reception for contemporary developments in Boston. He once wrote to a sculptor in Paris who wanted to know whether to show his work in Boston, "by all means show your things in Boston. . . . As for selling them, that you need not expect. But if you can get up a lecture on the shape of dishes used by the Greeks in which to mix plaster, you will have plenty of chances to deliver it, that subject being, at this moment, of surpassing importance to this city." (as quoted in Helen M. Knowlton, *The Art Life of William Morris Hunt* [Boston, 1899] p. 97).

2. See cat. no. 42.

3. Hunt's first self-portrait, painted in France in 1848 and 1849, shows him in the *chapeau montagnard* worn by the Republicans after the revolution of 1848 (Museum of Fine Arts, Boston). The present example is the second portrait; a third self-portrait (now lost) was painted in 1871, and the fourth (Museum of Fine Arts, Boston) was painted in 1879, the year of his death.

GEORGE PETER ALEXANDER HEALY (1813-1894)
active in Boston 1832–1834, and occasionally after 1855

44. *Orestes Brownson*

Signed and dated center right: *G. P. A. Healy/Chicago 1863*

Oil on canvas, 55¼ x 43½ in. (140.2 x 110.5 cm.)

Gift of Mrs. Louisa Healy. 95.1368

PROVENANCE: Louisa Healy (wife of the artist), Chicago, after 1863.

EXHIBITIONS: Annual exhibition, National Academy of Design, New York, 1863, no. 181; "G. P. A. Healy," Art Institute of Chicago, 1913, no. 13.

BIBLIOGRAPHY: M. Bigot, *G. P. A. Healy* (Chicago, n.d.), p. 50; Marie de Mare, *G. P. A. Healy, American Artist* (New York, 1954), pp. 209-210; Lawrence E. Scanlon, "Eakins as Functionalist," *College Art Journal* 19 (Summer 1960), p. 325; *American Paintings in the Museum of Fine Arts, Boston* (Boston, 1969), no. 540.

Like Chester Harding, his rival for portrait commissions in Boston in the 1830s, Healy parlayed Yankee ingenuity and modest talent into an international reputation. He first came to prominence in Boston, his birthplace, through a brash trick: he purportedly cajoled Mrs. Harrison Gray Otis, who was then Boston's leading socialite, into sitting for him (although she had never before heard of Healy) by saying to her: "I want to paint a beautiful woman. Will you sit for me?"[1] Amused and flattered, she consented, and became his loyal sponsor thereafter, financing his trip to France in 1834. There he first studied with Baron Gros and then with Thomas Couture; the same charm that captivated Mrs. Otis soon attracted European royalty, and in the 1840s and '50s Healy was commissioned to paint King Louis Philippe of France and Charles I and Elizabeth of Bulgaria, as well as Franz Liszt, the poet and diplomat Lord Edward Robert Bulwer Lytton, and other international figures. Healy enjoyed similar success in America when he returned in 1855. Buchanan, Lincoln, and Grant sat for him, as did Henry Clay, H. W. Longfellow, and other prominent Americans. Although most of these portraits are the dark, lifeless images typical of the Brown Decades, the best of them are marked by sensitive characterization despite conventional, if informal poses.

Healy painted the quixotic religious leader Orestes Brownson (1803–1876) in Chicago in 1863, at the end of the latter's career; the Civil War had ended the spirit of optimism that gave credence to his utopian philosophies. Brownson, a powerful voice in New England social reform from the 1830s, began his career as a Presbyterian minister, subsequently led a Universalist congregation, and then in 1836 founded his own church, the "Society for Christian Union and Progress," with parishioners drawn from the working classes in Boston. He used the pulpit not only to preach religious reform but also to attack inherited wealth, organized Christianity, and the penal code. In 1838, he founded *The Boston* (later *Brownson's*) *Quarterly Review,* to which Bronson Alcott, Margaret Fuller, and other social philosophers were frequent contributors; the *Review* enjoyed wide circulation until about 1844, when Brownson's conversion to Catholicism cost it many of its New England and nearly all of its southern subscribers. Nonetheless, Brownson continued to be an outspoken advocate of social reform and became a powerful spokesman for the abolitionist movement in the 1850s.[2]

Healy shows the sixty-year-old Brownson to be a man of powerful bulk and personal magnetism. His leonine head is rendered in bright light against a dark background; he squints piercingly out at the viewer. The books to his left were no doubt meant to refer to Brownson's career, but they are nondescript; of greater interest is the chair in which he sits. Like Brownson, it is a relic from an earlier time, having been made about thirty years before the portrait was painted. The chair, a heavy mahogany structure with gilded sphinx-like figures supporting the arms, is in the French-inspired Empire style, which made frequent use of Greek and Egyptian motifs and was the first of the many eclectic "revival" styles to gain currency in the nineteenth century. But by the 1860s, Egyptian forms in furniture were passé. Healy's use of this Egyptian Revival chair, its bulk a match for the sitter's, is a deliberate archaism, for like Brownson, it represents values and ideas that were not yet history, but neither were they any longer current.

1. Marie de Mare, *G. P. A. Healy, American Artist* (New York, 1954), p. 22.
2. Henry F. Brownson, "Orestes Brownson," *Catholic Encyclopedia* (New York, 1908), vol. 3, pp. 1-3.

WILLIAM P. BABCOCK (1826-1899)
exhibited in Boston 1855–1870

45. *Girl with a Pink Bonnet*

Signed and dated lower left: *WP* (in monogram) *Babcock '65*

Oil on canvas, 13¾ x 10¾ in. (35.1 x 27.3 cm.)

Gift of Miss Emma E. Hicks. 29.48

PROVENANCE: Emma E. Hicks, Milton, Mass.

Babcock was one of the first of his generation of Bostonians to seek an artistic education in France. He entered the *atelier* of Thomas Couture in 1847, a few months after his fellow Bostonian William Morris Hunt began to study there, but shortly thereafter he moved to Barbizon to work alongside Jean-François Millet. Babcock introduced Hunt to Millet around 1853, and together the two Bostonians were responsible for popularizing Millet's works in America. Although Babcock's work was exhibited frequently at the Boston Athenaeum and the National Academy of Design during the 1850s and '60s, he remained at Barbizon for the rest of his life, painting landscapes, still lifes, and figure subjects of uneven quality. More valuable was his contribution as agent and intermediary for his Boston patrons and French artist-friends.

As a painter, Babcock's closest ties were with Boston, which traditionally supported its native sons; from his Barbizon home he remained abreast of current artistic events in Boston, participating, for example, in the first exhibition of the francophile Allston Club, organized by his friend Hunt in 1866. Although few are known today, Babcock's paintings were enthusiastically sought in his own time by collectors such as Henry Sayles, who also patronized Hunt and Millet. His connection with two of Boston's favorite painters no doubt enhanced Babcock's popularity; in addition, he was widely admired for his sensuous use of color, a taste which Washington Allston had generated in Boston

some fifty years earlier. Even the arch-Ruskinian James Jackson Jarves praised his color, though pointing out his difficulties in drawing: "His sense of color . . . is an infusion direct from original life. It is a madness, a wild passion, a splendid frenzy; Babcock is color-drunk. It would be hasty to say that he cannot draw or model, but he will not heed design while fury of color is upon him."[1] In *Girl with a Pink Bonnet,* however, Babcock's drawing is unusually skillful: although the girl's smock is summarily treated, her head is well formed and well modeled. His palette illustrates the "fanaticism of color" Jarves attributed to him: his tones are rich, high-keyed (though they have turned somewhat acid over time), and harmonious, the pale pinks and oranges expressive of his subject's languorous charm.

Babcock's image resembles the work of his mentor Millet, both in early romantic paintings such as *Young Woman at a Window* (1844–1845; Art Institute of Chicago), in which a young turbaned peasant woman gazes suggestively at the viewer, and the more serious compositions of the 1850s and '60s such as *Peasant Grafting a Tree* (1855; private collection) in which the personality of the peasant woman is expressed not through her feminine charms but through her labor. In technique and in facial type *Girl with a Pink Bonnet* is close to the softly painted latter group of Millet's works; in its intimacy and simplicity of composition it reflects the former. But Babcock's picture possesses none of the vibrant sensuality of Millet's paintings of the mid-1840s nor the epic naturalism of his later works. Like similar compositions by William Morris Hunt, this subject represents the Victorian feminine ideal, clothed in a peasant's smock and turban.

1. James Jackson Jarves, *The Art Idea,* ed. Benjamin Rowland, Jr. (Cambridge, Mass., 1960), p. 186.

JOSEPH FOXCROFT COLE (1837-1892)
active in Boston ca. 1857–1860; 1863–1865; 1870–1872; 1877–1892

46. *Valley of the Rambouillet,* ca. 1865-1870

Signed lower left: *J. Foxcroft Cole*

Oil on canvas, 22¼ x 36 in. (56.6 x 91.4 cm.)

Gift of the Misses Louisa W. and Marian R. Case. 20.597

PROVENANCE: S. F. van Choate, Boston; Louisa W. and Marian R. Case, Boston.

EXHIBITIONS: "Art in Transition: A Century of the Museum School," Museum of Fine Arts, Boston, 1977, no. 2.

BIBLIOGRAPHY: *American Paintings in the Museum of Fine Arts, Boston* (Boston, 1969), no. 236.

Rambouillet, a small town about twenty-nine miles southwest of Paris, had been a watering place for the French royal family since the fifteenth century: Francis I spent the last years of his life there, it was used by two of the sons of Louis XIV, and it was Louis XVI's favorite retreat (although Marie Antoinette disliked it). The chateau at Rambouillet became national property under the Republic, but during the Second Empire, when Foxcroft Cole was in France, it was renovated as a residence for the imperial family. During this time, Rambouillet became a tourist attraction; the parks surrounding the chateau were hailed as "the finest in the environs of Paris," surpassing even those at nearby Versailles in size, variety, and natural beauty.[1] But for Cole, who sought at Rambouillet the kinds of subject matter French artists of the preceding generation had painted at Barbizon, the interest was not the residences and manicured parks of the aristocracy, but the surrounding countryside, with its uncultivated forests and occasional peasant dwelling, and the opportunities for *plein-air* painting that such settings presented.[2]

Cole's relationship to the artists who painted at Barbizon would be longstanding. Like so many young Boston painters at the time of the Civil War, he sought his artistic education in Paris, studying first with Emile Lambinet, the popular Normandy landscape painter, in the early 1860s. Returning to Boston in 1863, he met William Morris Hunt, a great supporter of the Barbizon painters, who urged him to return to Paris to seek further training from those masters. Through Hunt (who bought several of Cole's paintings himself), Cole sold enough of his own work to finance a second trip to Paris in 1865. He became a pupil of Charles Jacque, who had left Barbizon in 1854 but continued to be associated with the other Barbizon artists during the 1860s, and through him Cole became acquainted with Daubigny, Corot, Diaz, and others, whose work he later promoted in America through the Vose Galleries of Providence.

Charles Jacque's work had less effect on Cole than did that of Constant Troyon and Charles Daubigny. *Valley of the Rambouillet* is closest to the work of Daubigny, whose massing of houses, coloristic detail in the foreground, and long, low horizon line Cole emulates here. However, the central position of the farmhouse, blocking the view into the distance, differs from Daubigny's composition of this type, in which a succession of diagonals leads the eye into space. The emphasis on a picturesque motif and the arrangement of forms across the picture plane are typical of many Americans' interpretation of the Barbizon vision, and derive from William Morris Hunt's landscapes of the early 1850s (e.g., *By the River,* ca. 1850–1855, Museum of Fine Arts, Boston). And unlike his Barbizon mentors, who viewed the woods of Barbizon and its peasant occupants as primeval, harsh, and unyielding, often presenting them from an intimate perspective,[3] Cole chose to paint a domesticated scene—a snug, prosperous-looking farmhouse, surrounded by tidy meadows—from the detached perspective of a stroller in the countryside, and we feel his approval at the productivity of the farmhouse and the industry of its inhabitants.

1. Karl Baedecker, *Paris and Environs: Handbook for Travelers* (Leipzig, 1888), p. 295.
2. Presumably a guidebook to the environs of Paris, like the Baedecker quoted above, led Cole to Rambouillet, for neither the Barbizon artists nor any of Cole's American colleagues seem to have painted there.
3. Robert L. Herbert, *Barbizon Revisited* (Boston, 1962), p. 66.

THOMAS R. ROBINSON (1835-1888)
active in Boston ca. 1860–1888

47. *Woods and Equestrienne,* ca. 1870

Oil on canvas, 29½ x 36¼ in. (74.9 x 92.0 cm.)

Gift of the Isaac Fenno Collection. 18.400

PROVENANCE: Isaac Fenno, Boston.

EXHIBITIONS: "Centennial Celebration," Brockton Public Library, Brockton, Mass., 1967.

Robinson's greatest contribution to the arts in Boston stemmed from his activity as the Paris agent for Seth M. Vose, the Providence (and later Boston) dealer who was instrumental in fostering the taste for Barbizon painting in Boston. Robinson had visited Paris three times as a student before becoming Vose's agent: in 1854, after some training in mechanical drawing in Providence and a few weeks at Cummins Art School in New York, he went to Paris and entered the *atelier* of Auguste Bonheur, where he remained for three years. Robinson went to France twice more in the late 1850s and early '60s, and was greatly influenced by the realist painter Gustave Courbet. Through his acquaintance with Courbet, he gained access to the studios of many avant-garde painters, including the landscapists working at Barbizon, and in the 1860s began working with Vose to bring their paintings to America. Robinson also supplied Barbizon pictures directly to the elite St. Botolph Club and to Henry C. Angell and other Boston collectors, who obliged Robinson by buying some of his own paintings as well.

In the early years of his artistic career, Robinson confined himself for the most part to animal paintings, works that were often marred by crude drawing and by insufficient attention to the landscape background. Later, repeated exposure to French landscapes (and the greater enthusiasm in Boston for landscape than for animal painting) prompted Robinson to pursue that genre. *Woods and Equestrienne* is one of Robinson's more successful efforts. Although prob-

ably painted in New England, it was inspired by his mentor Courbet's numerous views of the forest near Ornans, which won great acclaim in the Salons of the mid-1860s.

In the most famous of these, *Covert of Roe-Deer by the Streams of Plaisir-Fontaine, Doubs* (1866; Louvre, Paris), Courbet converted a wild stream and thicket into a sheltered, domesticated covert,[1] and Robinson achieved a similar effect in *Woods and Equestrienne,* in which the handsome horse, fashionably attired rider, and little white dog seem to transform the rugged New England countryside into an English park. The composition of *Woods and Equestrienne* mirrors that of the Courbet: the prominent stand of trees in the left foreground, painted with a crusty impasto that suggests both the texture of the bark and the light filtering through the trees, is balanced in both pictures by another large tree in the middle distance at right. Between the two groups of trees in Robinson's picture is a rough road across which the horsewoman travels, her dark form nearly enveloped by the large boulder behind her. In Courbet's composition, this central element is a stream, leading the viewer's eye deep into the covert, but like so many American interpretations of mid-century French painting (see cat. no. 46), Robinson articulated this carefully constructed receding perspective as a frieze-like arrangement. The green tonalities of *Woods and Equestrienne* also reflect Courbet's Ornans landscapes, as does the highly textured surface. But much of the lushness and sensuality of Courbet's painting is lost here, for the brushstrokes are rather nervous and spiky, and the expanding, deepening space of Courbet's composition becomes tight and closed in Robinson's work.

1. In a letter to his agent, Courbet wrote, "This winter I hired some deer and made it [the stream] into a covert: there's a little doe in the middle, like a lady receiving company in her drawing-room. Her mate stands beside her, it is all quite delightful, and they are finished like diamonds." Quoted in *Gustave Courbet* (Grand Palais, Paris and Royal Academy, London, 1978), p. 169.

139

WINCKWORTH ALLAN GAY (1821-1910)
active in Boston 1850–1874; 1877; ca. 1884–1894

48. *Landscape (Farmhouse at Rye Beach, New Hampshire)*

Signed and dated lower right: *W. Allan Gay/1870*

Oil on composition board, 9⅞ x 19 in. (25.0 x 48.2 cm.)

Bequest of Mrs. Edward Wheelwright. 13.468

PROVENANCE: Edward Wheelwright, Boston.

Winckworth Allan Gay enjoyed enormous popularity in Boston throughout his career. After studying drawing for several years with R. W. Weir at West Point, Gay first exhibited at the Boston Athenaeum in 1846; he showed there frequently in the 1850s and '60s after a four-year sojourn in Italy, Switzerland and Holland and several months in the Paris studio of Constant Troyon. Gay's pictures were avidly collected by Bostonians during those years, especially by those who were interested in the French aesthetic and collected paintings by the Barbizon masters, *Farmhouse at Rye Beach* was bought from Gay by Edward Wheelwright, an amateur painter who studied with Jean-François Millet at Barbizon in the 1850s and later became one of Boston's most sensitive critics of French paintings.

Although Gay was one of the first of many Bostonians to travel to Barbizon and study with a French master, he seems to have embraced the Barbizon style and approach to subject matter only in part. His landscapes—many of which were painted along the shore at Cohasset, south of Boston, or Maine or New Hampshire—more closely reflect the tighter, more precise style of painters like John F. Kensett and especially A. T. Bricher, both of whom were working in this part of New England in the 1860s. Gay's broad, horizontal composition shows a bucolic scene: the end of a summer day, with the sun casting long shadows over the rocky New England field. The focal point of the composition is the comfortable-looking farmhouse behind a grove of trees. Gay imbues this farmhouse with a sense of prosperity and well-being that distinguishes it from the more ramshackle and impoverished-looking cottages found in many Barbizon landscapes; nor does he suggest—as, for example, Millet would—the hardships of the farmer's labor. The pale pink and yellow tones of Gay's sunset sky are reminiscent of Kensett's and other Luminists' work; the panoramic view of the smooth horizon, punctuated by white daubs representing sailboats, resemble Kensett's sweeping views of the Newport coast.

ELIHU VEDDER (1836-1923)
exhibited in Boston 1866–1868; 1874

49. *The Questioner of the Sphinx*

Signed and dated lower right: *Elihu Vedder/1863*

Oil on canvas, 36⅜ x 42⅛ in. (92.4 x 107.0 cm.)

Bequest of Mrs. Martin Brimmer. 06.2430

PROVENANCE: Martin Brimmer, Boston, ca. 1863.

RELATED WORKS: *Questioner of the Sphinx*, 1875, oil on canvas, Worcester Art Museum; *The Sphinx on the Seashore*, 1879-1880, oil on canvas, Fine Art Museums of San Francisco; *The Sphinx*, 1890, oil on canvas, Mr. and Mrs. Edgar P. Richardson, Philadelphia; *Questioner of the Sphinx*, 1898, crayon, American Academy of Arts and Letters, on loan to Mark Twain House, Hartford.

EXHIBITIONS: Annual exhibition, National Academy of Design, New York, 1863, no. 173; "Forty-fourth Exhibition of Paintings," Boston Athenaeum, 1868, no. 286; "Literature and Poetry in Painting since 1850," Wadsworth Atheneum, Hartford, 1933, no. 75; "Paintings and Drawings by Elihu Vedder," Smithsonian Institution (Traveling Exhibition), 1966, no. 7; "19th-Century America," Metropolitan Museum of Art, New York, 1970, no. 126; "American Narrative Painting," Los Angeles County Museum of Art, 1974, no. 70; "The Art of Elihu Vedder," Hyde Collection, Glens Falls, N.Y., 1975; "The Art of Elihu Vedder," National Collection of Fine Arts, Washington, 1978, no. 28.

BIBLIOGRAPHY: Henry T. Tuckerman, *Book of the Artists* (New York, 1870), p. 451; Ernest Radford, "Elihu Vedder and His Exhibition," *Art Journal* 51 (April 1899), p. 102; Elihu Vedder, *Digressions of V* (Boston, 1910), p. 460; James Thrall Soby and Dorothy Miller, *Romantic Painting in America* (Museum of Modern Art, New York, 1943), p. 29; *American Paintings in the Museum of Fine Arts, Boston* (Boston, 1969), no. 991; Regina Soria, *Elihu Vedder: American Visionary Artist in Rome* (Rutherford, N.J., 1970), pp. 38, 40, 283; Patricia D. Pierce, "Deciphering Egypt: Four Studies in the American Sublime" (Ph.D. dissertation, Yale University, 1980), pp. 55-76.

"My idea in the sphinx was the hopelessness of man before the immutable laws of nature."[1] In Vedder's famous picture, a fearful Arab kneels at the mouth of the sphinx, seeking answers to the mysteries of life. This image departs from the Greek myth, in which the sphinx questions men on the road to Thebes, allowing only those with sufficient wisdom and self-knowledge to answer her riddle, to pass. Rather, as indicated by the impassive statue, the huddled human form, and the empty sand in which a skull and architectural ruins are half-buried, the theme in Vedder's picture is the futility and transitoriness of man's endeavor in the face of nature's power. Earlier in the century, in the poem "Ozymandias," Shelley had attached this theme to the legend of the sphinx; in the next several decades the sphinx and other Egyptian images would become popular in romantic art and literature in Europe and America.[2]

Although he had not yet been to Egypt when he painted *Questioner of the Sphinx*, Vedder had ample opportunity to know the actual appearance of the statue, situated near the pyramids of Gizeh and a major attraction for all travelers through Egypt and the Holy Land. Excavations in the area made the site even more popular, and it was described in countless travel books and reproduced with fair archaeological accuracy in works such as W. H. Bartlett's *The Nile*

Boat; or Glimpses of the Land of Egypt (London, 1849). Vedder no doubt saw Egyptian statuary in the Louvre when he was in Paris in the late 1850s, and at the New-York Historical Society, which acquired a major collection of Egyptian art in 1864, but as he himself claimed in his autobiography, a historically accurate representation of the statue's features was not his concern. Rather, "it is their unwritten meaning, their poetic meaning, far more eloquent than words can express, and it sometimes seemed to me that the impression would only be dulled or lessened by a greater unveiling of their mysteries."[3]

Vedder was preoccupied by the image of the sphinx throughout his career, and would paint numerous replicas. The present painting is the most successful of these, although Vedder called it "a large sketch, more carefully studied later." He produced a smaller *Questioner of the Sphinx* (Worcester Art Museum) for one of his Boston patrons in 1875; in 1879, he painted *The Sphinx on the Seashore* (Fine Arts Museums, San Francisco), which is a total reworking of the theme, for it uses the sphinx to represent threatening female sexuality. In 1890, after his first (and only) trip to Egypt, he painted his most archaeologically correct image of the sphinx (collection Mr. and Mrs. Edgar P. Richardson, Philadelphia). Of all these versions, the first is most successful in presenting the sphinx as an emblem of the unknowable and infinite power of nature.

In 1863, the *Questioner of the Sphinx* was bought from Vedder for $500 by Martin Brimmer, a staid Boston lawyer who would become one of the artist's most faithful patrons. Brimmer was one of several prominent Bostonians who bought Vedder's work during the 1860s, when he was little appreciated in New York. James Jackson Jarves, himself an important collector and respected art critic, found Boston's taste for Vedder symptomatic of "a radical difference of aesthetic feeling between New York and Boston"[4] for, to his mind, Vedder's work was highly intellectual, and demanded a cultivated audience (such as he felt was present in Boston but not in New York). In fact, it was their appreciation of dreamy romantic subjects instilled by Washington Allston earlier in the century, as much as their supposed sophistication, that accounts for Bostonians' interest in Vedder. Nonetheless, Jarves rightly identified Boston's taste for a kind of latter-day romanticism, found in the works of Vedder and John La Farge and William Morris Hunt, that was the beginning of the divergence of its artistic interests from the mainstream represented by New York.

1. Elihu Vedder, in Venice, letter of September 7, 1884 to an unidentified woman. "Century Collection of Manuscripts." New York Public Library.
2. The many appearances of the Sphinx in nineteenth-century American literature, and several pictorial representations of the Sphinx prior to Vedder's are discussed in Patricia D. Pierce, "Deciphering Egypt: Four Studies in the American Sublime" (Ph.D. dissertation, Yale University, 1980), pp. 55-76.
3. Elihu Vedder, *Digressions of V* (Boston, 1910), p. 451.
4. James Jackson Jarves, *The Art Idea* (Boston, 1864), pp. 249-250.

JOHN LA FARGE (1835-1910)
active in Boston in the 1870s and '80s

50. *Halt of the Wise Men,* ca. 1868

Oil on canvas, 32⅝ x 42⅛ in. (83.0 x 107.0 cm.)

Gift of Edward W. Hooper. 90.151

PROVENANCE: Edward W. Hooper, Boston.

RELATED WORKS: "Halt of the Wise Men," watercolor on paper, Princeton University Art Museum; "Halt of the Wise Men," wood engraving, published in *Riverside Magazine for Young Children* 2 (December 1868), p. 528.

EXHIBITIONS: "La Farge and His Descendants," Wildenstein and Co., New York, 1931, no. 4; "John La Farge," Metropolitan Museum of Art, New York, 1936, no. 21; "American Painting," Cleveland Museum of Art, 1937, no. 116; "Romantic America," Columbus Gallery of Art, Columbus, Ohio, 1948, no. 30; "John La Farge," Macbeth Gallery, New York, 1948, no. 1; "Old Favorites Revisited" Municipal Art Gallery, Los Angeles, 1959, no. 29; "American Painting from 1865-1905," Toronto Art Gallery, 1961, no. 46; "American Traditional Painters," J. B. Speed Art Museum, Louisville, Ky., 1962; "John La Farge," Graham Gallery, New York, 1966, no. 29.

BIBLIOGRAPHY: William Howe Downes, "American Paintings in the Boston Art Museum," *Brush and Pencil* 6 (1910), p. 210; Royal Cortissoz, *John La Farge* (Boston, 1911), opp. p. 74; Ruth B. Katz, "La Farge as Painter and Critic," (Ph.D. dissertation, Harvard University, 1951), p. 105; *American Paintings in the Museum of Fine Arts, Boston* (Boston, 1969), no. 702; Helene Barbara Weinberg, "John La Farge—The Relation of his Illustrations to his Ideal Art," *American Art Journal* 5 (May 1973), pp. 69-70; Barbara T. Ross, *American Drawings in The Art Museum, Princeton University* (Princeton, 1976), no. 67.

Although incapacitated for nearly two years by a near-fatal attack of lead poisoning, John La Farge, living in New York, embarked upon several major, if disparate, projects in 1868. Work on *Paradise Valley, Newport* and *The Last Valley* (both in private collections), his most ambitious and adventurous landscapes to date, was almost completed; these pictures, exhibited over the next six years in New York, Boston, Philadelphia, and Paris, would gain wide critical acclaim.[1] At the same time, La Farge returned to an earlier interest in book illustration, and produced a series of imaginative drawings for *The Riverside Magazine for Young People.* A wood engraving of *Halt of the Wise Men,* based on La Farge's watercolor (now Princeton University Art Museum), appeared in the second issue of *Riverside,* accompanying the story "The Vision of John the Watchman." La Farge subsequently drew upon the watercolor for this composition.

The New Testament theme of *Halt of the Wise Men,* unusual in American art at this time, was nonetheless consistent with La Farge's desire to establish himself as a painter of works of monumental scale and heroic subject matter. The time he spent in France (1856–1857) furthered his belief in the traditional hierarchy of the arts; consequently, he sought to express himself in grand religious and historical subjects, despite his greater talent as a still-life painter. In France, too, he found ample precedent among the work of contemporary artists for such subject matter. Religious painting was increasingly visible in France after mid-cen-

tury, when the government commissioned large numbers of such subjects, and when religious pictures appeared in the Salons as well as in churches.[2] La Farge, impressionable and eclectic, would absorb the lessons of such paintings as he would those of the Pre-Raphaelite works he witnessed the next year. *Halt of the Wise Men* reflects his eager absorption of French painting from Delacroix to the Barbizon painters.

The barren setting of La Farge's picture (although believed to represent an actual view of the sea from Paradise Rocks, Newport, the setting of many small landscapes La Farge painted beginning in 1859) has antecedents in the religious paintings of Corot (e.g., *Hagar in the Wilderness,* 1835, Metropolitan Museum of Art, New York, which was in Corot's studio while La Farge was in Paris), Chassériau (e.g., *The Curse of Cain,* private collection, Paris) and others. The palette of La Farge's composition differs markedly from that of *Paradise Valley,* painted in bright, pastel tones. In this work, the high-pitched colors—strident reds and acid blues against a brown-green ground—are a somewhat subdued reflection of Delacroix's palette, just as La Farge's subject is a quieter echo of Delacroix's late, passionate religious pictures.[3] As in *Paradise Valley* and many of the small Newport landscape sketches, La Farge here used a high horizon line and a tilted ground plane. This device, often attributed to the influence of Japanese prints (but here equally likely reflecting the example of Corot, Millet [e.g., *The Sower,* Museum of Fine Arts, Boston], and other Barbizon painters), is used to separate the figures from the landscape and push them forward toward the viewer, emphasizing their isolation. La Farge invested these figures with a mystical quality underscored by their exotic dress, a device he adopted from the works of Delacroix, Horace Vernet, and others who in the 1830s began dressing their religious figures in Arab garb. Ostensibly for historic verisimilitude, this was, in fact, intended to demonstrate the archaic dignity of these characters, and for La Farge, such detail lent conviction to his spiritual message. The design of *Halt of the Wise Men,* with figures crowded to one side on a hill in the extreme foreground of the picture, emphasizes La Farge's theme, a theme as yet unarticulated in American art, but common in French paintings of the period: man abandoned in a troubled world, searching for spiritual comfort.

1. *The Last Valley* was shown at the National Academy of Design in New York in 1870, in Boston in 1872 (Henry James praised it for its poetic qualities), at the Paris Salon of 1874, and at the Centennial Exposition in Philadelphia in 1876.

2. Elisabeth Kashey, "Religious Art in Nineteenth Century France," *Christian Imagery in French Nineteenth Century Art* (Shepherd Gallery, New York, 1980), p. 21.

3. While La Farge was in Paris, Delacroix was occupied with the decoration of the Chapel of the Holy Angels at Saint-Sulpice. The dramatic compositions that resulted from Delacroix's last great effort surely made a strong impression on La Farge, whose decorations for Trinity Church, Boston some twenty years later were no less heroic, if quieter in mood.

WILLIAM RIMMER (1816-1879)
active in Boston 1831–1866; 1870–1879

51. *Flight and Pursuit*

Signed and dated lower left: *W. Rimmer/1872*

Oil on canvas, 18⅛ x 26⅜ in. (46.0 x 67.0 cm.)

Bequest of Edith Nichols. 56.119

PROVENANCE: Col. Charles B. Nichols, Providence, R.I., by 1880; Miss Edith Nichols, Providence.

RELATED WORKS: Pencil sketch for central figure, inscribed at bottom "Oh for the Horns of the Altar" (Yale University Medical Library, New Haven).

EXHIBITIONS: "Exhibition of Sculpture, Oil Paintings and Drawings by Dr. William Rimmer," Museum of Fine Arts, Boston, 1880, no. 22; "William Rimmer," Whitney Museum of American Art, New York, 1946, no. 18; "Painting in America, the Story of 450 Years," Detroit Institute of Arts, 1957, no. 117; "A Rationale for Modern Art," American Federation of Arts, New York, 1959; "American Painting from 1865–1905," Toronto Art Gallery, 1961, no. 52; "19th-Century America," Metropolitan Museum of Art, New York, 1970, no. 117; American Narrative Painting," Los Angeles County Museum of Art, 1974, no. 45.

BIBLIOGRAPHY: Truman H. Bartlett, *The Art Life of William Rimmer* (Boston, 1882), p. 127; Lincoln Kirstein, "The Rediscovery of William Rimmer," *Magazine of Art* 40 (March 1947), pp. 94, 95; *American Paintings in the Museum of Fine Arts, Boston* (Boston, 1969) no. 831; Charles A. Sarnoff, "The Meaning of William Rimmer's *Flight and Pursuit*," *American Art Journal* 5 (May 1973), pp. 18-19; Marcia Goldberg, "William Rimmer's *Flight and Pursuit*: An Allegory of Assassination," *Art Bulletin* 58 (June 1976), pp. 234-240; Ellwood C. Parry III, "On Finding a Few French Connections in American Nineteenth-Century History Paintings" (Hamline Press, Minneapolis, 1977), pp. 5-10.

Flight and Pursuit was painted in 1872, the year after Rimmer was fired as Director of the School of Design for Young Women at New York's Cooper Union for the Advancement of Science and Art. Like most of his works, it illustrates an intensely personal vision, and was never shown publicly in his lifetime. Rimmer may have been reluctant to submit it to public scrutiny, especially after his failure in New York and the criticism many of his earlier works received.

On a preliminary pencil sketch for the central figure in the painting (Yale University Medical Library, New Haven) Rimmer wrote: "Oh, for the Horns of the Altar!" That inscription is an allusion to I Kings 1:50 ("And Adonijah feared because of Solomon, and arose, and went, and caught hold on the horns of the altar"), an episode in the story of King David in which Adonijah, David's fourth son, and Joab, his nephew, conspire to usurp the throne from Solomon, David's designated heir. David discovers their plot and sends executioners after them; each man in turn flees to the altar, and finds sanctuary from his assassins there. Rimmer's image has variously been interpreted as an allegory of the pursuit and capture of John Surratt, one of Lincoln's assassins;[1] an allusion to recent political assassinations in the Near East which had captured the public's imagination;[2] and most likely, as a reflection of Rimmer's own troubled psyche.[3] Like Adonijah, Rimmer felt himself to be an outsider, never accepted by Boston's patrons, mocked by its

critics, and denied important commissions. The paranoia this picture illustrates may also reflect Rimmer's father's delusion that he was the rightful heir to the French throne and was being pursued by the assassins of Louis XVI. Although it is unlikely that Rimmer shared this delusion, the painting may express his understanding of his father's insanity, and his recognition of the same tendencies within himself.

The sources proposed for Rimmer's eerie image are as numerous and varied as are the interpretations of its meaning. Most plausible are the suggestions that Rimmer drew his figures from the compositions of French academic artists of the preceding generation. He probably knew J-L Gérôme's *Pasha's Runners* from a photogravure; it may have been his model for the pair of running figures and the Moorish setting. Decamp's *Night Patrol in Smyrna* (ca. 1860; Metropolitan Museum of Art, New York) was in New York in the 1870s; it shows figures running past Turkish buildings.[4] These associations suggest that Rimmer, long considered an isolated genius, was aware of current artistic trends in Europe. In addition, Rimmer's precise, linear style, his habit of painting thinly and with barely visible brushstrokes, and the dependence of his forms on the outlines beneath is like Gérôme's technique, and different from the Barbizon-influenced style then prevalent in Boston.

The content of *Flight and Pursuit* is, however, not very like that of the French academics, and indicates Rimmer's affinity for another sensibility. Gérôme was, after all, a narrative and history painter; however exotic and idealized his subjects might have been, they always departed from an actual event or observed reality. Although Rimmer used similar settings to suggest the exotic, *Flight and Pursuit* portrays not an event but an idea; it is an image that has substance not in the physical universe but in the mind. The wraith-like forms, the rhythmic pairing of figures, and the reduction of the composition to simply outlined, pale, monochromatic forms, are all devices that dematerialize the image and remove it from the real world. Rimmer's setting, too, invokes something unreal: the architecture is like a stage set, composed of a series of parallel planes with light falling from an undisclosed source between layers of space. The alternating zones of light and dark, and the archways that repeat seemingly to infinity, create an ambiguous and unsettling space. In his formal allegiance to the academic tradition, combined with his treatment of fantastic, indeed nightmarish subjects, Rimmer has much in common with the artists associated with the *symboliste* movement in France, such as Gustave Moreau, Odilon Redon, and Gustave Doré. Apparitions, eerie shadows, and undefined spaces frequently appeared in their work, and they, too, exploited the mysterious qualities of Moorish settings, so popular in the 1870s, as backdrops for ominous events. Although he may not have known Moreau's or Redon's works directly, Rimmer surely had seen Doré's illustrations, which were popular in Boston in the 1870s.[5] He was not, however, dependent on these artists; rather, the bizarre and horrific content of *Flight and Pursuit* is the expression of a kindred spirit.

Flight and Pursuit offers a refinement of themes that Rimmer had treated in some of his earlier works. His sculptures
of St. Stephen (1860), The Falling Gladiator (1861), and
The Dying Centaur (1861), and his paintings Hagar and
Ishmael (1857-1858) and Evening: Fall of Day (1869) are
all images of victims, of figures who come to grief for causes
external to themselves. In Flight and Pursuit, it is not the
victim's dramatic fall that is emphasized, but his terror at the
thought of ghostly pursuers. It is both an image of paranoia,
and a subtle interpretation of the nature of paranoia.

Rimmer suggests here that the victim and his pursuers
are aspects of a single personality. The foreground figure,
a bandit, appears to be an agent of some conspiracy against
unidentified persons. Close on his heels is the shadow of an
unseen figure. The uncertainty Rimmer creates—whether
that figure is a fellow conspirator, or the discoverer of the
plot who now pursues the pursuer—heightens the anxiety
of the vision. Running parallel to the bandit in the middle
distance is his Doppelgänger, a shrouded, semi-transparent
figure who glances ominously over his shoulder at the
viewer. These figures, both horrific and neither real, sug-

gest that the unnamed force pursuing the bandit is part of
himself, that he is pursued by his own imagination.

1. Marcia Goldberg, "William Rimmer's Flight and Pursuit," Art
Bulletin 58 (June 1976), pp. 234-240.
2. Ellwood C. Parry III, "On Finding a Few French Connections
in American Nineteenth-Century History Paintings" (Hamline
Press, Minneapolis, 1977), pp. 5-6, 9-10.
3. Charles A. Sarnoff, "The Meaning of William Rimmer's Flight
and Pursuit," American Art Journal 5 (May 1973), pp. 18-19.
4. Goldberg (op. cit.) proposed Gérôme's Death of Caesar (1859;
Walters Art Gallery, Baltimore) as Rimmer's source; Parry (op.
cit.) mentions The Pasha's Runners as a closer parallel. I thank
Alexandra Murphy of the Paintings Department, Museum of
Fine Arts, Boston, for bringing the Decamps to my attention.
5. Ghostly shadows that suggest a threatening presence occur
frequently in Dorés work, for example, in his illustrations for
Dante's Inferno ("Dante and Virgil before the tomb of Fari-
nata") or for Legend of the Wandering Jew by Pierre Dupont
("He roams through the Countryside"; Paris, 1856). An interesting parallel for Rimmer's setting of repeating Moorish-style
arches suggesting an infinite eerie space is to be found in
Moreau's Salome Dancing before Herod (ca. 1870; Los Angeles County Museum of Art).

GEORGE INNESS (1825-1894)
active in Medfield 1860–1864; 1874–1876

52. *Lake Nemi*

Signed and dated lower right: *Inness Nemi 1872*

Oil on canvas, 30 x 44⅞ in. (76.0 x 114.0 cm.)

Gift of the Misses Hersey. 49.412

PROVENANCE: Mr. and Mrs. S. D. Williams, Roxbury, Mass., 1872; Ada Hersey, Roxbury, 1905

EXHIBITIONS: "American Light: The Luminist Movement," National Gallery of Art, Washington, 1980, fig. 182.

BIBLIOGRAPHY: Alfred Trumble, *George Inness, N.A., A Memorial* (New York, 1895), p. 45; LeRoy Ireland, *The Works of George Inness* (Austin, Texas, 1965), no. 560; *American Paintings in the Museum of Fine Arts, Boston* (Boston, 1969), no. 654; Nicolai Cikovsky, Jr., *George Inness* (New York, 1971), fig. 46.

Lake Nemi and the surrounding Alban hills were visited by many artists in the nineteenth century. Richard Wilson painted there in the 1750s; J. M. W. Turner, inspired by Claude's golden views of this area, came to Lake Nemi twice, in 1819 and 1828. Among the Americans to tour Italy, Sanford Gifford stopped at Nemi in 1856; his richly painted view of the site is a paean to Turner's Italian pictures. Inness arrived in Rome in the spring of 1870 and stayed there for four years, producing many pictures of the Italian countryside. He visited Albano, a village seventeen miles southwest of Rome, in the summer of 1872, painting many pictures at the site and especially at nearby Lake Nemi.[1] As did so many artists before him, Inness found Nemi spectacularly beautiful: the lake fills the crater of an extinct volcano, and is over 1,000 feet above sea level. This image of Nemi is the richest of the many views of the site Inness painted that summer. It is reminiscent of the paintings of Claude: the landscape is bathed in golden light, the haze softens the outline of trees, and the scene is imbued with a spiritual quality that surpasses pure description.

Artists and tourists were attracted to Lake Nemi not only because of its celebrated beauty but also because of the myths associated with the area. Roman poets called the lake the mirror of Diana; the area was sacred to the goddess, for on the shore of the lake stood a great, wealthy temple to which many of her worshipers made pilgrimages. It was also the site of a strange and bloody ritual persisting through the decline of Rome, which governed the succession to the priesthood of Diana. The chief priest was required to wander alone through the sacred grove of Diana at Nemi, always watchful for his fellow priests, who could succeed to his office only by killing him. The murderer of the high priest then became high priest himself, retaining that position until he was killed by another.[2]

The description of Lake Nemi recorded in travel accounts of the period indicate that Inness took no great liberties with the topographical features of the site. Key elements of Inness's landscape, such as the steep hillside at Nemi, the mirror-smooth lake and the mist rising from it, and the forest coming just to the edge of the stone retaining wall, are all mentioned in contemporary guidebooks. The area immediately surrounding Nemi was little inhabited in the 1870s, although Albano and other nearby towns were described as noisy and colorful; it would seem that the eerie emptiness of Nemi pleased Inness more than the festival atmosphere of the neighboring villages which so delighted his fellow travelers. Priests, now Catholic rather than pagan, still remained at Nemi in Inness's time, and at least one tourist described them in an irreverent fashion, indicating his ignorance or indifference to the eerie legend: "Priests in black, looking always like a sort of ecclesiastical crow, such silly solemnity in their faces, so much slow flap to new petticoats and the brims of their hats . . ."[3]

Inness, however, was not indifferent; the sunny beauty of the lake and its horrible legend affected him equally. He included in his pastoral landscape a solitary monk who is armed now with a cane rather than a sword, and who like his predecessors walks slowly toward the lake as though reenacting the old legend. Because of his presence, the brilliant landscape becomes ominous, the soft light and palpable atmosphere suggestive of a lazy summer day take on a dreamlike, mythic meaning. The panoramic view, and the endless haze that obscures all detail other than the two white birds soaring over the lake also contribute to the sense of timelessness and mystery. Inness believed that art should represent not only the surface appearance of nature, but its soul, its emotional and spiritual content. This conviction is nowhere better demonstrated than here, where Inness eclipses the present with the mythic past and reveals the sylvan glory and sinister history of Lake Nemi.

1. LeRoy Ireland lists eight views of Lake Nemi painted during Inness's residence in Rome in the 1870s (*The Works of George Inness* [Austin, Texas, 1965], nos. 537, 538, 560, 561, 572, 573, 574, 623). A ninth painting, dated 1857, is described as *Lake Nemi or Lake Como* (Ireland, no. 132).
2. Sir James Frazer, *The Magic Art* (New York, 1935), vol. I, p. 9.
3. "H. H." (Helen Maria Hunt), *Bits of Travel* (Boston, 1872), p. 113.

53. *Kearsarge Village*

Signed and dated lower right: *G. Inness 1875*

Oil on canvas, 16⅛ x 24 in. (40.9 x 61.0 cm.)

Gift of Miss Mary Thacher in memory of Mr. and Mrs. Henry C. Thacher and Miss Martha Thacher. 30.102

PROVENANCE: Mary Thacher, before 1930.

RELATED WORKS: "November in the Adirondacks," Ireland, cat. no. 1158; ca. 1885), formerly with Chapellier Galleries, New York.

EXHIBITIONS: "The Oil Paintings Illustrated," Museum of Fine Arts, Boston, 1932; "Two Centuries of Art in New Hampshire," New Hampshire Historical Association, Concord, N.H., 1966; "Painting in the White Mountains," bicentennial exhibition, Tamworth, N.H., 1966; "Nineteenth-Century American Paintings from the Storerooms," Museum of Fine Arts, Boston, 1979.

BIBLIOGRAPHY: LeRoy Ireland, *The Works of George Inness* (Austin, Texas, 1965), no. 751; *American Paintings in the Museum of Fine Arts, Boston* (Boston, 1969), no. 657; Nicolai Cikovsky, Jr., *George Inness* (New York, 1971), fig. 57.

In the summer of 1875, Inness visited the White Mountains of New Hampshire, which had come to rival the Catskill Mountains in New York as a mecca for artists and vacationers. Inness, who lived in the Boston suburb of Medfield between 1860 and 1864 and again in 1875 and 1876, spent that summer in North Conway, on the eastern border of New Hampshire, and traveled as far north as the Mount Washington area to find subjects for his paintings. Kearsarge Village and North Kearsarge mountain, depicted here, are about one and one-half miles northeast of North Conway; although compared to Mount Washington, North Kearsarge is a small and rather unspectacular peak, it was nonetheless the inspiration for the most dramatic of the pictures Inness painted of the area.

In *Kearsarge Village,* Inness depicted a summer storm moving across North Conway meadow. During his career, he painted many pictures of nature in a moment of dramatic change; this subject had also been popular with Thomas Cole, Frederic Church, and other painters of the Hudson River School. But Inness's treatment of the subject reflects his exposure to French painting more than his affinity with those New York painters: rather than concentrating on topographical details and atmospheric effects, Inness here used the intense and rapidly changing light of a thunderstorm as the basis for experiments with color and composition. The picture is in fact an essay on the color green: Inness built his composition around successive variations on the color, from the deep gray-green of the pine trees in the foreground to the paler hue of the stand of birch trees in the middle distance; he also used a medium-valued yellow-green on the hillside and a startling turquoise for the pond, the last an unusual color that was a favorite of Corot's but was rarely used by American artists. Variations on shades of blue define a subsidiary theme: the dark blue-black of the storm clouds at left is juxtaposed with a brighter tone indicating patches of blue sky at right, painted over the clouds in a single, broad stroke.

FRANK DUVENECK (1848-1919)
exhibited in Boston 1875

54. *The Old Professor*

Signed and dated upper left: *FD* (in monogram) *Munich/1871*

Oil on canvas, 24 x 19⅛ in. (61.0 x 48.5 cm.)

Gift of Martha B. Angell. 19.96

PROVENANCE: Henry C. Angell, Boston, 1875; Martha B. Angell, Boston, 1916.

RELATED WORKS: "The Professor," wood engraving after Duveneck by Frederick Jüngling, 1880, published in the *American Art Review* 11 (1881).

EXHIBITIONS: Spring exhibition, Boston Art Club, 1875; "13th Exhibition," Charitable Mechanics Association, Boston, 1878, no. 36; "Paintings by Mr. Frank Duveneck and Mr. L. H. Meakin of Cincinnati, Mr. J. C. Steele of Indianapolis, and Mr. J. H. Sharp of Chicago," St. Botolph Club, Boston, 1903, no. 17; "Triumph of Realism," Brooklyn Museum, New York, 1967, no. 39.

BIBLIOGRAPHY: Henry James, "Art," *Atlantic Monthly* 35 (June 1875), pp. 751–753; Henry C. Angell, *Records of William Morris Hunt* (Boston, 1881), pp. 23-24; ———, "Our Pictures and About Them," (unpublished MS, Archives, Museum of Fine Arts, Boston, 1909), p. 1; F. Weitenkampf, *American Graphic Art* (New York, 1912), p. 156; Norbert Heerman, *Frank Duveneck* (Boston, 1918), p. 4; Alan Burroughs, *Limners and Likenesses* (Cambridge, Mass., 1936), fig. 163; *Exhibition of the Works of Frank Duveneck* (Cincinnati Art Museum, 1936), p. 71; Mahonri Sharp Young, "The Two Worlds of Frank Duveneck," *American Art Journal* 1 (1969), pp. 93-94; *American Paintings in the Museum of Fine Arts, Boston* (Boston, 1969), no. 372; F. W. Bilodeau, *Frank Duveneck* (Chapellier Gallery, New York, 1972), n.p.

Duveneck painted *The Old Professor* in Munich, where he went in 1870 to study at the Royal Academy. The Academy at that time offered a standard curriculum of painting and drawing classes; it was unusual, however, in that these classes emphasized the "study head" (the making of portrait studies from models) rather than the study of the nude. In the 1870s, the Academy was divided into two factions: a group centered around the director, Karl von Piloty, who favored the painting of historical subjects in an academic manner, and another, dominated by Wilhelm Diez, a popular professor of technique, and strongly influenced by the work of Wilhelm Leibl. The latter, which advocated a broad, sketch-like style, strong colors, and thick impasto rather than pristine finish, included most of the Americans studying in Munich at the time, including Duveneck.

Duveneck's *Old Professor* is one of the best of the portrait heads he painted in this vigorous, anti-academic manner. The model for the picture was not a professor but a local pharmacist, Clement von Sicherer. Von Sicherer had been painted by Leibl about 1865 (private collection, Schweinefurt); a few years later, several other Munich artists also painted his portrait, possibly as part of a classroom exercise.[1] The bust-length, frontal pose that Duveneck chose for his portrait study was used frequently by artists in the so-called Leibl circle, who found it direct and thus an appropriate vehicle for the straightforward realism for which they were striving. At the same time, such a format suggests that the subject is not an individual but a type; these

two seemingly contradictory impulses were successfully balanced in *The Old Professor*. Duveneck counteracted the stolidity of the pose with dramatic lighting, brightly illuminating the right side of von Sicherer's face while casting the left into deep shadow. Duveneck's broad, blunt strokes animate the picture surface and give the head a sculptural presence. And pervading the whole is the quality of "unfinish" so valued by artists of the Leibl circle: the sketchlike appearance of *The Old Professor* was intended to expose the powerful structure of the picture; it also imbued the figure with a lifelike quality, and the play of light over the animated surface suggests a figure capable of motion.

Although Duveneck had shown his work several times in Munich, where it excited both admiration and outrage, he won little recognition in America until 1875, when he sent six paintings to the spring exhibition of the Boston Art Club. The paintings caused an immediate sensation: one critic wrote excitedly of "the discovery of an unsuspected man of genius;"[2] Henry James, writing in *Atlantic Monthly*, praised the pictures for their abruptness and their fearless realism. He clearly viewed them as defining a new—and positive—artistic direction: "Their appeal is that of a progressive man, and should be met with encouragement."

The present picture was one of the six Duveneck exhibited that spring. James's description of it provides an insightful formal analysis, and probably was the source of its inaccurate title:

> *The Head of a Professor is exceedingly powerful. The old fellow scowls out of the canvas with a pedagogic ferocity which might well call back to the stoutest heart some memory of boyish tremors from a similar cause. The relief into which the face is thrown, by the management of light and shade and the liberal application of thick paint to the illuminated portions, is high and startling; the small canvas is fairly blistered with the pigment that goes to the construction of he rough chin, protuberant cheeks, and war-worn nose while the connecting piece of the spectacles is literally buried in the substance of this latter feature.[3]*

The Old Professor was purchased from the 1875 exhibition by Henry Angell, a prominent collector of French painting and a close friend of the Boston artist William Morris Hunt. In Angell's biography of Hunt, he speaks of the painter's enthusiasm for the picture, and so suggests an explanation for the immediate popularity of Duveneck's work in Boston. In the 1860s and '70s, Hunt was the most popular artist in the city, and guided its taste for contemporary pictures. It was he who first brought the "cult of the unfinish" to Boston, who kindled Boston's interest in works by foreign and foreign-trained artists, and who advocated an emotional and spontaneous painting style.

1. Alfred Langer, *Wilhelm Leibl* (Leipzig, 1961), p. 19.
2. "Notes," *The Nation* 20 (June 3, 1875), p. 376.
3. "Art," *The Atlantic Monthly* 35 (June 1875), p. 751.

GEORGE FULLER (1822-1884)

active in Boston and Deerfield, Mass., 1842–1848; 1860–1884

55. *The Dandelion Girl (By the Wayside)*

Signed and dated lower left: *G. Fuller, 1877*

Oil on canvas, 50¼ x 40⅜ in. (127.9 x 102.5 cm.)

Gift of Dr. and Mrs. George Faulkner, through the Trustees of the Faulkner Hospital. 11.2802

PROVENANCE: George Faulkner, Jamaica Plain, Mass., by 1884.

EXHIBITIONS: "Thirteenth Exhibition," Charitable Mechanics Association, Boston, 1878, no. 250; "Memorial Exhibition of the Works of George Fuller," Museum of Fine Arts, Boston, 1884, no. 121 (as *By the Wayside*); "Centennial Exhibition of the Works of George Fuller," Metropolitan Museum of Art, New York, 1923, no. 1; "American Art in the Barbizon Mood," National Collection of Fine Arts, Washington, 1975, no. 35.

BIBLIOGRAPHY: J. J. Enneking, "Fuller's Methods in Painting," *George Fuller His Life and Works* (ed. J. B. Millet, Boston, 1884), pp. 72–73, 90; Marianna van Rensselaer, *Six Portraits: Della Robbia, Correggio, Blake, Corot, George Fuller, Winslow Homer* (Boston, 1889), p. 196; William Howe Downes, "George Fuller's Pictures," *International Studio* 75 (July 1922), p. 267; William I. Homer and David M. Robb, Jr., "Paintings by Fuller," *Art Quarterly* 24 (Autumn 1961), p. 289; *American Paintings in the Museum of Fine Arts, Boston* (Boston, 1969), no. 423.

Although he is little known or appreciated today, George Fuller was enormously popular in Boston in the 1870s and '80s. At that time, French art, especially Barbizon painting, was very much in vogue, and Fuller, who worked for much of his life as a farmer in Deerfield and did not begin to exhibit his paintings until he was over fifty, was compared to the French painters Millet and Corot, who were mythologized as peasant-artists, men who achieved fame later in life and who were said to have brought to their art a nobility of purpose and wisdom gleaned from the land. Critics who wrote about Fuller tended to concentrate on his biography rather than his art; they saw him, like Millet, as an isolated genius, a martyr to his art, and found "something morally heroic in this art born of adversity. . . ."[1]

At the same time, Fuller was hailed as Boston's great discovery, as a native son who represented the best of America's values. He came to prominence at a time of great nationalistic spirit; his first exhibition at Doll and Richards occurred in the year of the Centennial, and he was hailed accordingly as a truly native genius, an artist who was self-taught, and so untainted by European influences. Such praise disregarded the five months Fuller spent in Europe in 1859, and his exposure to all the French art then exhibited and collected in Boston; it focused instead on his New England heritage and his similarity to Washington Allston and other revered artists of Boston's past.

The Dandelion Girl was painted in Deerfield in 1877 and exhibited to great acclaim in Boston the following year. The subject developed a theme on which Fuller had been working for fifteen years, using various local girls as models, to arrive at a type conceived in his imagination. The type was intended as ideal, visionary, and was so seen by Fuller's critics, who found paintings such as this to be the epitome of "womanly grace and child-like innocence."[2] *The Dande-*

lion Girl and her sisters were viewed as symbols of the New England adolescent: pure, simple, and unworldly.

Later critics associated pictures like *The Dandelion Girl* with the works of Albert Pinkham Ryder, who also painted his own personal mythology, worked in isolation, and developed his own unorthodox techniques. Like Ryder, Fuller constantly reworked his paintings, rubbing out forms, painting them over and producing a thick, crusty surface. Fuller acknowledged his difficulties as a draftsman, but along with critics of his day believed that the awkwardness of his drawing gave a valuable freshness to his pictures. Concerning the clumsily drawn cow in the middle of *Dandelion Girl*, he said he "would not have changed her for the most graceful cow in the country."[3]

The popularity of *The Dandelion Girl* was due not only to the admired innocence of its creator and the honest awkwardness of his technique but also to the events and values underlying its nostalgic subject matter. By the 1870s, Bostonians had been collecting French landscapes and "peasant pictures" for two decades, and the image of a young woman tending farm animals shown in large scale against steeply rising terrain was a familiar one. Although *The Dandelion Girl* has some formal connection to Millet's work, with which it was compared, it is closer in spirit to the work of more conservative French artists such as Jules Breton, Charles Jacque, and Edouard Frère. Like Millet, these artists painted numerous pictures of life in the fields; young shepherdesses and cowgirls were particularly popular themes. However, unlike Millet, whose brutalized yet heroic peasants reflect the social disaffection that followed the Revolution of 1848 in France, these artists had a romantic vision of peasant life, and presented their heroes and heroines as pretty, charming, and content.

This sentimental, overly rosy view of rural life was shared by Fuller, who refrained from showing the difficulties and frustrations of farm work, which he knew well, and the brutalizing effect of such toil, especially on children. Rather, he shows the Dandelion Girl stealing a moment of childish pleasure from her work of tending the cows: making a wish, she blows on a dandelion. An idealized, prettified figure, her appeal is one of nostalgia: New England after the Civil War was rapidly evolving from a rural to an industrial community, and images like this one present in poetic terms a treasured mode of life that was rapidly disappearing.

1. Frank Jewett Mather, *Estimates in Art, Series II, Sixteen Essays, on American Painters of the Nineteenth Century* (New York, 1931), p. 105. See also Marianna van Rensselaer (*Six Portraits*, Boston, 1889, p. 236) who said of Fuller ". . . I found him so exactly what a lover of his pictures would have wished." Much of the information referred to here concerning Fuller's reputation in the 1870s and '80s, was gathered by Tanya Boyett, whose contribution I gratefully acknowledge.

2. Josiah B. Millet, ed., *George Fuller His Life and Works* (Boston, 1886), p. 71.

3. John J. Enneking, "Fuller's Methods in Painting," in ibid., p. 73.

HENRY BACON (1837–1912)
active in Boston, with frequent and extended trips to Europe, from 1860

56. *On Shipboard*

Signed and dated lower left: *Henry Bacon 1877*

Oil on canvas, 19¾ x 29 in. (50.2 x 73.7 cm.)

Gift of Mrs. Edward Livingston Davis. 13.1692

PROVENANCE: Mrs. Edward Livingston Davis, 1913.

EXHIBITIONS: Salon de 1877, Paris, no. 84 (as "En pleine mer; la Pereire, paquebot transatlantique"); "The Social Scene in Paintings and Prints from 1800–1935," Whitney Museum of American Art, New York, 1935, no. 4; "Off for the Holidays," Wadsworth Atheneum, Hartford, 1955, no. 7; "Nineteenth-Century American Paintings from the Storerooms," Museum of Fine Arts, Boston, 1979.

BIBLIOGRAPHY: Mantle Fielding, *Dictionary of American Painters, Sculptors, and Engravers* (Philadelphia, 1926), p. 14; *American Paintings in the Museum of Fine Arts, Boston* (Boston, 1969), no. 76; Hermann Warner Williams, Jr., *Mirror to the American Past* (Greenwich, Conn., 1973), pp. 210–212.

After the Civil War, the "grand tour" of Europe became a required component of the education of the wealthier classes. Henry Bacon, a Massachusetts-born artist who made many trips to the Continent, depicted such travels in paintings and watercolors of European and Near-Eastern subjects. He also described the crossing in a number of shipboard scenes; these usually featured young women shown strolling on the deck, leaning over the side rails to look for land, or, as here, reading, dozing, and playing ring toss and other games.

Bacon went to France in 1864 and enrolled in the Ecole des Beaux-Arts. He studied there with Alexandre Cabanel and later with Edouard Frère, both of whom were representatives of conservative, academic painting in France. From these masters, Bacon learned to paint in a highly finished manner; the smooth brushstrokes, softly outlined figures, and rich colors also derive from the French Academic tradition. The unusual composition of *On Shipboard* reflects the structural experiments of these artists in the 1860s and '70s; Degas and, in a less adventurous manner, James Tissot, Cabanel, and Carolus-Duran were working with a new compositional mode that promoted a greater intimacy between the viewer and the scene depicted.[1] Figures were placed in the foreground, close to the picture plane, the scene was often viewed obliquely, and certain elements of the picture were cropped. In *On Shipboard*, Bacon borrows this device with great success: the photographic cropping of the scene, the shifting of key figures to the sides of the composition, and the resulting emphasis given to the empty foreground, create an immediate and realistic image.

Bacon did not invent the shipboard theme, although he helped to popularize it by exhibiting many such subjects at both the Salons in Paris and at the National Academy of Design in New York. His inspiration likely came from both American and European sources. In 1867, Winslow Homer published an illustration entitled *Homeward Bound* in *Harper's Weekly*; in this image, he recorded his observations of his journey home from France in 1867.[2] As Bacon would do ten years later, Homer used the oblique angles and cropping effects then being developed in French painting. Perhaps even more influential were Tissot's paintings of shipboard scenes, such as *The Last Evening* (1873; Guildhall Art Gallery, London) or *The Ball on Shipboard* (1874; Tate Gallery, London). The latter, which was exhibited at the Royal Academy in 1874, features the same isolated figure groups and empty area in the center of the composition that distinguish Bacon's picture.

1. *The Second Empire, 1852–1870: Art in France under Napoleon III,* (Philadelphia Museum of Art, 1978), p. 265.
2. *Harper's Weekly* 11 (December 21, 1867), pp. 808–809.

WINSLOW HOMER (1836-1910)

active in Boston ca. 1855–1859; in Boston frequently thereafter

57. *Boys in a Pasture*

Signed and dated lower right: *Winslow Homer N.A./1874*

Oil on canvas, 15¼ x 22½ in. (38.7 x 57.1 cm.)

Charles Henry Hayden Fund. 53.2552

PROVENANCE: Mr. Tinker, Dublin, Ireland, after 1874; Miss Tinker, Dublin (his granddaughter); Patrick O'Connor, Dublin, before 1953.

EXHIBITIONS: "American Realists," Art Gallery of Hamilton, Hamilton, Ontario, 1961, no. 28; "Triumph of Realism," Brooklyn Museum, 1967, no. 70; "The Good Life: Exhibition of American Genre Painting," St. Petersburg, Fla., 1971.

BIBLIOGRAPHY: Barbara N. Parker, "*Boys in a Pasture* by Winslow Homer," *Bulletin of the Museum of Fine Arts, Boston* 52 (December 1954), p. 89; Lloyd Goodrich, *Winslow Homer* (New York, 1959), pl. 25; Albert Ten Eyck Gardner, *Winslow Homer, American Artist: His World and His Work* (New York, 1961), p. 30; *American Paintings in the Museum of Fine Arts, Boston* (Boston, 1969), no. 562; John Wilmerding, *Winslow Homer* (New York, 1972), pp. 88-89, 108; Gordon Hendricks, *The Life and Work of Winslow Homer* (New York, 1979), pp. 110, 114.

Boys in a Pasture was probably painted at Walden, New York, at the summer home of Lawson Valentine, a friend of Homer's and a business associate of his brother Charles.[1] It is one of many compositions featuring children in a bucolic setting Homer produced in the 1870s. In those years, Homer viewed nature as benign and hospitable, a romantic vision that was underscored by the innocence of its youthful inhabitants and a style that carefully balanced the ideal and the real.

Among the earliest conceptions of this theme are *Snap the Whip* (1872; Butler Art Institute, Youngstown, Ohio), in which a group of boys plays a favorite childhood game in a broad sunny field, and the contemporary *Nooning* (Wadsworth Atheneum, Hartford), like *Boys in a Pasture* an intimate scene in which a boy pursues his daydreams in a lush meadow. During the early '70s, Homer also made several drawings and watercolors like *Three Boys on a Beached Dory* (1873; Museum of Fine Arts, Boston) which were eventually adapted for *Boys in a Pasture*. In this drawing and in other sketches of the period, Homer refined his approach to the subject: in each case he avoided portrait-like rendering by showing the boys with their faces averted or with their hats casting shadows to mask their faces. Similarly he suppressed any narrative content, and instead showed the figures as possessing a kind of mythic permanence, being large, motionless, sculpturesque forms located in the foreground and center of the composition. The figures in *Boys in a Pasture*, so skillfully drawn and naturally posed, are nonetheless icons of youthful innocence.

It was common practice for Homer to derive wood engravings from compositions already completed in oil or watercolor,[2] and in so doing, to give the image an anecdotal quality not present in the paintings. This was the case with a composition adapted from *Boys in a Pasture*: the engraving *On the Meadow,* which appeared in *Harper's Weekly* of September 19, 1874. There the boys' poses are altered to show them facing a third figure, creating an image of animated conversation rather than reverie.

In *Boys in a Pasture*, the sun-dappled foreground, created by a complex pattern of long, thin, single strokes and flecks of pigment sprinkled over a thin layer of color, is subtly rendered; the rich impasto and brilliant white of the first boy's shirt, laid in with a few sure strokes, contrasts effectively with the more delicately painted landscape. The composition of the painting has roots in mid-nineteenth century French art especially the work of the Barbizon painter Jean-François Millet, which Homer knew well in France and America. The high horizon line, the tilting up of the ground plane, pushing the figures toward the viewer, and the suppression of anecdotal detail are devices used here, as they are in Millet's work (e.g. *The Gleaners*, 1857; Louvre, Paris), to increase the iconic prominence and power of the figures. However, the content of Homer's painting—the optimistic view of nature, coupled with a romantic image of children who in the 1870s are the almost exclusive inhabitants of Homer's pictorial world—does not yet match the deep and poignant sentiment of *The Gleaners* or Millet's other works; such profundity would come in the 1880s, in the paintings made at Prout's Neck.

1. Gordon Hendricks, *The Life and Work of Winslow Homer* (New York, 1979), p. 110.
2. John Wilmerding, *Winslow Homer* (New York, 1972), p. 88.

58. *The Fog Warning*

Signed and dated lower left: *Winslow Homer 1885*

Oil on canvas, 30 x 48 in. (76.2 x 121.6 cm.)

Otis Norcross Fund. 94.72

PROVENANCE: With Doll and Richards, Boston, 1886; Laura Norcross and Grenville H. Norcross, Boston, 1893–1894.

EXHIBITIONS: Exhibition, Doll and Richards, Boston, 1886; "World's Columbian Exposition," Chicago, 1893, no. 576; "Twelfth Annual Exhibition," Carnegie Institute, Pittsburgh, 1908, no. 156; "Winslow Homer Memorial Exhibition," Museum of Fine Arts, Boston, 1911; "Homer," Philadelphia Museum of Art, 1936, no. 15; "Survey of American Painting," Carnegie Institute, Pittsburgh, 1940, no. 172; "Winslow Homer," Worcester Art Museum, 1944, no. 11; "American Heritage," Denver Art Museum, 1948, no. 44; "Winslow Homer," National Gallery of Art, Washington, 1958, no. 51; "Winslow Homer," Museum of Fine Arts, Boston, 1959, no. 47; "Directions in 20th-Century American Painting," Museum of Fine Arts, Dallas, 1961, no. 1.

BIBLIOGRAPHY: William Howe Downes, "American Painting in the Boston Art Museum," *Brush and Pencil* 6 (1900), pp. 202-204; Frederick W. Morton, "The Art of Winslow Homer," *Brush and Pencil* 10 (1902), pp. 50, 54; F. W. Coburn, "Winslow Homer's Fog Warning," *New England Magazine* n.s. 38 (1906), pp. 616-617; Leila Mechlin, "Winslow Homer," *International Studio* 34 (1908), p. cxxxv; Christian Brinton, "Winslow Homer," *Scribner's Magazine* (January 1911), p. 19; William Howe Downes, *The Life and Works of Winslow Homer* (Boston, 1911), pp. 137-140, 183; Kenyon Cox, *Winslow Homer* (New York, 1914), pp. 32, 36, 45; James Thrall Soby and Dorothy Miller, *Romantic Painting in America* (New York, Museum of Modern Art, 1943), p. 32; Lloyd Goodrich, *Winslow Homer* (New York, 1944), pp. 90-91, 100, 134, 180; Albert Ten Eyck Gardner, *Winslow Homer, American Artist* (New York, 1961), p. 214; *American Paintings in the Museum of Fine Arts, Boston*, (Boston, 1969), no. 564; John Wilmerding, *Winslow Homer* (New York, 1972), pp. 136-137, 148; Gordon Hendricks, *The Life and Work of Winslow Homer* (New York, 1979), p. 183-184, 195.

After living for two years at Cullercoats, a tiny English fishing village near Tynemouth and Newcastle on the North Sea, Homer returned to America in 1883 and settled at Prout's Neck, Maine. There he began a series of dramatic seascapes which are among his best-known works. Like Cullercoats, Prout's Neck was a small, rustic village, sparsely populated, and was not yet the fashionable resort it would become at the turn of the century. Homer may have chosen to live there because of the primordial violence of the rugged coast line, and because it afforded him the opportunity to paint undisturbed. In his paintings of the 1880s and '90s, Homer developed a subject which has appeared intermittantly in his work of the previous decade. *The Fog Warning* is one of the first major statements of this theme: man's heroic, and potentially tragic, struggle with his environment.

For the most part, Homer's paintings of the 1870s show nature as benign, and the sea as a place for pleasure and excitement (e.g., *Breezing Up*, 1876; National Gallery of Art, Washington). But a few images, such as *Waiting for Dad* (1873; collection Mr. and Mrs. Paul Mellon, Upperville, Va.), exhibit the ominous ambiguity that characterized Homer's later pictures. At Cullercoats, Homer was affected by developments in contemporary British marine painting, and accordingly his work became more picturesque and anecdotal. In watercolors such as *Watching the Tempest* (1881; Fogg Art Museum, Harvard University, Cambridge) and *Hauling the Net, Tynemouth* (1881; Art Institute of Chicago), he used local figures and landmarks as a foil for the power and drama of the sea. However, in some of those images, culminating in *Inside the Bar, Tynemouth* (1883; Metropolitan Museum of Art, New York), he reduced the narrative and topographical detail, and focused on the figures, especially the wives of the fishermen, and their stoic response to the sea.

The Prout's Neck paintings of the mid-'80s took on an increased seriousness as Homer arrived at a mature conception of the relationship between man and nature. These works focus on the fishermen themselves, and on their isolation and endurance in the face of the drudgery of daily tasks and the constant resistance of the sea. Originally called *Halibut Fishing* but retitled by Homer to emphasize the potential tragedy of the subject, *Fog Warning* is one of a series of pictures in which Homer balanced the sense of the sea's expanse and the heroic fortitude of the fishermen with an intimation of danger;[2] it is, in William Howe Downes's words, "a suggestion of peril in terms of studied restraint."[3] Contributing to the somber, desolate tone of the picture is Homer's muted palette: gray, slate blue, pale rose in the sky and on the bellies of the fish; dull browns are used for the sculpturesque form of the fisherman and his boat. Eliminating the anecdotal features found in many of the Cullercoats seascapes, Homer arrived at a composition of elemental simplicity—the man in his dory, the tiny ship on the horizon, and the cloud of fog whose shape counterbalances that of the fisherman. Homer's long, rhythmic brushstrokes render with great mastery the cresting of the waves and the violent rocking movement of the boat; the swell on which the dory rises pushes the boat up, toward the viewer, underscoring the critical distance between the fisherman and the safety of his ship on the horizon. The fisherman's averted face emphasizes his isolation, and his features are indistinct, his strong profile representative rather than particular. By these devices Homer suggests that his fisherman is fully integrated with nature; at the same time, the tensions between the heroic figure in the boat, the rolling sea, and the oncoming fog signal potential disaster.

1. *Harper's Weekly* (April 26, 1873), p. 345.
2. These works include *The Herring Net* (1885; Art Institute of Chicago), *Eight Bells* (1886; Addison Gallery of American Art, Phillips Andover Academy, Andover, Mass.), *The Life Line* (1884; Philadelphia Museum of Art), *Undertow* (1886; Sterling and Francine Clark Art Institute, Williamstown, Mass.) and many watercolors.
3. William Howe Downes, *The Life and Works of Winslow Homer* (Boston, 1911), p. 139.

FREDERIC PORTER VINTON (1846-1911)
active in Boston 1862–1911

59. *Samuel H. Russell*

Signed and dated lower left: *Fred.ᶜ P. Vinton/1880*

Oil on canvas, 54 x 34 in. (137.3 x 86.2 cm.)

Bequest of Edith, Lady Playfair. 33.531

PROVENANCE: Samuel H. Russell, Boston; Edith, Lady Playfair (his daughter), Edinburgh.

BIBLIOGRAPHY: *American Paintings in the Museum of Fine Arts, Boston* (Boston, 1969), no. 997.

Frederic Porter Vinton and John Singer Sargent were Boston's leading portraitists in the late nineteenth century. The two were not rivals; Sargent, who first came there in 1887 (about ten years after Vinton began working), used Vinton's Exeter Street studio during his early visits to the city. Sargent's Boston clients were, for the most part, women whom he painted in a flashy continental style, while Vinton specialized in men's portraits, painted in a dark and dramatic manner that conveyed the dignity and forcefulness of his sitters' personalities.

Samuel Russell was one of the first of Boston's "upper crust" to be painted by Vinton; among his other clients were Thomas Gold Appleton and Charles Francis Adams. Like William Morris Hunt, with whom he studied in the 1860s and whose studio he occupied after Hunt's death in 1879, Vinton was admired because he offered Bostonians the opportunity to be painted in the latest European portrait styles. Unlike Hunt, however, he did not disparage his portrait work, although he painted landscape with equal facility.

Samuel H. Russell bears witness to Vinton's eclectic training in Europe, where he went to study in 1876 with Léon Bonnat, a Parisian portraitist popular with expatriate Bostonians. However, this subject reflects not the Bonnat manner but rather an earlier, more robust prototype developed in France at mid-century. The strong light and thick, almost sculpted paint were first used by Courbet (see his *Portrait of Alfred Bruyas*, 1853, Musée Fabre, Montpellier) and later by Manet, as were the conventions of costume Vinton exploits so successfully here: the dark, luxurious coat set off by a bright collar and the exquisitely painted kid gloves held at the waist. Vinton's painting technique developed during his brief sojourn in Munich, made at the advice of Frank Duveneck, whom he met in Paris in 1876. Although he was not happy in Germany, he did learn from Karl von Piloty (a leading figure at Munich's Royal Academy) and especially from Duveneck the device of a scumbled, distressed backdrop painted in a rich monochrome over a light ground. The free brushwork and general emphasis on paint texture also reflects the technique of the artists in Munich, as does his practice of building tones from light to dark.

In this portrait, Vinton's characterization of his stern, aristocratic sitter is especially adept; his painterly interest, however, was in the working out of subtle color relationships. Especially skillful is the painting of the coat: the deep green of the sleeve is juxtaposed with the brown-black of the collar, through which small areas of red ground have been allowed to show through to give warmth and softness to the fur. Vinton enlivens his painting with brilliant coloristic accents such as the Holbeinesque yellow-brown gloves and the collar with purplish tie and gold stick pin, and the daring use of flecks of pink, white, and blue-gray in the hair. As with the work of his Boston contemporary Dennis Bunker, Vinton's ability as a colorist is the key to the apparent dichotomy in his style. Beginning about 1890, following a trip to France, Vinton began to experiment with Impressionism, and painted a number of landscapes (e.g., *La Blanchisseuse*, 1890, Museum of Fine Arts, Boston) whose bright palette and casual subject matter contrast markedly with the severe formal portraits for which he is best known.

FREDERICK CHILDE HASSAM (1859-1935)
active in Boston ca. 1875–1883; 1886

60. *Grand Prix Day*

Signed and dated lower left: *Childe Hassam Paris—1887*

Oil on canvas, 24 x 34 in. (61 x 78.7 cm.)

Ernest W. Longfellow Fund. 64.983

PROVENANCE: Celian M. Spitzer, Toledo, Ohio, ca. 1900; Sidney Spitzer, Toledo, 1919; with Hirschl & Adler Galleries, New York, 1964.

EXHIBITIONS: "Exhibition and Private Sale of Paintings by Mr. Childe Hassam," Noyes, Cobb & Co., Boston, 1889, no. 16; "Childe Hassam: A Retrospective Exhibition," Corcoran Gallery of Art, Washington, 1965, no. 5; "War Memorial Dedication Exhibition," Boston, 1965; "19th-Century America," Metropolitan Museum of Art, New York, 1970; "Childe Hassam," University of Arizona Musuem of Art, Tucson, 1972, no. 26; "Retrospective of a Gallery: Twenty Years," Hirschl & Adler Galleries, New York, 1973, no. 52; "Impressionism: French and American," Museum of Fine Arts, Boston, 1973, no. 111; "American Impressionist Paintings," National Gallery of Art, Washington, 1973–1974, no. 29; "Celebration," Carnegie Institute, Pittsburgh, 1974–1975, no. 12; "Masters of American Impressionism," Coe Kerr Gallery, New York, 1976, no. 10; "Paris-New York. A Continuing Romance," Wildenstein Gallery, New York, 1977, no. 69; "American Impressionism," Henry Art Gallery, Seattle, 1980.

BIBLIOGRAPHY: *American Paintings in the Museum of Fine Arts, Boston* (Boston, 1969), no. 498; Donelson Hoopes, *The American Impressionists* (New York, 1972), pp. 66-67; Mahonri Sharp Young, "Purple Shadows in the West," *Apollo* 93 (October 1973), pp. 309-310.

The Grand Prix de Paris is one of the oldest and most prestigious horse races in Europe. Beginning in 1863, it was held annually in late June at the Hippodrôme de Longchamp, a course built in 1857 in the southwest corner of the newly annexed Bois de Boulogne, Paris's equivalent of Hyde Park. Hassam shows not the race but its fashionable preliminaries: families from the residential district centered in the Boulevard Haussmann and the Champs-Elysées gathering at the Etoile to ride out to the races.

Hassam painted *Grand Prix Day* the year after he arrived in Paris. He repeated the composition in pastel (exhibited in 1891 at Doll and Richards Gallery, Boston; present location unknown) and in oil (New Britain Museum of Art, Connecticut); the latter version won a bronze medal at the Salon of 1888. These works mark a radical change in direction from his earlier compositions, which are painted in the warm brown and green tones characteristic of the Barbizon-influenced style then prevalent in Boston. Hassam was attracted to the paintings of the Impressionists as soon as he came to Paris; as is apparent in *Grand Prix Day,* he was able to incorporate into his own style the lively brushwork,

vibrant palette, and concern for light and atmosphere characteristic of those works, and used these stylistic traits in an innovative manner to represent aspects of contemporary urban life. He gravitated almost immediately to the quarter of Paris that had provided Manet, Caillebotte, Degas, and others with subject matter: the eighth *arrondissement,* which had recently been developed by Baron Haussmann, Napoleon III's Prefect of the Seine and chief city planner.[1] Hassam, like his French counterparts, painted images of upper-middle-class recreation there.

As in Manet's and Degas's pictures of Longchamp from the preceding decade,[2] Hassam was as concerned with capturing an aspect of the passing urban scene as with depicting the excitement of the race, for he set his subject not on the course at the Bois de Boulogne, but rather at the Etoile, which had become, in accordance with Baron Haussmann's plans, the new, fashionable center of Paris.[3] The key element in Hassam's representation of the bustle and conviviality of modern urban life in *Grand Prix Day* is his organization of space. His arrangement owes a debt to Degas and Caillebotte, for like them, he composed his scene in a very unacademic, untraditional way, using devices that produce a vision analogous to that of a candid photograph. By stretching a band of trees across the picture plane, and at the same time diminishing their scale from right to left, he created tension between receding and horizontal movement. The empty foreground, the lack of any real compositional focus, and the abrupt cropping of the image create a scene that is exciting because of its unconventionality, and approximates for the viewer the unselective and sweeping vision of a participant in the pageant of Grand Prix Day.

1. Anthony Sutcliffe, *The Autumn of Central Paris* (London, 1970), p. 169. The major painter of the new Paris was Gustave Caillebotte, who lived and worked in the eighth *arrondissement.* Of *Rue de Paris; Temps de Pluie* (1877; Art Institute of Chicago), which may well be Caillebotte's masterpiece, J. Kirk T. Varnedoe has noted: "Every street here was pierced, and every building built, within the artist's lifetime" (*Gustave Caillebotte, A Retrospective Exhibition* [Museum of Fine Arts, Houston, 1976], no. 25).

2. See, for example, Manet's *Race Track near Paris (Courses à Longchamp)* (1864; Art Institute of Chicago) and his watercolor *Race Course at Longchamp* (1864; Fogg Art Museum, Cambridge). Degas painted numerous scenes of horse races, among them *Before the Start* (ca. 1875, private collection, Switzerland), *Racehorses at Longchamps,* and *Carriage at the Races* (both ca. 1871; Museum of Fine Arts, Boston).

3. Sutcliffe, op. cit. See also David H. Pinckney, *Napoleon III and the Rebuilding of Paris* (Princeton, 1958) especially pp. 62-63 and 98-99.

61. *Charles River and Beacon Hill,* ca. 1890-1892

Signed lower right: *Childe Hassam*

Oil on canvas, 18 7/8 x 20 7/8 in. (48.0 x 53.0 cm.)

Arthur Gordon Tompkins Fund. 1978.178

PROVENANCE: With Doll and Richards Gallery, Boston, 1893; Frederick Amory, Boston; Margot Amory Ketchum, Boston, by 1916–1948; Phillips Ketchum, Boston, 1948–1978.

EXHIBITIONS: "Exhibition and Private Sale of Paintings by Childe Hassam," Doll and Richards Gallery, Boston, 1893, no. 27.

Boston is depicted here from a vantage point along the Charles River, looking east toward Beacon Hill over the present-day Storrow Drive. The artist stood just beyond Massachusetts Avenue at the point where the river bends northward and the land mass widens, providing a dramatically foreshortened view into the city. At the end of the vista, the gold dome of the State House gives definition to the skyline and arrests the eye's rapid progression along the embankment toward the buildings of Beacon Hill. Along the roadway at the right are the backs of houses along lower Beacon Street in the then recently developed Back Bay.

Like Paris, from which Hassam had returned only a year or two before executing this picture, Boston had grown dramatically in the years after mid-century, when the filling of the Back Bay began. For this painting, he chose a vantage point at the edge of the construction, at the place separating the newly built streets of the city from the undeveloped marshland and the suburbs beyond. While Hassam was painting, Frederick Law Olmsted was effecting plans to extend Commonwealth Avenue northwestward along the river and to develop the Back Bay Fens, then a noxious swamp, into a park that would create a "ring of green" linking the Boston Common with parks in the outlying regions of Dorchester and Jamaica Plain.[1] Hassam thus depicted the moment at which Boston was transformed from a small colonial town to a cosmopolitan center.

Hassam painted *Charles River and Beacon Hill* in the early 1890s, when he was living in New York City but was making frequent trips to Boston and rural New England. Like other works of this period, it exhibits stylistic traits reflecting the Impressionist painting Hassam had seen in Paris: fairly broad, broken brushstrokes, concern with the effects of light and atmosphere, and a radical approach to composition. The climatic conditions he chose to record here—those of a gray, blustery spring morning—called for a subdued palette based on tones of gray and brown; none-

theless, Hassam used brilliant touches of color, such as the bright blue overcoat worn by the man leaning over the railing, and the yellow dome of the State House, to enliven the surface.

Hassam's composition in *Charles River and Beacon Hill* is most unusual, and again reflects the paintings he saw in France. Like Degas and Caillebotte, he was masterful in the use of empty space, and exploited it as a vehicle for commentary on the urban scene. Here the whole center of the painting is empty. Instead, there is a road leading from the artist's vantage point straight into the heart of the scene; other pictorial elements are arranged as though part of a perspective diagram, and converge at a point close to the center of the picture. This compositional device was borrowed from paintings Hassam saw in Paris. During the 1870s, Degas and Caillebotte both experimented with this sort of "tunnel perspective," and it may be that paintings such as Caillebotte's *Pont d'Europe* (1876 Musée du Petit Palais, Geneva) inspired Hassam to use the railing, whose vertical members are placed at diminishing intervals to define accelerating recession into space.[2] As Hassam did here, the French painters used casual, seemingly unplanned cropping of the picture to create a sense of immediacy and the impromptu, suggesting what a viewer might ordinarily see as he walked down the street.

Like the artists who painted Baron Haussmann's new Paris, Hassam in *Charles River and Beacon Hill* showed the new Boston in its most important period of transition. He chose an unremarkable, yet significant viewpoint to capture the random activity of the city, while at the same time alluding to historic changes in its social fabric. He made clear that the momentous and the incidental were inseparable in the new city; with the seemingly casual placement of the figure in the blue overcoat, who looks neither at the artist nor at the new city behind him but rather gazes out at the river in a moment of private introspection, Hassam indicates the anonymity of the new urban life.

1. For a discussion of the development of the Back Bay, and of the appearance of Boston about 1890, see Walter Muir Whitehill, *Boston, A Topographical History* (Cambridge, Mass., 1963), chapter 7, especially pp. 180-181.
2. Caillebotte's painting was shown in the Third Impressionist exhibition in 1877 and remained in the artist's possession thereafter. It is interesting to compare Hassam's painting with Caillebotte's, for both contain a figure leaning over the railing who directs the viewer's eye against the hurtling perspective and who looks away from the new city and out over the unchanging river.

JOHN SINGER SARGENT (1856-1925)

active in Boston 1887–1888; 1890; 1895; 1903; 1916–1918; 1919–1920; 1921; 1923–1924

62. *Oyster Gatherers of Cancale*, 1877

Signed lower right: *J. S. Sargent/Paris*

Oil on canvas, 16¼ x 24⅛ in. (41.3 x 61.2 cm.)

Gift of Mary Appleton. 35.708

PROVENANCE: Samuel Colman, Newport, R.I.; Mary Appleton, Boston, before 1905.

RELATED WORKS: *The Oyster Gatherer,* 1877, Fine Arts Museum of San Francisco (preparatory study); *Study for Oyster Gatherers of Cancale,* 1878, location unknown; *Oyster Gatherers of Cancale,* 1878, Corcoran Gallery of Art, Washington.

EXHIBITIONS: "First Exhibition," Society of American Artists, New York, 1878, no. 23 (as *Fishing for Oysters at Cancale)*; "Memorial Exhibition of the Works of the Late John Singer Sargent," Museum of Fine Arts, Boston, 1925, no. 13; "Exhibition of Works by John Singer Sargent and Mary Cassatt," Society of the Four Arts, Palm Beach, Fla., 1959, no. 3; "Painters by the Sea," California Palace of the Legion of Honor, San Francisco, 1961; "Impressionism: French and American," Museum of Fine Arts, Boston, 1973, no. 128; "American Art in the Making," Smithsonian Institution (traveling exhibition) 1975, no. 59; "Young Painters of America," *Scribner's Monthly* 20 (1880), p. 12; William Howe Downes, *John S. Sargent: His Life and Work* (Boston, 1925), pp. 8, 120; Evan Charteris, *John Sargent* (New York, 1927), p. 281; Charles Merrill Mount, *John Singer Sargent: A Biography* (New York, 1955), p. 442; David McKibbin, *Sargent's Boston* (Boston, 1956), pp. 20-21; *American Paintings in the Museum of Fine Arts, Boston* (Boston, 1969), no. 856; Richard Ormond, *Sargent* (London, 1970), p. 235.

Painted in 1877, when Sargent was only twenty-one, *Oyster Gatherers at Cancale* is the preparatory version for a larger picture of the same subject (now in the Corcoran Gallery of Art, Washington) that Sargent submitted to the Salon of the next year. He was awarded an Honorable Mention for the picture, and from that point began to assert himself as an independent master: he would shortly leave the *atelier* of Carolus-Duran (although he would always remain close to his teacher) and was to receive his first major portrait commission the following year.

The present painting is one of several works Sargent began in the summer of 1877, when he was traveling through Brittany with fellow students Eugène Lachaise and Carroll Beckwith. Brittany's rugged, beautiful seacoast had already begun to attract many painters: Boudin had been there in the mid-1860s; Monet and Renoir would come in the 1880s to be followed by Gauguin, Serusier, and other Post-Impressionists. Several artists closer to the academic tradition also worked there, finding the unspoiled terrain an ideal background for pictures representing the labors and rituals of the Breton peasants. Although depictions of France's rural poor had outraged the public when introduced by Millet in the 1850s, they were quite popular by Sargent's time, especially when the peasants were shown as handsome figures, ennobled by their toil.[1] Having lived in Paris in the 1870s, Sargent was well versed in that tradition; his oyster gatherers, though not sentimentalized, were acceptable to the conservative Salon: they are proud, erect figures silhouetted against the sky; their costumes are ragged and picturesque.

Far more compelling than his interpretation of his subject matter is Sargent's technique: his figures are solidly drawn, his composition—a procession of vertical figures against broad stretches of sand and sky—is marked by the unerring sense of design that distinguishes his masterpieces. The color of *Oyster Gatherers* is equally effective; it is composed almost entirely of shades of blue, gray, and brown, with glittering white highlights that animate the surface. Here Sargent's free brushwork and his brilliant color harmonies evoke the silver light and damp, tangy air of the Atlantic coast town even more expressively than in the more richly colored and tightly painted final version.

About a month before the large *Oyster Gatherers* was shown in Paris, Sargent sent the smaller version to the 1878 exhibition of the Society of American Artists in New York. It was subsequently bought by the landscape painter Samuel Colman, whose explanation for his purchase of a work by an unknown artist in a style quite different from his own was a prescient tribute to Sargent's genius: "I wanted to have it near me to key myself up with. I am afraid that I may fall below just such as standard, and I wish to have it hanging in my studio to reproach me whenever I do."[2]

1. Richard Ormond, *Sargent* (London, 1970), p. 17.
2. G. W. Sheldon, *American Painters* (New York, 1879), p. 72.

63. *Mrs. Fiske Warren and her Daughter Rachel*

Signed and dated lower left: *John S. Sargent 1903*

Oil on canvas, 60 x 40⅜ in. (152.5 x 102.5 cm.)

Gift of Mrs. Rachel Warren Barton and the Emily L. Ainsley Fund. 64.693

PROVENANCE: Fiske Warren, Boston, 1903; Mrs. Fiske Warren, Boston, 1938; Mrs. Rachel Warren Barton and Hamilton Warren (her children), 1961.

EXHIBITIONS: Exhibition of Recent Paintings by John Singer Sargent, Museum of Fine Arts, Boston, 1903; "100th Anniversary Exhibition," Pennsylvania Academy of the Fine Arts, Philadelphia, 1905, no. 729; "Twentieth Anniversary Exhibition of American Oil Paintings and Sculpture," Art Institute of Chicago, 1907, no. 315; "Fifteen Annual Exhibition of Oil Paintings," Worcester Art Museum, 1912, no. 45; "Fourth Exhibition of Oil Paintings by Contemporary American Artists," Corcoran Gallery of Art, Washington, 1912, no. 33; "International Exhibition," Carnegie Institute, Pittsburgh, 1913, no. 249; "Retrospective Exhibition of Important Works by John Singer Sargent" Grand Central Art Galleries, New York, 1924, no. 11; "Memorial Exhibition of the Works of the late John Singer Sargent," Museum of Fine Arts, Boston, 1925, no. 80; "Memorial Exhibition of the Work of John Singer Sargent," Metropolitan Museum of Art, New York, 1926, no. 42; "American Painting from 1860 until Today," Cleveland Museum of Art, 1937, no. 168; "Private Collections in New England," Museum of Fine Arts, Boston, 1939, no. 122; "Half Century of American Art" Art Institute of Chicago, 1939, no. 141; "Sargent's Boston," Museum of Fine Arts Boston, 1956, no. 38; "New England Art from New England Museums," Brockton Art Center, Brockton, Mass., 1969.

BIBLIOGRAPHY: R. V. S. Berry, "John Singer Sargent," *Art and Archaeology* 18 (1924), p. 103; William Howe Downes, *John S. Sargent: His Life and Work* (Boston, 1925), p. 210; L. Mechlin, "John Singer Sargent," *Magazine of Art* 16 (1925), p. 284; Charles Merrill Mount, *John Singer Sargent: A Biography* (New York, 1955), pp. 241-245, 329; *American Paintings in the Museum of Fine Arts, Boston* (Boston, 1969), no. 868; Richard Ormond, *Sargent* (London, 1970), p. 57.

Born Margaret Osgood and called Gretchen, Mrs. Fiske Warren (1871–1961) was the daughter of a wealthy doctor from Chelsea, Massachusetts. She was educated in Europe, first in Germany (hence her nickname) and then in France, where her family resided in the 1880s. She married Fiske Warren, the fourth son of the founder of the S. D. Warren Paper Company, in 1891, and thus became connected with a family admired both for its wealth and for its remarkable art collections.[1] In her lifetime, Mrs. Warren herself was known for her abilities in several fields: she was an accomplished singer and actress, and was active as a poet, serving as president of the New England Poetry Society in 1928. Her salons were famous in Boston; she entertained a variety of prominent figures including William James, Robert Frost, Clarence Darrow, and Booker T. Washington. She is pictured here with her eldest daughter Rachel, born in 1892.

When Sargent painted Mrs. Warren on his fourth trip to Boston, he was producing between twenty and twenty-five portraits a year. For full-sized pictures like this one, he usually adhered to the conventions of formal portraiture and created grand images that elicited comparison with Van Dyck. Mrs. Warren is shown in three-quarter-length view, sitting on a large chair, her hands folded in her lap, her gaze directed toward the viewer. Her daughter leans on her shoulder in a gesture of filial devotion, but her expression is somewhat detached and melancholy. The portrait clearly indicates the social caste and type of the sitters, as high-style portraiture was meant to do, yet it also invites speculation about the character of the sitters, and about the relationship between mother and daughter.

In *Mrs. Fiske Warren and her Daughter Rachel*, Sargent employed several devices he had developed in earlier portraits. He elongated the sitter's torso and idealized her features to enhance her aristocratic demeanor (photographs of Mrs. Warren and her daughter made at the sittings for this portrait show the women to be neither as handsome nor as vapid as Sargent portrayed them). As he had for several other women's portraits, Sargent dictated Mrs. Warren's costume—he insisted on painting her wearing pink (perhaps to complement her fair coloring) and, having no suitable dress of her own, she borrowed one from her sister-in-law that was several sizes too large.[2] The element of fantasy and romance that gave his earlier costume pieces such as *El Jaleo* (1882; Isabella Stewart Gardner Museum, Boston) or *Javanese Dancing Girl* (1889; private collection, Connecticut) their exotic quality is also present, in a more calculated way, in this portrait. Painted in Isabella Stewart Gardner's new museum at Fenway Court in Boston, first opened to the public that year, Mrs. Warren is posed in a high-backed Renaissance-style chair; behind her are seen all the brilliant and bizarre accoutrements of Mrs. Gardner's Gothic Room, including a *Madonna and Child* in painted terracotta by the early Renaissance sculptor Jacopo della Quercia.

Above all, the painting is dazzling for its technique: the sweeping strokes suggest that the portrait was rapidly executed, as though Sargent were setting down his spontaneous impression of the sitter. The color scheme is bold—pinks, lavenders, and pale blues in the two women's dresses, deep brown, green, and gold in the background—and the dashing strokes of paint are supplemented by dramatic use of the palette knife: in the arm of the chair, for example, a thick white stroke edged in blue-green is paired with a darker brown one to describe the fall of a beam of light. The women's faces, however, are painted with smooth strokes in florid, overheated colors, and contrast markedly with the treatment of their dresses. The disparity in handling is at the heart of Sargent's interpretation of his sitters, combining brilliance and fluidity of surface with intimations of psychological tension.

1. The S. D. Warrens were pioneer collectors of Barbizon art and later assembled a distinguished collection of old master paintings. Edward Warren, his brother, was a brilliant collector of classical statuary, pottery, and other objects, and advised first the Museum of Fine Arts' and later the Metropolitan Museum's developing classical departments.
2. Richard Ormond, *Sargent* (London, 1970), p. 63.

64. *An Artist in his Studio*, 1904

Signed upper right: *John S. Sargent*

Oil on canvas, 22 x 28½ in. (66.0 x 71.7 cm.)

Charles Henry Hayden Fund. 05.56

PROVENANCE: Purchased from the artist, 1905.

EXHIBITIONS: "Winter Exhibition," New English Art Club, London, 1904, no. 103 (as *His Studio*); "Retrospective Exhibition of Important Works by John Singer Sargent," Grand Central Art Galleries, New York, 1924, no. 14; "Memorial Exhibition of the Works of the late John Singer Sargent," Museum of Fine Arts, Boston, 1925, no. 77; "Memorial Exhibition of the Work of John Singer Sargent," Metropolitan Museum of Art, New York, 1926, no. 45; "The Scientific Methods of Examination of Works of Art," American Academy of Arts and Sciences, Boston, 1950; "Exhibition of Works by John Singer Sargent and Mary Cassatt," Society of the Four Arts, Palm Beach, Fla., 1959, no. 13; "The Private World of John Singer Sargent," Corcoran Gallery of Art, Washington, 1964, no. 67.

BIBLIOGRAPHY: William Howe Downes, *John S. Sargent: His Life and Work* (Boston, 1925), p. 212; Evan Charteris, *John Sargent* (New York, 1927), p. 287; Charles Merrill Mount, *John Singer Sargent: A Biography* (New York, 1955), p. 448; *American Paintings in the Museum of Fine Arts, Boston* (Boston, 1969), no. 869; Richard Ormond, *Sargent* (London, 1970), pp. 254-255.

An Artist in His Studio presents a variation on a theme with which Sargent experimented several times in the 1880s. In *Paul Helleu Sketching with His Wife* (1889; Brooklyn Museum), *Claude Monet painting at the Edge of a Wood* (1887–1889; Tate Gallery, London), and *Dennis Miller Bunker Painting at Calcot* (1888; collection Daniel T. Terra, Evanston, Ill.) Sargent depicted his friends painting out-of-doors, with their wives or other companions as somewhat bored spectators. In the late 1880s, Sargent was experimenting with *plein-air* painting and Impressionist technique, but after the turn of the century his interests shifted; conse-

quently, this composition, if freely brushed, is more solidly drawn than his earlier treatments of the theme and is set indoors. The artist is shown working alone, inside his small hotel room, with a series of Barbizon-like landscape sketches propped against his unmade bed.

The artist, formerly believed to be Jean-François Raffaelli, has recently been identified as the Italian genre and landscape painter Ambrogio Raffele (1845–1928), who was with Sargent in 1904 at Purtud in the Val d'Aosta, Italy, where this was probably painted, and returned with him to that picturesque site in 1907.[1] By this time, Sargent was beginning to refuse portrait commissions in order to devote more time to landscapes and subject pictures, which he painted in both watercolor and oil. Although his skill in representing light in this picture is a natural outgrowth of the *plein-air* studies Sargent made throughout his career, it was augmented by his experiments with watercolor, which accounts for his even greater boldness in the use of white.

An Artist in His Studio is an especially rich pictorial *tour-de-force*, an essay, not without satiric aspects, on the art of painting. Beginning with the perennial favorite theme, the picture within a picture, Sargent showed no less than five paintings: scattered around the room are four sketches on artist's board, some of which seem to be studies, made out-of-doors, for the larger canvas, a somewhat pedestrian bucolic scene. The crumpled sheets, painted white with blue and brown strokes defining contours, form a brilliant drapery study. The painter, contemplating his canvas, sits in shadow at the foot of the bed, his brushes fanned out before him. Light pours in over his shoulder, throwing his hand into deep shadow against his palette, on which the daubs of bright pigment are made vividly tangible by Sargent's thick impasto.

1. Richard Ormond, *Sargent* (London, 1970), pp. 254-255.

173

DENNIS MILLER BUNKER (1861-1890)
active in Boston 1885–1889

65. *The Pool, Medfield*

Signed and dated lower left: *D. M. Bunker/1889*

Oil on canvas, 18⅜ x 24¼ in. (46.7 x 61.7 cm.)

Emily L. Ainsley Fund. 45.475

PROVENANCE: Arthur T. Cabot, Boston; Trustees of the estate of Arthur T. Cabot, 1912.

EXHIBITIONS: "Dennis Miller Bunker," Museum of Fine Arts, Boston, 1943, no. 15; "American Painting from 1865 to 1905," The Art Gallery of Toronto, 1961, no. 8; "American Traditional Painters," American Federation of Arts, New York, 1962; Boston Painters," Museum of Fine Arts, Boston, 1971; "Revealed Masters: 19th-Century American Art," American Federation of Arts, New York, 1974, no. 12; "Impressionism: French and American," Museum of Fine Arts, Boston, 1973, no. 93; "Dennis Miller Bunker Rediscovered," New Britain Museum of Art, New Britain, Conn., 1978, no. 34.

BIBLIOGRAPHY: R. H. Ives Gammell, *Dennis Miller Bunker* (New York, 1953), pp. 56-57, pl. 17a; *American Paintings in the Museum of Fine Arts, Boston* (Boston, 1969), no. 187.

Dennis Bunker matured early as an artist. By 1889, when he painted *The Pool, Medfield,* he had been exposed to a variety of artistic styles, beginning with the bravura technique of William Merritt Chase, with whom he studied at the Art Students' League, and the academic style of J.-L. Gérôme, under whose tutelage he worked at the Ecole des Beaux-Arts in Paris in the early 1880s. He spent several summers with Abbott Thayer and with John Singer Sargent, both only slightly older than he; their works served as catalysts for Bunker at different moments of his development. In 1889, Bunker, then only twenty-nine years old, had been exhibiting at the National Academy of Design for nine years; he was well known in Boston, was working on several important portrait commissions,[1] and was teaching at the newly founded Cowles Art School. During this period he adopted and discarded several different styles reflecting the influence of his numerous teachers and peers, and although when he died in 1890 he had not yet settled upon his own distinctive style, Bunker's technical ability was considerable and his paintings surprisingly sophisticated and successful.

The Pool, Medfield is one of a series of landscapes Bunker painted at Medfield, a small town about fifteen miles southwest of Boston, during the summers of 1888 and 1889. Most of the work he produced during the two preceding years had been portraits or figure paintings, and he went to Medfield to develop his skills as a landscape painter. He was especially interested in recording the changing appearance of landscape under different conditions of light and atmosphere. Although the weather there was consistently good, and so led Bunker to speak disappointedly about the lack of variety and challenge, he nonetheless described Medfield with affection as "a funny charming little place, about as big as a pocket-handkerchief with a tiny river, tiny willows and a tiny brook."[2]

The brook was the subject of several compositions Bunker painted those summers; they mark a departure from his earlier, Barbizon-inspired landscapes painted in 1884 and 1885. They are full-fledged Impressionist paintings, executed with a secure knowledge of the French painters' innovations in color and composition. Bunker was first exposed to *plein-air* painting in the early 1880s in Paris, where the works of the Impressionists were frequently exhibited; his experiments with a lighter palette and looser brushwork were further encouraged by John Singer Sargent, with whom he traveled and painted in England in the summer of 1888.

In *The Pool, Medfield,* Bunker emulates the Impressionists' technique of juxtaposing long, blunt strokes of pure color—for example, strokes of green dragged over bright blue in the foreground of *The Pool, Medfield*—in order to create on canvas the appearance of nature with colors that are not, strictly speaking, naturalistic. Academic drawing, such as Bunker would have learned from Gérôme, was set aside in favor of a technique whereby individual strokes and daubs of pure color combine visually to represent whole objects, as is the case in the middle ground, where yellow and pink strokes suggest wildflowers. Most radical was Bunker's composition, which echoes Monet's paintings of the meadows along the Seine painted in the early 1880s and especially Manet's marine paintings of the 1860s.[3] In those works, the artists showed a vertical slice of space, in which distance is compressed and peripheral views limited in order to create a greater sense of immediacy and proximity to nature. Bunker, whose composition here is especially close to Monet's *Champ de Blé* (1881, Cleveland Museum of Art), uses the same devices for a similar effect: little panoramic vision is allowed for; rather, the stream widens rapidly just at the spectator's feet, and the unusually high horizon line and tipped-up ground plane accelerate the rapid recession into space traced by the stream. The result is a lively tension between the pattern of brushstroke and color on the surface of the canvas and a compelling recession into distance, where the eye is caught by the little yellow house (possibly Bunker's boarding house) on the horizon.

1. For example, the portraits of John Lowell Gardner II (Portland Museum of Art, Portland, Me.), Samuel Endicott Peabody (Groton School, Groton, Mass.), and George Augustus Gardner (Museum of Fine Arts, Boston).

2. Dennis Bunker, quoted in R. H. Ives Gammell, *Dennis Miller Bunker* (New York, 1953), p. 56.

3. Most instructive is Manet's innovative construction of space in *The Battle of the Kearsarge and the Alabama* (1864; Philadelphia Museum of Art), which was exhibited in 1884 at Durand-Ruel's Gallery in Paris, where Bunker undoubtedly saw it. Monet used high horizons and compressed spaces frequently during the 1880s; paintings such as *Meadow at Giverny in Autumn* (Museum of Fine Arts, Boston) are close to Bunker's work in both spatial organization and compositional elements.

66. *Jessica*

Signed and dated lower left: *D. M. Bunker. 1890*

Oil on canvas, 26⅛ x 24 in. (66.4 x 61.2 cm.)

Gift by contribution. 91.130

PROVENANCE: Mrs. Alpheus Hardy, Boston, 1890; Gift by contribution, 1891.

EXHIBITIONS: "Catalogue of an Exhibition of the Pictures of Dennis Miller Bunker," St. Botolph Club, Boston, 1891, no. 18; "Dennis Miller Bunker," Museum of Fine Arts, Boston, 1943, no. 8; "Dennis Miller Bunker," Museum of Fine Arts, Boston, 1945, no. 4; "American Painting from 1800–1915," Maryhill Museum of Fine Arts, Maryhill, Washington, 1956; "In Summer's Light," Crapo Gallery, Swain School of Design, New Bedford, Mass., 1967.

BIBLIOGRAPHY: W. H. Downes, "American Paintings in the Boston Art Museum," *Brush and Pencil* 6 (1900), pp. 208, 210; R. H. Ives Gammell, *Twilight of Painting* (New York, 1947), pl. 47; ————, *Dennis Miller Bunker* (New York, 1953), pp. 54-55; *American Paintings in the Museum of Fine Arts, Boston* (Boston, 1969), no. 188; Charles B. Ferguson, *Dennis Miller Bunker (1861–1900) Rediscovered* (New Britain, Conn., 1978), pp. 3, 21, 22, no. 38.

In the late 1880s, Bunker spoke about the artistic climate in Boston with increasing frustration and bitterness. He believed that New York City was the only place in America that he could find the excitement and stimulation he had once known in Paris, and in the winter of 1889 he moved there, establishing his studio at 3 Washington Square North. His old friend Abbott Thayer and the pastelist and painter Thomas Dewing were in residence in the same building, and his close relationship with them over that winter may well have rekindled Bunker's interest in figure painting.

When he moved to New York, Bunker gave up the lucrative portrait commissions that had been his mainstay in Boston. Instead, he turned to working with professional models, as was the practice of many of his contemporaries in New York. One of these models posed for *Jessica* and may well have contributed her name to the title of the painting.[1] There is no evidence to suggest that Jessica was either a portrait of some now-forgotten patron of Bunker's or inspired by some literary or dramatic character; rather, the subject reflects the vogue for idealized female figures that was prevalent at the end of the nineteenth century.

Like Dewing, Thayer, George DeForest Brush, and other artists who portrayed delicate young women as embodiments of purity and virtue, Bunker rendered Jessica as a graceful and somewhat wistful figure who represents a feminine ideal. The type to which she belongs appeared in painting at about the same time that Henry Adams was writing his *Education,* and illustrates the character of Adams's "Virgin"; that is, a woman whose timeless beauty preserves the values of an earlier era, and whose grace and serenity enable the world around her to maintain a certain morality, harmony, and equilibrium in the face of disturbing forces of change.

Artists of the Renaissance Revival like Thayer and Brush, who painted this subject repeatedly in the late nineteenth century, often expressed the notion that the ideal woman was a timeless, universal figure by clothing her in vaguely antiquarian dress. In contrast, Bunker's conception of the type is closer to an actual portrait. Jessica's features, though softly painted, are carefully delineated and individualized; her surroundings and her expression suggest a personality characterized by gentleness and restraint. She wears a dress of the period and stands before an ebony mirror, a fashionable piece of furniture in the 1890s. Despite the contemporaneity of her clothes and furnishings, the mood of the painting is nostalgic and subdued. Jessica's dress is rather plain, and she wears no jewelry, an indication that she is not dressed to go out; her hair is arranged in an old-fashioned style. Her downcast eyes, which gaze neither in the mirror nor out at the viewer, suggest that she is occupied with her own thoughts. The black dress, her meditative expression, and the vagueness of her surroundings create a somber, almost mournful mood.

Although the striking profile view and bold color contrasts of *Jessica* were common features of many Renaissance Revival images of the period, here Bunker was inspired by a different model: the notorious *Madame X* (1884; Metropolitan Museum of Art, New York), which his friend John Singer Sargent had exhibited in the Salon of 1884 (where Bunker first saw it) and kept in his studio thereafter. In *Jessica,* Bunker emulated that figure's severe and aristocratic profile silhouetted against a plain, dark ground, albeit in a more modest, even domestic fashion. Bunker's work is far less stylized, less calculated, less extreme than Sargent's masterpiece, although his color scheme is equally austere, his sense of design as abstract. He seems to have taken Sargent's sophisticated image and reformed it into a vision that was in keeping with the idealized and introspective view of the American woman of his time. It is not known whether Bunker was satisfied with *Jessica,* but the differences between his picture and its inspiration may well have served as an ironic reminder of the differences between the dull, provincial world of Boston (from which he had just fled but which this picture, with its emphasis on gentility rather than eroticism, suggests he had not entirely escaped) and the brilliant climate in Paris, which he had known only too briefly.

1. After his marriage to Eleanor Hardy in October 1890, Bunker would use only his wife as a model. That "Jessica" is not Eleanor Bunker, and thus was painted before the winter of 1890, is indicated by Mrs. Bunker (later Mrs. Charles Platt) in a letter written to W. G. Constable in December 1942 (Paintings Department files, Museum of Fine Arts, Boston), and is confirmed by comparing "Jessica" with the figure of Mrs. Bunker in *The Artist's Mirror* (1890; Metropolitan Museum of Art, New York).

JOHN J. ENNEKING (1838-1916)
active in Boston 1868–1872; 1876–1916

67. *The Rundy House on the Neponset River,* 1890

Signed lower right: *Enneking*

Oil on canvas, 26¼ x 36 in. (66.5 x 91.5 cm.)

Gift of Morton C. Bradley, Jr. in memory of Robert C. Vose. 1976.753

PROVENANCE: With Vose Galleries, Boston; Morton C. Bradley, Jr., Arlington, Mass.

EXHIBITIONS: "Colonial Dames of Massachusetts Prize Exhibition," Boston, n.d.; "John J. Enneking, American Impressionist," Brockton Art Center, Brockton, Mass., 1972, no. 35.

The Neponset River, which flows near Enneking's home in Hyde Park, southwest of Boston, was the setting for many of his paintings in the 1880s and '90s. An ardent conservationist, Enneking painted landscapes dramatizing the purity of nature he worked hard to preserve during those years. He specialized in autumnal scenes, frequently without figures or with figures nearly obscured by foliage, as here. Enneking's subject in *The Rundy House*—a modest homestead hidden in dense woods, viewed from an intimate perspective—and his green-brown palette, reflect the works of the Barbizon School, the major artistic influence in Boston from the 1860s; his acquaintance with the Barbizon painter Charles Daubigny in France in the 1870s may also have influenced his vision. However, his technique of freely brushed, scumbled paint, resulting in a heavily impastoed surface, is not Barbizon but rather, can be attributed to a brief period of study in 1872 at the Royal Academy in Munich, and also to the influence of the much-admired figure painter George Fuller, with whom he shared a studio in the 1880s. In Enneking's later pictures, composition was dominated by technique, and individual forms were absorbed by the thickly brushed surface pattern in a manner that is often called Impressionist but is, in fact, closer to the mystical late works of George Inness and Ralph Blakelock. Here the balance between linear and painterly values has been maintained, so that forms retain their integrity and space recedes legibly without loss of textural richness on the picture surface.

Although little known today, at the turn of the century Enneking was greatly admired, as Fuller had been, for his expression of traditional New England rural values and for his noble ideals:

He possessed a rich vein of nature sentiment, and he found means to express this in an eloquent and forceful manner . . . His autumnal sunset and twilight scenes have a solemnity of feeling that is most striking in its appeal to the sensibilities of the observer, and they embody the mild and gentle melancholy of the season perhaps more perfectly than the pictures of any other American landscapist.[1]

1. William Howe Downes, obituary of John J. Enneking, *Boston Evening Transcript* (November 17, 1916).

JOHN APPLETON BROWN (1844-1902)
active in Boston 1865-1902

68. *Early Summer*, ca. 1890

Signed lower left: *Appleton Brown*

Oil on canvas, 29⅛ x 36¼ in. (74.0 x 92.0 cm.)

Gift of the Estate of Mrs. G. H. Champlin. 11.1279

So strong was William Morris Hunt's influence in Boston that, on his example, young painters automatically chose Paris, rather than any other city in Europe, for their artistic education. After only a year in Boston's Studio Building, where Hunt, George Inness, and E. W. Longfellow were working, Brown went to Paris in 1866. There he made copies of old master paintings in the Louvre (as generations of Bostonians had before him), then studied with the landscape painter Emile Lambinet. However, his early work was less indebted to Lambinet than to the Barbizon painters Daubigny and especially Corot, whose subtle palette and feathery paint textures he emulated. His interest in Barbizon painting was reinforced by a second trip to France in 1875, when he painted at Ville d'Avray, where Corot had worked, and exhibited at the Salon. When he returned to Boston, he was embraced by local patrons of the arts, who were eagerly buying Barbizon paintings and were also collecting the work of American artists who painted in the Barbizon manner.

The zenith of Brown's popularity coincided with Boston's first exposure to Impressionist landscape in the late 1880s. Paintings like *Early Summer,* with its high-keyed palette, grainy brushstrokes, and irregularly textured surface (with the coarse weave of the canvas exploited for additional textural effect) does parallel, albeit in a conservative way, Monet's Giverny landscapes of the 1880s. Also similar is the depiction of a view that, except for the small house nearly hidden by shrubbery in the far distance, is totally devoid of human presence; was neither symbolic nor sociological (as earlier American and French landscape had been) but merely suggests the effects of light in nature at a particular season and moment.

Brown's contact with Impressionism came through artists working at Broadway, in Worcestershire, England, where he spent the spring and summer of 1886. Those painters—John Singer Sargent, Frank D. Millet, and Charles Parsons—were experimenting with Impressionist techniques (loose brushwork, bright palette, informal composition, and above all, painting out-of-doors), while retaining a solidity of form and drawing that distinguished their work from that of their French counterparts. This fidelity to drawing and solid design is equally evident in *Early Summer,* giving the landscape a monumental and permanent, rather than a transitory aspect. In Boston, Dennis Miller Bunker (who worked at Broadway in 1888) used a palette and technique similar to Brown's: both painted with cool greens and deep blues and purples, and enlivened the broad foregrounds of their pictures with daubs of white, lavender, and yellow. But whereas Bunker's colors in paintings like *The Pool, Medfield* (cat. no. 67) were robust, Brown's were pastel-like and silvery; where Bunker tilted up his ground plane to provide a close inspection of the lush meadow, Brown's viewpoint was more panoramic and more traditional.

Brown was widely praised in his own time; his view of nature was compared not with that of other painters but with poets such as Keats and Wordsworth. Presumably the comparisons referred to those poets' most felicitious moments, for Brown was admired above all for his sunny temperament and good cheer, which was believed to have found perfect expression in his works. Called "Appleblossom Brown" because of his predilection for spring scenes with blossoming trees (as here), his work won favor for precisely that mood of optimism and sense of well-being that seems somewhat saccharine today:

No trace is discernible of Nature's harsher moods, of tempest, strife, cold, darkness, sullen hours, frowning aspects, melancholy portents. His brush was ever busy with the smiling, luminous, sweet and serene phases of the rural world.[1]

1. William Howe Downes, obituary of John J. Enneking, *Boston American Magazine of Art* 14 (August 1923), p. 436.

MAURICE PRENDERGAST (1859-1924)

active in Boston ca. 1887–1914 (made frequent trips to Europe during this time)

69. *Race Track*, ca. 1900

Signed lower right: *Prendergast*

Oil on canvas, 23 x 20⅝ in. (58.5 x 52.4 cm.)

Emily L. Ainsley Fund. 62.321

PROVENANCE: Charles Prendergast; Mrs. Charles Prendergast, Westport, Conn.

EXHIBITIONS: "Impressionism: French and American," Museum of Fine Arts, Boston, 1973, no. 123; "Maurice Prendergast: Art of Impulse and Color," University of Maryland Art Gallery, College Park, Md., 1976, no. 30; "Early Twentieth-Century Landscape Paintings," Alpha Gallery, Boston, 1979.

BIBLIOGRAPHY: *American Paintings in the Museum of Fine Arts, Boston* (Boston, 1969), no. 816.

Behind Prendergast's idyllic view of a summer day spent at the race track lies an intensely ambitious artistic vision. In paintings like this one, and in the similarly constructed watercolors of the period, Prendergast was striving to create a new style, one independent of the traditional rules of picture making, and so free of narrative content and of the formal trappings of painterly illusionism. Yet he differed from his fellow modernists working in France and America, who used abstraction to define more completely and objectively the elements and attitudes of contemporary life. Instead, Prendergast used those elements—the women in white dresses and parasols, the little children playing on the beach—as a point of departure, repeating them endlessly over the surface of his picture in order to achieve a rich, decorative abstraction.

The subject of this picture, the race track, was part of a larger theme of urban recreation that was the starting point for most of Prendergast's designs. At the turn of the century he was back in Boston, living with his brother Charles, having spent most of the previous decade in France and Italy. He found in New York City and New England subjects similar to those he had been painting in Paris and Venice, and produced many watercolors and a few oils of Central Park, Franklin Park in Boston (where he probably witnessed this scene), and resorts along the coast of Maine. A sporting subject—however tangential the actual sport is to the picture—is somewhat unusual in Prendergast's oeuvre; he customarily painted quieter pastimes such as bathing or strolling in the park, and here he showed not the excitement of the race but rather some moment before or after the event begins.[1]

During his many years in Paris, Prendergast came to know the works by painters such as Degas, Manet, and Caillebotte who also painted the recreation of the new urban middle class. Although contemporary critics called him a Boston Impressionist,[2] neither his style nor his approach to subject matter were significantly affected by those French masters. Degas, Caillebotte, and others, eager to document the new industrial Paris, filled their paintings with the landmarks of Baron Haussmann and through various pictorial devices indicated the motion and energy of the fast-paced, modern city. In contrast, Prendergast's figures in *Race Track* are static and hieratic; there is no sense of specific time and place. Nor does he use devices such as the photographic close-up views and cropping with which the Impressionists suggested the casualness and sudden intimacy of daily life. Such techniques were alien to Prendergast's experience, for unlike Degas and Caillebotte, he was painting a world to which he did not belong, from which he was excluded because of his class, his lack of education, and his poverty. His distance from his scenes of middle-class leisure is reflected in his style.

Rack Track is peopled with generalized, faceless, almost pictographic figures, most of whom are turned away from the viewer. They are arranged in a frieze-like manner across the picture plane, shown frontally or in strict profile. Even the horses in the middle ground are motionless silhouettes; the two placed perpendicular to the picture plane are facing away from the viewer; not charging toward him as Manet would have done to dramatize the excitement of the race. And despite the gradual diminuation of forms, the illusion of recession into space is countered by the sharply tipped-up ground plane and the repeating patterns of color and shape that the eye perceives as a decorative design on the picture surface.

1. A sketch of ball players (no. 61, 1899 watercolor notebook, Museum of Fine Arts, Boston) shows the same emphasis on the spectators, not the sport.
2. *San Francisco Chronicle*, May 13, 1900, as discussed in *Maurice Prendergast: Art of Impulse and Color*, (University of Maryland Art Gallery, College Park, Md., 1977), p. 42.

70. *Woman in a Brown Coat,* ca. 1908

Signed lower left: *Prendergast*

Oil on canvas, 26 x 23¼ in. (66.0 x 59.1 cm.)

Gift of Mrs. Charles Prendergast in honor of Perry T. Rathbone. 68.585

PROVENANCE: Charles Prendergast; Mrs. Charles Prendergast, Westport, Conn.

EXHIBITIONS: "Maurice Prendergast, Charles Hopkinson, Charles Hovey Pepper," Copley Society, Boston, 1911.

Prendergast's model for *Woman in a Brown Coat* was probably Edith Lawrence King (1884–1975), whom he painted on at least two other occasions between 1908 and 1913. In both of those paintings (*Portrait of a Girl with Flowers,* Metropolitan Museum of Art, New York, and *La Rouge,* Anna E. Wilson Memorial Collection, Lehigh University, Bethlehem, Pa.), Prendergast shows King seated with a vase of flowers in the background, as here, combining his renewed concern for figure painting with experiments in still life. He would be increasingly occupied with those genres in the 1910s, yet none of his images of King are conventional portraits, and his concern for rendering likeness was subordinate to his interest in color and decorative pattern. In *Woman in a Brown Coat,* King's features are generalized and relatively expressionless, while the portrait exhibits remarkable coloristic freedom. Prendergast's palette consists of deep tones of blue, green, and rust-brown, a subdued harmony animated by touches of blood red in King's jaw, eyebrows, and sleeve, and pale yellow and lavender on her cheek. Prendergast was also more interested in surface design than in indications of volume or three-dimensional space: the all-over pattern of large, square brushstrokes, reminiscent of Cézanne's technique, flattens the image into a lively mosaic; the dashing outline of the lapel of her coat, the contour of her broad-brimmed hat, and the strong curves of the vase of flowers are rendered with a linear flourish more decorative than descriptive.

Prendergast probably became acquainted with King while she was teaching at the Buckingham School in Cambridge, Mass. They shared an interest in decoration: while at Buckingham School, King and fellow-teacher Dorothy Coit began designing costumes and scenery for children's plays, an activity which led them to found the King-Coit School of Acting and Design (later the King-Coit Children's Theater) in New York in 1923. During those years, King was also developing her talents as a painter. She traveled to Capri about 1910 and worked with Prendergast there, and exhibited several watercolors in a style quite similar to Prendergast's at the Armory Show in 1913.[1]

1. Doreen Bolger Burke, *American Paintings in the Metropolitan Museum of Art* (New York, 1980), vol. 3, pp. 340-343.

EDMUND CHARLES TARBELL (1862-1938)
active in Boston 1881–1882; 1886–1917; 1925–1938

71. *Edward Robinson*

Signed and dated lower left: *Edmund C. Tarbell 1906*

Oil on canvas, 44 x 34 in. (111.7 x 86.4 cm.)

Charles Henry Hayden Fund. 06.1895

PROVENANCE: Purchased from the artist, 1906.

EXHIBITIONS: "Twentieth Annual Exhibition," Art Institute of Chicago, 1907, no. 370; "Edmund Tarbell," Montross Gallery, New York, 1907, no. 3; "Twenty-Third Annual Exhibition," Herron Museum of Art, Indianapolis, 1908, no. 73; "Exhibition of Paintings by Ten American Painters," Pennsylvania Academy of the Fine Arts, Philadelphia, 1908, no. 79; "Edmund Tarbell," Corcoran Gallery of Art, Washington, 1908, no. 28; "Annual Exhibition," National Academy of Design, New York, 1909; "Paintings by Edmund Tarbell," Copley Society, Boston, 1912, no. 36; "Edmund Tarbell," Montross Gallery, New York, 1912, no. 13; "Edmund Tarbell," M. Knoedler and Co., New York, 1918, no. 26; "Nineteenth Anniversary Show," Copley Society, Boston, 1966.

BIBLIOGRAPHY: *American Paintings in the Museum of Fine Arts, Boston* (Boston, 1969), no. 965.

Trained first in law and then in archaeology, Edward Robinson (1858–1931) was appointed assistant curator in classical archaeology at the Museum of Fine Arts, Boston, in 1885. He brought to this position several years of exposure to classical art in Greece and Italy and more formal academic training at the University of Berlin. Two years after his initial appointment, he was made the first curator of the newly formed Department of Classical Antiquities. During the next fifteen years he bought many important original objects for the Museum and expanded its collection of plaster casts, which he believed were an important aspect of the institution's educational responsibilities. Robinson became director of the Museum in 1902 and developed the initial plans for its new building on Huntington Avenue, but a dispute with the trustees over the use and placement of the plaster cast collection in the new galleries caused him to submit his resignation in 1905. Later that year, he became assistant director, and in 1910, director, of the Metropolitan Museum in New York, a position he held until his death.[1] In 1906, the trustees of the Museum of Fine Arts

commissioned one of the city's leading portraitists, Edmund Tarbell, to paint Robinson and Charles Greeley Loring (1905; Museum of Fine Arts, Boston), Robinson's predecessor as director.

Tarbell was a founding member of the Ten American Painters and a leading figure among the artists associated with the Boston School. Like many of his colleagues, his first formal training came from Otto Grundmann and Frederic Crowninshield at the School of the Museum of Fine Arts. In 1881 he and his friend Frank Benson went to Paris and enrolled at the Académie Julian; more important for their education were their travels in England, Italy, and Germany. In 1885, Tarbell returned to Boston, where during the next decade John Singer Sargent, Dennis Bunker, and the portraitist Frederic Vinton dominated the artistic community. By the 1890s, Tarbell was well known as a painter of figure subjects in an Impressionist manner, and began to receive many important commissions. He painted this portrait at the height of his career.

Tarbell depicted Edward Robinson in his study, with the books and papers that were the attributes of his position in the background. The three-quarter length, seated pose and dark setting Tarbell used were characteristic of the style of portraiture that had been popular in Boston since the 1880s; as in the formal portraits by his predecessors Vinton and Bunker, his sitter's face is strongly illuminated and details of costume and setting are minimized to focus attention on Robinson's intense expression, the indication of his forceful personality. Tarbell's fluid technique—the freely applied long individual strokes of color, particularly noticeable on Robinson's vest and on the pile of books and papers behind him—marks a departure from his Impressionist manner of the 1890s and reflects the influence of John Singer Sargent, who had been painting in Boston in 1903, and whose portrait of Robinson (1903; Metropolitan Museum of Art, New York) no doubt deeply affected Tarbell's own image.

1. Walter Muir Whitehill, *Museum of Fine Arts, Boston, A Centennial History* (Cambridge, Mass., 1970), p. 146.

72. *Reverie (Katherine Finn)*

Signed and dated lower left: *Tarbell—1913*

Oil on canvas, 50¼ x 34⅛ in. (127.5 x 86.7 cm.)

Bequest of Georgina S. Cary. 33.400

PROVENANCE: Georgina S. Cary, Boston, by 1915.

EXHIBITIONS: "Panama-Pacific International Exposition," San Francisco, 1915, no. 3950; "American Painting 1875–1925," Maryhill Museum of Fine Arts, Maryhill, Wash., 1956, no. 22; "Painting by 19th and 20th-Century American Artists," Percy Whitney Art Center, Fairhope, Ala., 1968; "Turn of the Century Boston Impressionists," State Street Bank and Trust Co., Boston, 1968; "60th Anniversary Celebration," Guild of Boston Artists, Boston, 1974; "Beginnings," Guild of Boston Artists, Boston, 1979.

BIBLIOGRAPHY: R. H. Ives Gammell, *Twilight in Painting* (New York, 1946), pl. 60; *American Paintings in the Museum of Fine Arts, Boston* (Boston, 1969), no. 967.

By 1913, when Tarbell painted *Reverie,* he was well known in Boston as a portraitist and figure painter. His model for this picture, Katherine Finn (1893–1918), was a student at the School of the Museum of Fine Arts, where Tarbell had been on the faculty since 1889. She came to Tarbell's attention through his student Georgina Cary, for whom she had posed; he subsequently asked Finn to pose for him for several pictures painted in 1912 and 1913.[1] Having found a congenial model, Tarbell was able to develop the popular turn-of-the-century theme of a young woman in a fashionable interior setting, and at the same time to experiment with styles and techniques distinct from his own. This image of woman as both an ideal and a decorative object, indicated by her handsome generalized features, thoughtful expression, and filmy white dress, appeared in the works of Abbott Thayer, Thomas Dewing, and other artists associated with the Beaux-Arts style, as well as in the paintings of Tarbell's Boston School colleagues Frank Benson and Joseph DeCamp.

Although *Reverie* was painted the year the Armory Show came to Boston, Tarbell was unaffected by the radical modern paintings in the exhibition, and instead chose to paint a work reflecting the influence of Post-Impressionist artists like Edouard Vuillard, whose decorative, patternistic images of women in interiors he had known since his days at the Académie Julian, and especially of J. A. M. Whistler, who in the 1860s had inaugurated the theme of handsome, contemplative women dressed in white.[2] Like Whistler's *White Girl* (1862; National Gallery of Art, Washington), Tarbell's painting of Katherine Finn is more an ideal composition than a portrait; it is, in fact, a pure study of mood. Under Whistler's influence, Tarbell abandoned both the academic manner of his portraiture and the Impressionistic style of his earlier figure subjects, and instead emphasized decorative design. The figure is pushed far to the right in the composition, and turns toward the center, her elbows resting on a pillow, an odd pose that was deliberately contrived. The profile view, which Whistler frequently employed, and the graceful gesture of resting the chin on the back of the hands distance the subject from the viewer, and emphasizes the mood of isolation and self-absorption. The spray of flowers, decoratively painted at upper right, is a self-conscious Whistlerian touch, and the Japanese screen in the background also reflect that master's influence.

Tarbell's technique in *Reverie* reflects that of another artist long influential in Boston: John Singer Sargent, whose most recent visit to that city resulted in a number of remarkable portraits. In *Mrs. Fiske Warren* (cat. no. 65), for example, Sargent painted with a light palette and a lively brushstroke, frequently dragging a dry brush over an already heavily impastoed surface. Such dry, crusty brushwork, very different from Tarbell's usual style, is apparent in *Reverie,* especially in the model's dress.

1. According to Patricia Jobe Pierce (letter to the author), Finn posed for *Young Lady with a Hat* and *Woman with a Corsage* in addition to *Reverie.*

2. Several major exhibitions of Whistler's work, including paintings such as *The White Girl* and *Purple and Rose: The Large Lijzen of the Six Marks* (1864; John G. Johnson Coll., Philadelphia) were held in the preceding decade, e.g., at Copley Hall, Boston, in 1904 and at the Metropolitan Museum in New York in 1910. Sargent's work was highly visible in Boston, and *Mrs. Fiske Warren* was shown in several public exhibitions during this period, including exhibitions in Worcester and at the Corcoran Gallery in Washington in which Tarbell and his friends participated.

FRANK W. BENSON (1862-1951)
active in Boston 1874-1951

73. *Eleanor*

Signed and dated lower left: *F. W. Benson/1907*

Oil on canvas, 25 x 30 in. (63.5 x 76.2 cm.)

Charles Henry Hayden Fund. 08.326

PROVENANCE: Purchased from the artist, 1908.

EXHIBITIONS: "Twentieth Annual Exhibition," Doll and Richards Gallery, Boston, 1907 (as *Lady in Pink);* "Ten American Painters," Pennsylvania Academy of the Fine Arts, Philadelphia, 1908, no. 4; "Frank Weston Benson," St. Botolph Club, Boston, 1910, no. 4; "Paintings, Etchings and Drawings by Frank W. Benson," Corcoran Gallery of Art, Washington, 1912, no. 13; "Frank W. Benson," Carnegie Institute, Pittsburgh, 1924, no. 8; "Frank W. Benson," Akron Art Institute, 1924, no. 15; "Frank W. Benson," Essex Institute, Salem, Mass., 1956, no. 7; "In Summer's Light," Crapo Gallery, Swain School of Design, New Bedford, Mass., 1967; "Boston Painters 1720–1940," Boston University School of Fine and Applied Arts, Boston, 1968, no. 7; "Impressionism: French and American," Museum of Fine Arts, Boston, 1973, no. 91; "Ten American Impressionists: Frank Weston Benson and Edmund C. Tarbell," University Art Galleries, University of New Hampshire, Durham, 1979, no. 14; "American Impressionism," Henry Art Gallery, Seattle, 1980.

BIBLIOGRAPHY: *American Paintings from the Museum of Fine Arts, Boston* (Boston, 1969), no. 96; Patricia Jobe Pierce, *The Ten* (Concord, N.H., 1976), p. 52.

Like several generations of Bostonians before him, Frank Benson sought his artistic education in Paris, where he profited both from academic training and from exposure to more innovative painting gleaned from attending dealers' shows and visiting artist-friends in their studios. He combined these two aspects of his education—the academic and the avant-garde Impressionist and Post-Impressionist styles—in a manner that would characterize the work of a group of early twentieth-century American artists known as the Boston School. The leading figures of this movement—Benson, Edmund Tarbell, and Joseph DeCamp—had similar European educations. They were also members of the Ten American Artists, a group of painters who broke away from the powerful Society of American Artists in 1897 and began to exhibit their paintings, all generally Impressionist in style, at Durand-Ruel's New York gallery. The association of the Ten continued intermittently for twenty years; the influence of the Boston School was even more enduring, for Benson, Tarbell, and DeCamp were all members of the faculty of the School of the Museum of Fine Arts from the 1890s to about 1912, and they taught their French-inspired painting style to several generations of Boston painters.

Benson frequently used members of his family as models, depicting them in sunny outdoor settings. Here he painted his daughter Eleanor at their summer home on North Haven Island in Penobscot Bay, Maine. This kind of subject—a young woman, dressed in white, gracefully posed before a brilliant landscape—was painted frequently by Benson and other Boston School artists, who found it ideally suited to their Impressionist style. Benson's interest in rendering the effects of direct sunlight was no doubt kindled by Impressionism; his subject is reminiscent of Monet's and Renoir's many paintings of the 1870s showing young women in garden settings. The broad brushstrokes and bright pastel colors of *Eleanor* are characteristically Impressionist, and Benson's rendering of the foliage with short, curved brushstrokes was inspired by paintings like Monet's *Antibes* pictures of the late 1880s, which had been shown in Boston in 1905 at a major Monet exhibition at Copley Hall. But rather than using light to dissolve form, as the Impressionists did in their landscapes, Benson reasserted the sculptural solidity of the figure, using color and light to define and model the central human presence that dominates his composition. Eleanor is placed in the immediate foreground, with light coming from behind her, silhouetting her figure. Although the dappling of her dress with silvery light is a favorite Impressionist device, the tighter, smoother brushwork in her face, the emphasis on profile, and the idealized presentation of the figure reflect the more academically inspired Beaux-Arts tradition that flourished in Europe and America in the 1890s.[1] Benson's adaptation of Impressionist brushwork to academic emphasis on the figure followed similar developments in France: in the 1880s, Renoir turned to figurative subjects and attempted a more tightly painted, classicizing style; a rendering of solid form through Impressionism was an interest of Cézanne's throughout his career. However, despite the popularity of Impressionist landscape in Boston from the late 1880s, figurative Impressionism was not well received there until after the turn of the century, when Boston School artists were exhibiting regularly.

Benson's paintings from this period, and the paintings and etchings of sporting subjects he made during the next two decades, were highly successful in their time; *Eleanor* was bought from the artist by the Museum of Fine Arts and exhibited frequently thereafter. Art critics found Benson's work an appealing alternative to "modern" painting by the Eight and others, which depicted the darker realities of urban life. Those artists were called "nonunderstandable" by one of Benson's supporters because their art reflected a "troubled, morbid" world; Benson's art, "refreshingly sane and gay," avoided those unpleasant realities and presented instead an uplifting view of genteel, middle-class life.[2]

1. See for example, Charles C. Curran, *On the Heights* (1909; Brooklyn Museum).
2. Anna Seaton-Schmidt, "Frank W. Benson," *American Magazine of Art* 12 (November 1921), p. 366.

74. *The Silver Screen*

Signed and dated lower right: *F. W. Benson/1921*

Oil on canvas, 36¼ x 44 in. (92.1 x 111.7 cm.)

A. Shuman Collection. 1979.615

PROVENANCE: F. L. Dunne, Boston, 1921; Alice M. Dunne, Boston, by 1938; Mr. and Mrs. John Dorsey, Wellesley, Mass.; with Vose Galleries, Boston, 1979.

EXHIBITIONS: "Eighth Exhibition of Contemporary Oil Paintings," Corcoran Gallery of Art, Washington, 1921; "Seventeenth Annual Exhibition," Pennsylvania Academy of the Fine Arts, Philadelphia, 1922; "Paintings, Watercolors and Etchings by Frank W. Benson," The Gage Gallery, Cleveland, 1922, no. 8; "Ten American Impressionists: Frank W. Benson, Edmund C. Tarbell," Museum of Fine Arts, Boston, 1938, no. 39; "Paintings by Frank W. Benson," Farnsworth Museum, Rockland, Me., 1973; "Frank Weston Benson and Edmund C. Tarbell" University Art Galleries, University of New Hampshire, Durham, 1979, no. 35.

BIBLIOGRAPHY: Jerrold Lanes, "Boston Painting 1880–1930," *Artforum* 10 (January 1972), pp. 49-50.

Although in its day Benson's *Silver Screen* might have been considered an Impressionist picture, it exemplifies for the contemporary viewer the aesthetic of the 1920s. The tightness and solidity of form, the emphasis on edges and outlines, and the bright artificial colors of *Silver Screen* are components of the Art Deco style, prevalent especially in the decorative arts of the 1920s and '30s. The crusty texture of Benson's brushwork marks a development from the looser, Impressionist technique he used at the turn of the century, and parallels the work of Luks, Lawson, and other members of the Eight, who used a thick building up of impasto as a substitute for painterliness.

Benson established his reputation as a painter of idealized figure subjects and sporting pictures, and began to paint still lifes only in the early 1920s. *The Silver Screen* is one of a series of large still-life compositions he painted between 1920 and 1925[1] that contain similar objects—a large Chinese jar, a bowl of fruit, an oriental-style jacket thrown over the patterned tablecloth, and a subtly colored folded screen in the background. The vogue for oriental art took hold in Boston in the late 1870s, about a decade after it had a dramatic impact on avant-garde painters in France; it first appeared in paintings at the turn of the century, when Benson and other Boston School painters used oriental objects as attributes of genteel interiors. By the 1920s, such objects were no longer exotic but were familiar to most educated Bostonians. However, in *The Silver Screen* the Chinese jar and jacket are not simply a nostalgic link with the aesthetic interests of the late nineteenth century; rather, Benson used them in a modern way, in a staged arrangement that exploits their unusual shapes and textures and emphasizes their sensuous, decorative qualities.

1. At least three other very similar still lifes are a part of this series; they are owned by the Corcoran Gallery of Art, Washington; Vose Galleries, Boston; and a private collector, San Francisco.

JOSEPH R. DE CAMP (1858-1923)
active in Boston 1881–1882; 1884–1923

75. *The Blue Cup*

Signed and dated lower left: *JOSEPH-DE-CAMP-1909*

Oil on canvas, 50⅛ x 41¼ in. (127.3 x 104.9 cm.)

Gift of Edwin S. Webster, Laurence T. Webster, and Mary H. Sampson, in memory of their father, Frank G. Webster. 33.532

PROVENANCE: Frank G. Webster, Boston, by 1924.

RELATED WORKS: Pencil drawing for *The Blue Cup*, squared, 11 x 9¼ in., Museum of Fine Arts, Boston; Pencil sketch for china on the table in *The Blue Cup*, 2½ x 4⅜ in., Museum of Fine Arts, Boston.

EXHIBITIONS: "DeCamp Memorial Exhibition," St. Botolph Club, Boston, 1924, no. 13; "Turn of the Century Boston Impressionists," State Street Bank, Boston, 1968; "Finished Studies and their Objects," Jewett Art Center, Wellesley College, Wellesley, Mass., 1972; "The Painter's America: Rural and Urban Life 1810–1910," Whitney Museum of American Art, New York, 1974, no. 31; "Boston Painters, 1720–1940," Boston University School of Fine and Applied Arts, Boston, 1976, no. 24; "Art in Transition: A Century of the Museum School," Museum of Fine Arts, Boston, 1977, no. 5.

BIBLIOGRAPHY: R. V. S. Berry, "DeCamp," *American Magazine of Art* 14 (1923), p. 186; *American Paintings in the Museum of Fine Arts, Boston* (Boston, 1969), no. 336; Patricia Jobe Pierce, *The Ten* (Concord, N.H., 1976), p. 68.

One of the founding members of the Ten American Painters, DeCamp, like his colleague and fellow midwesterner William Merritt Chase, went to Munich in the 1870s to study at the Royal Academy in association with Frank Duveneck. When DeCamp returned from Europe in 1880, he settled in Boston and enrolled at the School of the Museum of Fine Arts; he soon abandoned the dark-toned, broadly painted technique he learned in Germany in favor of the brighter palette and smooth brushstroke taught at the Museum School. Edmund Tarbell and Frank Benson, who were also living in Boston, became DeCamp's closest associates among the Ten, and his mature work shares with theirs the facile brushwork, softened contours, and genteel subject matter of the Boston School.

DeCamp's subject in *The Blue Cup*—a housemaid pausing from her dusting to examine a piece of fine porcelain—represents a theme common in the work of the Boston School, which focused on a refined world of exquisite objects, elegant gestures, and anecdotal events. As in *The Housemaid* (1910; Corcoran Gallery of Art, Washington) by William Paxton (DeCamp's former pupil at the Cowles Art School in Boston), oriental jars and bowls are prominent, reflecting the passion for collecting Japanese art that had affected Boston's wealthy citizens since the late 1870s.

Compared with the themes and aspirations of their contemporaries working in New York, the art of DeCamp and his colleagues was conservative, seeking to escape the increasingly mechanized realities of modern life and perpetuate instead the image of a more exclusive and timeless environment. Appropriately, their interest in progressive stylistic developments, particularly Impressionist technique, was tempered by an academic insistence on drawing and on the figure, and by a deliberate emulation of the old masters, especially Vermeer.

The Boston School's interest in Vermeer was kindled in Europe in the 1880s and '90s when many paintings by the Dutch master were on the art market; it culminated in 1913 with the publication of the first American study of Vermeer by Philip Hale, another of DeCamp's pupils.[1] DeCamp, working in Munich rather than Paris, had less opportunity to see Vermeers firsthand than did his colleagues; however, many were engraved, several were in German collections in the 1880's, and by 1892 Isabella Stewart Gardner had brought one to Boston.[2] The antecedents for DeCamp's subject in *The Blue Cup* are found in Vermeer's *Milkmaid* (1660–1661; Rijksmuseum, Amsterdam), *Woman with a Water Jug* (1662; Metropolitan Museum of Art of New York), and other images of women performing light domestic tasks. DeCamp's figure is monumental in comparison to Vermeer's; however, the contemplative mood and the love of texture and of the decorative object reflect the Dutch painter's influence. And although DeCamp painted with the loose, animated brushwork of the late nineteenth century and so achieved a hazy quality rather than Vermeer's brilliant clarity, his use of light was surely inspired by Vermeer: as in that master's *Woman with a Pearl Necklace* (1662–1665; Gemäldegalerie, Berlin-Dahlem), light streams in through a window and bathes the figure's face, arms, and torso, while the rest of the picture is seen in soft shadow.

1. Philip L. Hale, *Jan Vermeer of Delft* (Boston, 1913).
2. For detailed descriptions of the provenance of Vermeer's works, see Albert Blankert, *Vermeer of Delft* (Oxford, 1978).

THEODORE WENDEL (1859-1932)
active in Boston 1892–1896; in Ipswich, Massachusetts 1897–1932

76. *Bridge at Ipswich,* ca. 1908

Oil on canvas, 24¼ x 30 in. (61.6 x 76.2 cm.)

Gift of Mr. and Mrs. Daniel S. Wendel and Purchase, Arthur Gordon Tompkins Fund. 1979.179

PROVENANCE: Mr. and Mrs. Daniel S. Wendel, Ipswich, Mass.

EXHIBITIONS: "Theodore Wendel. An American Impressionist," Whitney Museum of American Art, New York, 1976, no. 15; "Beginnings," The Guild of Boston Artists, Boston, 1979; "American Impressionism," Henry Art Gallery, University of Washington, Seattle, 1980.

BIBLIOGRAPHY: John I. H. Baur, "Introducing Theodore Wendel," *Art in America* 64 (November-December 1976), pp. 102-105.

Wendel painted *Bridge at Ipswich* toward the end of his career, after he moved from Boston to Ipswich, Massachusetts, and shifted his subject matter from urban to small-town views. Here he depicted the Green Bridge, a local landmark that was one of three bridges across the Ipswich River. The prototypes for his subject were the bridges across the Seine at Paris and Argenteuil that figured prominently in the works of Monet and Pissarro, both of whom Wendel admired. In their work, bridges were intended either as emblems of modernism and encroaching industrialization, or, as in the paintings of the Paris bridges, as picturesque elements of a city view. Wendel's vision was affected by the latter images, and he showed the bridge at Ipswich as a monumental, decorative form harmonizing with the bucolic features of the little town. The loose brushwork and high-keyed palette also reflect the influence of the Impressionists, as does the high horizon, the steeply rising compressed space of the middle ground, and the absence of specific compositional focus.

Wendel was born in Midway, Ohio, and attended briefly the School of Design at the University of Cincinnati. In 1878 he and his friend Joseph DeCamp decided to continue their studies in Munich, which had replaced Düsseldorf as the training ground for young American artists in Germany. Wendel studied first at the Royal Academy, then dominated by the style and methods of Wilhelm Leibl, and in 1879 became one of Frank Duveneck's students. None of Wendel's work from this period has survived; paintings he pro-duced in subsequent years indicate that Duveneck's dark palette and lively brushwork had no lasting effect on Wendel's colors, his composition, or his subject matter.[1]

A trip to Paris in the 1880s changed the direction of Wendel's art, and he became one of the first American painters to adopt the subjects and something of the technique of the Impressionists. In Paris, he studied first at the Académie Julian, and then in the summer of 1886, worked at Giverny, where Monet was painting. Many other young artists would follow Wendel to Giverny, as the *Art Amateur* noted in 1887: "Quite an American colony has gathered, I am told, at Giverny, seventy miles from Paris on the Seine, at the home of Claude Monet, including our Louis Ritter, W. L. Metcalf, Theodore Wendel, John Breck and Theodore Robinson of New York. A few pictures just received from these men show that they have got the blue-green color of Monet's impressionism and 'got it bad'."[2] Despite his flippant tone, this critic accurately identified what Wendel and the others would derive from Monet. They did not adopt the Impressionist vision nor its concern for the dissolution of forms in light but rather appreciated some of the means by which that vision was realized: the sketchy handling, the energetic brushwork, and especially the color, strong and bright. These features would characterize Wendel's art for the rest of his life.

After his summers in Giverny, Wendel returned to America and settled in Boston, a sympathetic environment for an Impressionist painter. He taught painting at Wellesley College and at the Cowles Art School in Boston, and maintained a studio on Huntington Avenue, which burned in 1897 or 1898. Shortly thereafter, Wendel moved from Boston to Ipswich. Like Monet at Giverny or Pissarro at Pontoise, Wendel made the town of Ipswich his subject, painting again and again the activities of its citizens and its modest topographical and architectural features.

1. A detailed biography of Wendel is to be found in John I. H. Baur, "Introducing Theodore Wendel," *Art in America* 64 (November-December 1976), pp. 102-105.
2. "Greta," Boston Art and Artists," *The Art Amateur* 17 (October 1887), p. 93, as quoted in William H. Gerdts, *American Impressionism* (Henry Art Gallery, University of Washington, Seattle, 1980), p. 30.

LILIAN WESTCOTT HALE (1881-1963)
active in Boston ca. 1900–1952

77. *L'Edition de Luxe*

Signed and dated upper left: *Lilian Westcott Hale 1910*

Oil on canvas, 23¼ x 15 in. (59.0 x 38.1 cm.)

Gift of Mary C. Wheelwright. 35.1487

PROVENANCE: Andrew Wheelwright, Boston, 1911; Miss Mary Wheelwright, Boston, by 1935.

EXHIBITIONS: "Winter Exhibition," Copley Society, Boston, 1911; "Catalogue of the 106th Annual Exhibition of the Pennsylvania Academy of the Fine Arts," Philadelphia, 1929; "The Painter's America: Rural and Urban Life, 1810–1910," Whitney Museum of American Art, New York, 1974, no. 131; "Turn of the Century America: Paintings, Graphics, Photographs, 1890–1910," Whitney Museum of American Art, New York, 1977, no. 83; "American Impressionist Paintings," Danforth Museum, Framingham, Mass., 1978; "A Centennial Exhibition," Copley Society, Boston, 1979, no. 20.

BIBLIOGRAPHY: *American Paintings in the Museum of Fine Arts, Boston* (Boston, 1969), p. 293.

From its founding in 1877, the School of the Museum of Fine Arts was the training ground for many of Boston's best-known artists. When Lilian Westcott Hale studied there at the turn of the century, a group of painters associated with the Boston School, including her husband, the painter and critic Philip Hale, as well as Frank Benson and Edmund Tarbell, were on the faculty. The aesthetic they championed, based on a coupling of academic drawing with Impressionist technique applied primarily to figurative (rather than landscape) subjects, was perpetuated by several generations of artists. Lilian Hale's oeuvre reflects this training. Her portraits, for which she is best known, though freely brushed and often unconventionally composed, are still carefully delineated. Her genre scenes were set, as a rule, in interiors rather than out-of-doors, and featured attractive young women performing genteel domestic tasks or engaged in quiet pastimes.

Like Tarbell's *Girl Reading* (Museum of Fine Arts, Boston), painted the same year, *L'Edition de Luxe* shows a handsome, well-dressed woman, absorbed in a book—in this case, an album of colored prints. The image describes a world that is intimate, refined, and idealized; the figure is treated as part of the general *mise-en-scene* rather than as a specific expressive personality. This rarefied world of decorative femininity and upper-class leisure was a major theme in *fin-de-siècle* American painting in both Boston and New York, where William Merritt Chase and Thomas Dewing addressed the same subject; in Europe, artists from Whistler to Vuillard also painted interior scenes in which women functioned as ornaments, although their compositions were generally more abstract, their paint handling freer.

The palette and technique in *L'Edition de Luxe* are a restrained version of the paint handling found in the works of Monet, the Impressionist most admired by Boston painters. Hale's figure sits in a handsome room bathed in soft light that comes through the window behind her. The use of pale tones of strong, near-complementary colors in small strokes placed side by side—pink and green-blue in the window, yellow and gray-lavender in the sitter's dress—create the effect of flickering afternoon light; the muted pink strokes used throughout the canvas bind the composition together.

The room's accoutrements become in Hale's composition a series of beautifully painted still-life vignettes, such as the openwork porcelain bowl with branches of pink hawthorne; the delicate blossoms at lower right, reflected in the highly polished table, are reminiscent of still lifes painted by John La Farge several decades before. These decorative elements, oriental in flavor, reflect the taste for Japanese culture transmitted through prints and other objects of art that Boston collectors had imported since the 1870s, and that were favorite accessories of the Boston School painters. The composition, with its carefully planned asymmetry and its compressed space, also reflects these artists' interest in oriental art; the use of strong verticals and horizontals to hem in the figure suggest the artist's acquaintance with the work of Vuillard, who used similar devices in his interior scenes painted around the turn of the century.

WILLIAM MC GREGOR PAXTON (1869-1941)

active in Boston 1893–1941

78. *The New Necklace*

Signed and dated lower left: *Paxton/1910*

Oil on canvas, 35½ x 28½ in. (90.2 x 72.3 cm.)

Zoe Oliver Sherman Collection. 22.644

PROVENANCE: Zoe O. Sherman, Boston, 1912.

EXHIBITIONS: "13th Annual Exhibition of Paintings," Worcester Art Museum, 1910, no. 11; "3rd Exhibition of Oil Paintings by Contemporary American Artists," Corcoran Gallery of Art, Washington, 1911, no. 77; "106th Annual Exhibition," Pennsylvania Academy of the Fine Arts," Philadelphia, 1911, no. 553; "Paintings by American Artists," Copley Gallery, Boston, 1911; "24th Annual Exhibition of Oil Paintings and Sculptures by American Artists," Art Institute of Chicago, 1911, no. 272; "Paintings by William McGregor Paxton," St. Botolph Club, Boston, 1913, no. 2; "William McGregor Paxton, N.A.," Maryhill Museum of Fine Arts, Maryhill, Wash., 1946, no. 12; "Centennial Celebration," Brockton Public Library, Brockton, Mass., 1967; "The Painters' America: Rural and Urban Life 1810–1910," Whitney Museum of American Art, New York, 1974, no. 90; "150th Anniversary Exhibition," National Academy of Design, New York, 1975, p. 100; "William McGregor Paxton (1869–1941)," Indianapolis Museum of Art, 1978, no. 22; "The American Renaissance, 1876–1917," Brooklyn Museum, 1979, no. 223.

BIBLIOGRAPHY: *Worcester Art Museum Bulletin* 1 (September 1910), p. 3; Julia deWolf Addison, *The Boston Museum of Fine Arts* (Boston, 1940), pp. 52-53; Denys Sutton, "Cathay, Nirvana, and Zen," *Apollo* 84 (August 1966), p. 153; *American Paintings in the Museum of Fine Arts, Boston* (Boston, 1969), no. 794.

In 1892, the critic Thoré-Burger's collection of paintings, including several works by the seventeenth-century Dutch master Jan Vermeer, was sold at auction in Paris. William Paxton was then in his third year at the Ecole des Beaux-Arts, studying with J. L. Gérôme, and was also working at the more experimental Académie Julian. He was a witness to important old master sales, as well as to the many revolutionary exhibitions held in Paris in those years: the large show of Japanese prints held at the Ecole des Beaux-Arts in 1890, the annual showings of the Independents, and the first exhibition of the Impressionist and Symbolist Painters in 1891, which included paintings by Bonnard, Rousseau, Vuillard, and Signac. All of these events made an impression on Paxton and had a significant effect on his style.

Paxton returned to Boston in 1893. Although at first he had to supplement his income by designing newspaper advertisements, he soon was showing his paintings to increasing acclaim in both Boston and New York. He associated with the group of artists somewhat older than he known as the Boston School—Edmund Tarbell, Frank Benson, and Joseph DeCamp—first studying with them and in 1906 joining them on the faculty of the School of the Museum of Fine Arts. During this period he painted portraits and evolved the subject matter for which he would become famous: attractive young women in richly appointed interiors. *The New Necklace* was painted in 1910, during a period in which oriental accessories occur frequently in Paxton's pictures. Here the pink Chinese jacket is the main coloristic

feature in a painting otherwise based upon blues, browns, and golds; it recurs in several of Paxton's later works, as does the doll on the writing desk and the handsome folding screen.[1] These oriental objects, reflecting the taste for *japonisme* that had begun in Paris as early as 1861 and to which Paxton was exposed both in Gérôme's studio and in the works of the Nabis, are set against a backdrop of European luxury. The writing desk is a French secretary, reviving the style of the 1820s; the tapestry is antique, and the painting visible behind the folding screen is Titian's *Allegory of the Marchese del Vasto* (ca. 1530–1535; Louvre, Paris), which Paxton may have copied in Paris. That painting has been subject to numerous interpretations, all of which center on the theme of marriage and separation,[2] thus suggesting an anecdotal meaning for Paxton's picture: the woman in the pink coat is writing to her distant lover, and pauses to show her companion his latest gift.

But storytelling was not Paxton's chief interest in *The New Necklace*. Rather, he was absorbed by the juxtaposition of many different decorative patterns and the meticulous rendering of textures, by the creation of an atmosphere of luxury and refinement remote from the vulgarity of modern urban life, and above all, by the representation of a warm golden light. There are parallels for all of these features in the tradition of late nineteenth-century French painting, both academic and *avant-garde,* in which he was trained. Paxton's smooth brushwork and rich coloration were learned during his years with Gérôme. Like Bonnard and Vuillard, fellow pupils at the Académie Julian, he stressed decorative designs and blurred contours, and although he never incorporated the patternistic flatness of their work, the compression of space in *The New Necklace* shows Paxton's awareness of their example. Like them, he depicted the psychological content of daily life, yet the emphasis on material objects reveals a tendency toward superficiality paralleling the society pictures of "chic" European painters Alfred Stevens, James Tissot, and Paul Helleu.

A fundamental aspect of Paxton's experience in Europe, as important as his acquaintance with contemporary French painters, was his exposure to work of the old masters. He copied images by Titian and Ingres; more significant was his borrowing from the work of Vermeer. That artist, whose paintings were rediscovered by the French critic Théophile Thoré (Thoré-Burger) in the 1860s, was seen as a precursor of Impressionism because of his emphasis on bright color and the effect of sunlight; his work continued to fascinate artists in France through the end of the century. Several paintings by Vermeer were on the Paris art market in the 1880s and '90s, including three at the Thoré-Burger auction in 1892, one of which the Boston collector Isabella Stewart Gardner purchased. Paxton and his fellow artists of the Boston School found Vermeer's works especially intriguing, imitating his soft golden light and incorporating many of his motifs into their pictures. In Paxton's work, the activity of letter-writing, the device of including a picture within a

picture, the rich textures and patterns of the incidental objects, and the practice of including an object (here the chair on which the visitor's hat sits) in the immediate foreground of the composition are all derived from Vermeer, as is the motif of the necklace itself. However, whereas the world created by Vermeer seems no less natural for its perfection, Paxton's world is a hothouse, too mannered, too remote from everyday life, too elegant to be real.

1. The jacket appears in *The Blue Book* (1914; collection Brayton Wilbur, Jr., San Francisco) and *The Embroidered Jacket* (1916; estate of the artist); the doll is the featured motif in *The Figurine* (1921, National Collection of Fine Arts, Washington) and *1875* (1914; collection Mrs. Thomas A. McGovern, Chicago).

2. The interpretations of Titian's picture are summarized by Harold E. Wethey, *The Paintings of Titian*, III, London, 1975, no. 1.

INDEX